MATHS ON TARGET

Year 5

Stephen Pearce

Elmwood Press

First published 2008 by
Elmwood Press
80 Attimore Road
Welwyn Garden City
Herts. AL8 6LP
Tel. 01707 333232

Reprinted in 2009

ISBN 9781 902 214 931

Numerical answers are published in a separate book.

Typeset and illustrated by Tech-Set Ltd., Gateshead, Tyne and Wear.
Printed and bound in Spain on behalf of JFDi Print Services Ltd.

PREFACE

Maths on Target has been written for pupils in Year 5 and their teachers.

The intention of the book is to provide teachers with material to teach all the objectives as set out in the yearly programme in the renewed Primary Framework for Mathematics.

The structure of **Maths on Target** matches that of the renewed framework. It is arranged in five blocks, A–E, each of which consists of three units. To ensure progression throughout the year the units are best taught in the order in which they appear in both this book and the exemplar planning structure for Year 5 in the renewed framework.

	Block A	Block B	Block C	Block D	Block E
Term 1	Unit 1	Unit 1	Unit 1	Unit 1	Unit 1
Term 2	Unit 2	Unit 2	Unit 2	Unit 2	Unit 2
Term 3	Unit 3	Unit 3	Unit 3	Unit 3	Unit 3

Each unit in **Maths on Target** consists of lessons based upon the learning overview for that unit in the renewed framework. Each lesson is divided into four sections:

Introduction: the learning intention expressed as an 'I can' statement and, where necessary, clearly worked examples.

Section A: activities based upon work previously covered. This generally matches the objectives for Year 4 pupils. This section can be used to remind children of work previously covered, as well as providing material for the less confident child.

Section B: activities based upon the objectives for Year 5 pupils. Most children should be able to work successfully at this level.

Section C: activities providing extension material for the faster workers and for those who need to be moved quickly onto more challenging tasks. The work in this section generally matches the objectives for Year 6 pupils. Problems in Section C can also provide useful material for discussion in the plenary session.

The correspondence of the three sections A–C to the objectives for different year groups provides a simple, manageable structure for planning differentiated activities and for both the formal and informal assessment of children's progress. The commonality of the content pitched at different levels also allows for progression within the lesson. Children acquiring confidence at one level find they can successfully complete activities at the next level.

The author is indebted to many colleagues who have assisted him in this work. He is particularly grateful to Sharon Granville and Debra Turner for their invaluable advice and assistance.

Stephen Pearce

CONTENTS

A1 NUMBER SEQUENCES

I can find missing numbers in a sequence including those with negative numbers.

To find the rule that links the numbers study the gaps.

Examples

4	0	−4	−8	−12	The rule is *subtract 4*.
1	4	7	10	13	The rule is *add 3*.

A

Write the first six numbers in each sequence.

	Start at	Rule		Start at	Rule		Start at	Rule
1	23	+2	6	83	−7	11	21	+5
2	56	−8	7	59	+3	12	48	−6
3	125	+25	8	56	−7	13	19	+9
4	73	−5	9	5	+8	14	110	−20
5	47	+4	10	120	−3	15	21	+11

B

Complete these sequences by filling in the boxes. Write the rule each time.

1. 83 85 87 89 [ ] [ ] [ ]
2. −1 −3 −5 −7 [ ] [ ] [ ]
3. [ ] [ ] [ ] 175 225 275 325
4. [ ] [ ] [ ] 61 72 83 94
5. 68 64 [ ] [ ] [ ] 48 44
6. 325 350 [ ] [ ] [ ] 450 475
7. −24 −20 −16 −12 [ ] [ ] [ ]
8. −2 [ ] −10 [ ] −18 [ ] −26
9. [ ] 62 [ ] [ ] 47 42 37
10. 21 18 [ ] 12 [ ] 6 [ ]
11. 62 [ ] 48 [ ] [ ] 27 20
12. [ ] 49 42 [ ] 28 21 [ ]
13. 114 [ ] 316 [ ] 518 [ ] 720
14. [ ] −40 [ ] [ ] −25 −20 −15
15. 68 57 [ ] 35 [ ] 13 [ ]
16. −5 [ ] −15 [ ] [ ] −30 −35

C

Copy the sequences and write the next three numbers. What is the rule for each sequence?

1. 77 83 89 95
2. −2 −4 −6 −8
3. 0·1 0·3 0·5 0·7
4. 68 77 86 95
5. 25 20 15 10
6. 35 60 85 110
7. 3 1 −1 −3
8. 0·25 0·5 0·75 1·0
9. 132 121 110 99
10. 0·05 0·06 0·07 0·08
11. 54 62 70 78
12. 18 14 10 6
13. 48 38 28 18
14. 45 38 31 24
15. 64 52 40 28
16. 5 24 43 62
17. 19 13 7 1
18. 48 69 90 111

I can identify missing numbers in a sequence involving negative numbers.

Negative numbers (below zero) | Positive numbers (above zero)

−10 −9 −8 −7 −6 −5 −4 −3 −2 −1 0 1 2 3 4 5 6 7 8 9 10

A

Copy and complete.

1. −5 −4 ☐ ☐ ☐ 0 1
2. 3 2 ☐ ☐ ☐ −2 −3
3. ☐ ☐ ☐ −6 −4 −2 0
4. −14 −10 ☐ −2 ☐ 6 ☐
5. −7 −5 ☐ −1 ☐ 3 ☐
6. 5 3 1 −1 ☐ ☐ ☐

Count on

7. 4 from −3
8. 7 from −9
9. 8 from −5
10. 6 from −2
11. 5 from −5
12. 9 from −4

Count back

13. 7 from 4
14. 8 from −1
15. 12 from 6
16. 9 from 0
17. 6 from −4
18. 10 from 3

B

Copy and complete.

1. −11 −9 −7 −5 ☐ ☐ ☐
2. −11 −8 −5 ☐ ☐ ☐ 7
3. −6 −4 ☐ ☐ ☐ 4 6
4. −14 −10 ☐ ☐ ☐ 6 10
5. 5 3 1 ☐ ☐ ☐ −7
6. 8 6 4 2 ☐ ☐ ☐

Put each set of numbers in order, smallest first.

7. 7 −3 −6 9 3 −1
8. 9 −2 −8 1 4 0
9. 1 −4 −7 6 −1 2
10. −2 0 5 3 −3 −6

C

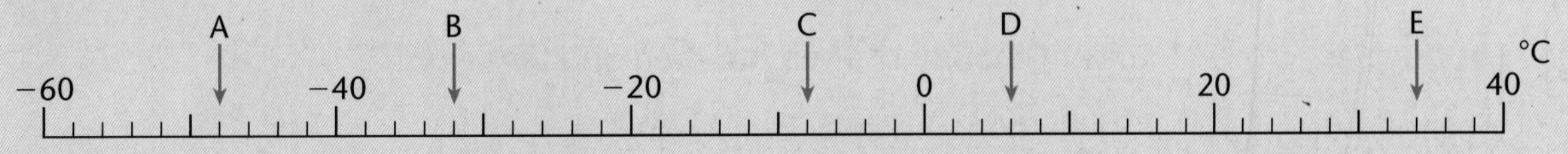

1. What temperatures are shown by the letters?
2. Give the difference in temperature between:
   a) C and D b) B and C c) C and E d) A and D.
3. What would the temperature be if it was:
   a) at A and rose 34°C? b) at D and fell 18°C? c) at C and fell 26°C? d) at B and rose 48°C?

I can read and write whole numbers.

Numbers are made up from digits.
There are ten digits, 0 1 2 3 4 5 6 7 8 and 9.
347 is a three-digit number, 3472 is a four-digit number, and so on.

The way we read a digit depends upon its place in the number.

2748 is two thousand seven hundred and forty-eight
27 485 is twenty-seven thousand four hundred and eighty-five
274 856 is two hundred and seventy four thousand eight hundred and fifty-six
2 748 563 is two million seven hundred and forty-eight thousand five hundred and sixty-three

TAKE CARE when a number has zeros in it.

3006 is read as three thousand and six.
600 502 is read as six hundred thousand five hundred and two

These figures show the distances between London and other cities around the world.
Write each distance in words.

1. Rome 1431 km
2. Chicago 6356 km
3. Beijing 8138 km
4. Copenhagen 952 km
5. Mexico City 8936 km
6. Cairo 3508 km
7. Lagos 5017 km
8. Singapore 10 852 km
9. Berlin 928 km
10. Caracas 7507 km

11. Copy the table, writing each distance in figures.

City	Distance to London (kilometres)
New York	five thousand five hundred and seventy-two
Moscow	two thousand four hundred and ninety-eight
Paris	three hundred and forty-two
Los Angeles	eight thousand seven hundred and fifty-eight
Johannesburg	nine thousand and seventy-one
Bombay	seven thousand one hundred and ninety
Rio de Janeiro	nine thousand two hundred and ninety-nine
Buenos Aires	eleven thousand one hundred and thirty-one
Calcutta	seven thousand nine hundred and sixty-one
Toronto	five thousand seven hundred and four

1. The table shows the areas of the largest seas and oceans in the world.
   Copy the table, writing each area in figures.

Seas	Area (square miles)
Pacific Ocean	sixty-four million one hundred and ninety thousand
Atlantic Ocean	thirty-three million four hundred and twenty thousand
Indian Ocean	twenty-eight million three hundred and fifty thousand
Arctic Ocean	five million one hundred and ten thousand
South China Sea	one million one hundred and forty-eight thousand
Caribbean Sea	one million and sixty-three thousand
Mediterranean Sea	nine hundred and sixty-six thousand five hundred
Baring Sea	eight hundred and seventy-five thousand seven hundred
Gulf of Mexico	five hundred and ninety-five thousand eight hundred
Sea of Okhotsk	five hundred and eighty-nine thousand eight hundred

The same areas are written here in square kilometres.
Write each area in words.

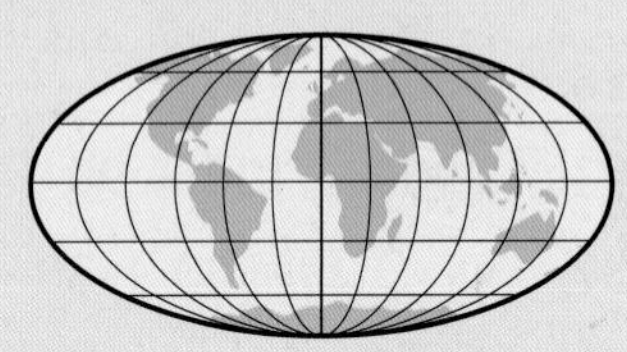

2. Pacific Ocean 166 240 000 km^2
3. Atlantic Ocean 86 560 000 km^2
4. Indian Ocean 73 430 000 km^2
5. Arctic Ocean 13 230 000 km^2
6. South China Sea 2 974 000 km^2
7. Caribbean Sea 2 753 000 km^2
8. Mediterranean Sea 2 503 000 km^2
9. Baring Sea 2 268 180 km^2
10. Gulf of Mexico 1 542 985 km^2
11. Sea of Okhotsk 1 527 570 km^2

C

The following figures show the populations of some European capital cities.
Write each population in words.

1. London 7 007 091
2. Brussels 953 175
3. Berlin 3 472 009
4. Budapest 2 002 121
5. Luxembourg 77 400
6. Vienna 1 806 737
7. Paris 9 319 367
8. Cardiff 302 747
9. Monaco 27 063
10. Rome 2 693 383
11. Athens 3 072 922
12. Sarajevo 529 021

13. Make as many five-digit numbers with a value of less than 26 000 as you can using these digits only.

    7 2 0 5 9

    Write each number in words and figures.

I can say what any digit represents in a number with up to seven digits.

The value of a digit depends upon its position in the number.

Example 1 423 698

M	HTh	TTh	Th	H	T	U
1	4	2	3	6	9	8

The 1 has a value of 1 000 000.
The 4 has a value of 400 000.
The 2 has a value of 20 000.
The 3 has a value of 3 000.
The 6 has a value of 600.
The 9 has a value of 90.
The 8 has a value of 8.

A

Copy and complete by writing the missing number in the box.

1. 369 = ☐ + 60 + 9
2. 1426 = 1000 + 400 + ☐ + 6
3. 2193 = 2000 + 100 + 90 + ☐
4. 4537 = ☐ + 500 + 30 + 7
5. 3858 = 3000 + ☐ + 50 + ☐
6. 672 = ☐ + ☐ + 2
7. 5724 = ☐ + 700 + ☐ + 4
8. 2917 = 2000 + ☐ + ☐ + 7
9. 1946 = ☐ + 900 + 40 + ☐
10. 1156 = 1000 + ☐ + ☐ + ☐
11. 8538 = ☐ + ☐ + ☐ + ☐
12. 3532 = ☐ + ☐ + ☐ + ☐

B

Write down the value of the digit underlined.

1. $3\underline{9}82$
2. $671\underline{5}$
3. $2\underline{4}\,360$
4. $38\,\underline{6}74$
5. $1\underline{8}5\,037$
6. $241\,\underline{4}26$
7. $1\,\underline{6}59\,249$
8. $1\,51\underline{8}\,598$
9. $\underline{3}\,460\,103$
10. $9\,772\,85\underline{1}$
11. $2\,3\underline{9}6\,910$
12. $3\,\underline{8}24\,672$
13. $75\underline{3}\,217$
14. $4\,805\,\underline{2}46$
15. $\underline{5}\,130\,909$

Add 4000 to:

16. 13 672
17. 100 813
18. 145 628

Add 30 000 to:

19. 243 497
20. 813
21. 1 545 628

Take 200 from:

22. 424 357
23. 1 173 884
24. 12 916

Take 100 000 from:

25. 432 176
26. 1 918 534
27. 6 259 019

C

Write the answers only.

1. 317 496 + 60 000
2. 1 854 031 + 9000
3. 2 007 193 − 4000
4. 62 584 − 20 000
5. 450 267 + 700 000
6. 3 194 805 − 2 000 000
7. 7 436 + 1 000 000
8. 5 219 320 − 4000
9. 1 329 754 − 300 000

Add 600 000 to:

10. 1 587 362
11. 204 189

Add 25 000 to:

12. 8174
13. 5

Take 7000 from:

14. 28 298
15. 142 165

Take 1100 from:

16. 1 211 471
17. 95 362

A1 ORDERING NUMBERS

I can compare and order numbers.

Example

Arrange 2581 2158 21 158 in ascending order.

Look at the highest value digits first and if they are the same compare the next highest value.

The correct order is 2158, 2581, 21 158.

2000	2000	20 000
↑	↑	↑
2581	2158	21 158
↓	↓	
500	100	

A

Put these sets of numbers in order, starting with the smallest.

1. 865 2836 683 2386
2. 5419 1945 5914 5149
3. 2743 3472 3247 3274
4. 1638 1386 1863 1836
5. 4785 4758 4578 4857

Copy and complete.

6. 378 + □ = 678
7. 9410 − □ = 7410
8. 2561 + □ = 2961
9. 584 − □ = 524
10. 2037 + □ = 5037
11. 6924 + □ = 8924
12. 560 − □ = 60
13. 3168 + □ = 7168
14. 4725 − □ = 4125
15. 639 + □ = 689

B

Put these numbers in ascending order.

1. 4738 3874 3478 4837
2. 52 287 52 783 53 872 53 827
3. 19 162 19 612 19 261 19 216
4. 16 006 10 606 16 060 10 660
5. 14 231 14 321 14 421 14 312

Copy and complete.

6. 35 684 + □ = 39 684
7. 619 207 − □ = 612 207
8. 1 873 410 − □ = 1 373 410
9. 25 836 − □ = 25 536
10. 159 870 + □ = 759 870

C

Work out the number that is halfway between each pair of numbers.

1. 3400 ⟷ 4400
2. 19 300 ⟷ 20 000
3. 25 280 ⟷ 25 380
4. 17 400 ⟷ 18 200
5. 16 680 ⟷ 16 740
6. 6940 ⟷ 7020

7. Use these digits once each.

   1 6 5 2 7 4 3 8

   Make two different 4-digit numbers which give:

   a) the largest possible total.

   b) the smallest possible total.

   c) the largest possible difference.

   d) the smallest possible difference.

I can multiply and divide whole numbers by 10, 100 and 1000.

Multiplying – digits move to the left
Dividing – digits move to the right

Examples

×/÷ by 10 – digits move 1 place	624 × 10 = 6240	58 000 ÷ 10 = 5800
×/÷ by 100 – digits move 2 places	36 × 100 = 3600	2000 ÷ 100 = 20
×/÷ by 1000 – digits move 3 places	72 × 1000 = 72 000	15 000 ÷ 1000 = 15

A

Multiply by:

10

1. 30
2. 187
3. 620
4. 714
5. 593
6. 58

100

7. 9
8. 16
9. 40
10. 58
11. 100
12. 62

Divide by:

10

13. 860
14. 90
15. 3000
16. 1530
17. 700
18. 5400

100

19. 6000
20. 3900
21. 6100
22. 400
23. 7300
24. 10 000

Copy and complete.

25. ☐ × 10 = 8600
26. ☐ ÷ 10 = 62
27. ☐ × 100 = 7000
28. ☐ ÷ 100 = 81
29. ☐ × 10 = 1390
30. ☐ ÷ 10 = 580
31. ☐ × 100 = 2400
32. ☐ ÷ 100 = 90

B

Write the answers only.

1. 987 × 10
2. 1700 ÷ 10
3. 860 × 100
4. 1400 ÷ 100
5. 52 × 1000
6. 30 000 ÷ 1000
7. 74 000 × 10
8. 49 000 ÷ 10
9. 1340 × 100
10. 28 000 ÷ 100
11. 147 × 1000
12. 650 000 ÷ 1000

Copy and complete.

13. ☐ × 10 = 21 600
14. ☐ ÷ 10 = 83 000
15. ☐ × 100 = 96 000
16. ☐ ÷ 100 = 7400
17. ☐ × 1000 = 80 000
18. ☐ ÷ 1000 = 1000

19. How many £10 notes make £15 000?
20. How many millilitres are there in 30 litres?

C

Copy and complete.

1. ☐ × 10 = 397 000
2. ☐ ÷ 10 = 400 000
3. ☐ × 100 = 99 000
4. ☐ ÷ 100 = 1500
5. ☐ × 1000 = 1 700 000
6. ☐ ÷ 1000 = 400
7. 6100 × ☐ = 610 000
8. 2 000 000 ÷ ☐ = 2000
9. 25 600 × ☐ = 256 000
10. 2 400 000 ÷ ☐ = 24 000
11. 370 000 ÷ ☐ = 37 000
12. 8100 × ☐ = 8 100 000

13. How many pounds is 1 million pence?
14. What is 100 km in centimetres?
15. What is $2\frac{1}{2}$ kg in grams?
16. There are 14 sweets in each packet. There are 100 packets in each box. How many sweets are there in 100 boxes?

A1 MULTIPLICATION FACTS

I can recall the multiplication and division facts to 10 × 10.

A

What is

1. 8 × 4
2. 4 × 7
3. 9 × 2
4. 6 × 6
5. 7 × 3
6. 3 × 9
7. 7 × 8
8. 6 × 3
9. 9 × 9
10. 7 × 5
11. 8 × 6
12. 5 × 4
13. 40 ÷ 5
14. 16 ÷ 8
15. 30 ÷ 10
16. 49 ÷ 7
17. 20 ÷ 2
18. 30 ÷ 6
19. 63 ÷ 7
20. 50 ÷ 10
21. 64 ÷ 8
22. 27 ÷ 3
23. 54 ÷ 9
24. 36 ÷ 4

B

Copy and complete.

1. □ × 2 = 14
2. □ × 7 = 42
3. □ × 3 = 24
4. □ × 8 = 72
5. □ × 6 = 42
6. □ × 9 = 72
7. □ ÷ 7 = 8
8. □ ÷ 5 = 6
9. □ ÷ 9 = 7
10. □ ÷ 6 = 9
11. □ ÷ 8 = 6
12. □ ÷ 4 = 7

Write the answers only.

13. 70 × 8
14. 600 × 3
15. 30 × 6
16. 400 × 9
17. 400 × 5
18. 50 × 7
19. 800 × 20
20. 70 × 70
21. 300 × 80
22. 600 × 60
23. 40 × 40
24. 50 × 90
25. 320 ÷ 4
26. 540 ÷ 9
27. 4000 ÷ 8
28. 7000 ÷ 10
29. 480 ÷ 6
30. 6300 ÷ 7
31. 400 ÷ 8
32. 2400 ÷ 4
33. 2100 ÷ 7
34. 420 ÷ 6
35. 810 ÷ 9
36. 6400 ÷ 8

C

Copy and complete.

1. □ × 40 = 24 000
2. □ × 60 = 1800
3. □ × 90 = 72 000
4. □ × 80 = 56 000
5. □ × 70 = 63 000
6. □ × 30 = 1500
7. □ ÷ 9 = 50
8. □ ÷ 5 = 600
9. □ ÷ 7 = 30
10. □ ÷ 6 = 900
11. □ ÷ 2 = 70
12. □ ÷ 8 = 600

Write the answers only.

13. 0·7 × 6
14. 0·9 × 8
15. 0·6 × 2
16. 0·8 × 7
17. 0·9 × 3
18. 0·6 × 9
19. 7 × 0·5
20. 3 × 0·9
21. 6 × 0·6
22. 4 × 0·7
23. 8 × 0·8
24. 7 × 0·4
25. 4·0 ÷ 8
26. 4·5 ÷ 5
27. 4·2 ÷ 7
28. 4·8 ÷ 6
29. 6·3 ÷ 9
30. 3·6 ÷ 4
31. 4·9 ÷ 7
32. 2·4 ÷ 3
33. 3·2 ÷ 8
34. 8·1 ÷ 9
35. 2·0 ÷ 2
36. 3·0 ÷ 6

I can choose a sensible strategy to work out a mental calculation.

Examples

ADDITION AND SUBTRACTION

Partitioning
328 + 63 = 320 + 60 + 8 + 3
= 380 + 11
= 391

279 − 45 = 279 − 40 − 5
= 239 − 5
= 234

Using Near Doubles
25 + 26
(25 × 2) + 1
50 + 1
51

Counting Up
403 − 186

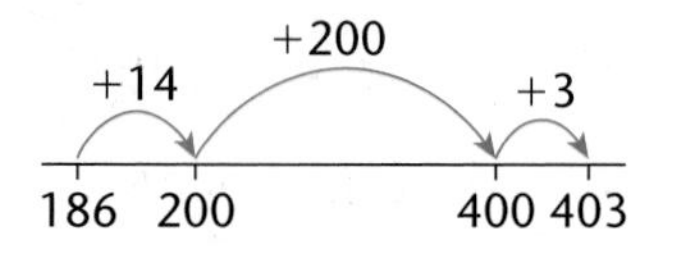

200 + 14 + 3 = 217

Using Nearest Multiple of 10/100/1000
264 − 78
264 − 80 + 2
184 + 2
186

Examples

MULTIPLICATION AND DIVISION

Using Factors
210 ÷ 14
210 ÷ 7 ÷ 2
30 ÷ 2
15

Partitioning
34 × 4
(30 × 4) + (4 × 4)
120 + 16
136

Multiplying Multiples of 10/100
60 × 20
(6 × 2 = 12)
60 × 20 = 1200

Multiplying by 19/21 etc.
23 × 19
(23 × 20) − (23 × 1)
460 − 23
437

A

Choose one method for each group of six problems.

1. 12 + 13
2. 21 + 22
3. 23 + 24
4. 14 + 13
5. 34 + 35
6. 11 + 13

7. 63 − 54
8. 402 − 285
9. 6000 − 5986
10. 72 − 38
11. 303 − 177
12. 5000 − 4974

13. 35 × 10
14. 52 × 10
15. 81 × 100
16. 174 × 10
17. 27 × 100
18. 64 × 100

19. 14 × 9
20. 16 × 9
21. 13 × 9
22. 11 × 11
23. 14 × 11
24. 18 × 11

25. 9 × 8
26. 9 × 6
27. 7 × 8
28. 84 ÷ 6
29. 64 ÷ 8
30. 48 ÷ 16

31. 13 × 3
32. 18 × 3
33. 24 × 3
34. 12 × 4
35. 19 × 4
36. 23 × 4

37. 63 + 29
38. 93 + 61
39. 84 + 28
40. 75 − 19
41. 193 − 71
42. 129 − 62

43. 24 + 47
44. 39 + 55
45. 57 + 26
46. 87 − 33
47. 96 − 22
48. 74 − 36

B

Choose one method for each group of six problems.

1. 239 + 54
2. 516 + 47
3. 627 + 38
4. 539 − 45
5. 618 − 67
6. 263 − 58

7. 17 × 19
8. 22 × 19
9. 26 × 19
10. 18 × 21
11. 23 × 21
12. 21 × 21

13. 503 − 194
14. 702 − 279
15. 614 − 396
16. 8004 − 5991
17. 6000 − 2982
18. 4000 − 3486

19. 34 × 4
20. 57 × 5
21. 42 × 6
22. 24 × 7
23. 28 × 8
24. 32 × 9

25. 60 × 30
26. 70 × 20
27. 30 × 200
28. 70 × 400
29. 30 × 50
30. 40 × 300

31. 15 + 16
32. 25 + 27
33. 35 + 34
34. 45 + 46
35. 15 + 14
36. 25 + 24

37. 15 × 6
38. 12 × 8
39. 13 × 12
40. 128 ÷ 8
41. 180 ÷ 12
42. 189 ÷ 9

43. 468 + 81
44. 467 − 71
45. 284 + 99
46. 4007 − 3006
47. 6005 + 2007
48. 3004 − 1997

C

Choose one method for each group of six problems.

1. □ ÷ 6 = 62
2. □ ÷ 7 = 86
3. □ ÷ 7 = 73
4. □ ÷ 8 = 59
5. □ ÷ 8 = 84
6. □ ÷ 9 = 86

7. 376 − □ = 57
8. 428 − □ = 143
9. 269 − □ = 86
10. □ + 189 = 446
11. 546 − □ = 152
12. □ + 168 = 533

13. 2·8 + □ = 5·6
14. 3·7 + □ = 7·6
15. 4·8 + □ = 9·4
16. 5·7 + □ = 11·5
17. 3·8 + □ = 7·4
18. 2·6 + □ = 5·3

19. 13 × 16
20. 25 × 18
21. 17 × 21
22. 189 ÷ 21
23. 288 ÷ 16
24. 306 ÷ 18

25. □ + 199 = 648
26. □ − 299 = 364
27. □ + 2986 = 8279
28. □ + 111 = 983
29. □ − 202 = 627
30. □ + 3012 = 5828

31. □ × 20 = 8000
32. □ × 50 = 3500
33. □ × 400 = 1200
34. □ × 60 = 42 000
35. □ × 300 = 2400
36. □ × 70 = 2800

37. □ ÷ 49 = 13
38. □ ÷ 51 = 12
39. □ ÷ 99 = 11
40. □ ÷ 101 = 14
41. □ ÷ 49 = 16
42. □ ÷ 99 = 15

43. 728 − □ = 291
44. 532 − □ = 176
45. 641 − □ = 383
46. 5000 − □ = 1784
47. 6004 − □ = 3965
48. 7005 − □ = 2974

I can use a written method for addition calculations.

Examples

```
  57       457       457      1457
+28      +  28     +928     + 961
  85       485      1385      2418
  1         1       1 1        11
```

A

Copy and complete.

1. 183 + 65
2. 456 + 27
3. 692 + 36
4. 305 + 78
5. 761 + 94
6. 496 + 53
7. 547 + 54
8. 337 + 149
9. 254 + 193
10. 529 + 256
11. 681 + 275
12. 738 + 217
13. In one month 384 adults and 65 children stayed at an hotel. How many people stayed at the hotel altogether?
14. In one hour 457 cars were counted passing a school going one way. Only 136 cars were counted going in the opposite direction. How many cars passed the school altogether?

B

Copy and complete.

1. 563 + 398
2. 849 + 728
3. 695 + 563
4. 974 + 672
5. 781 + 368
6. 837 + 649
7. 552 + 587
8. 1785 + 369
9. 1367 + 1295
10. 2948 + 727
11. 4279 + 1098
12. 4693 + 2156

11. Jackie's holiday cost £873. She spent a further £658. How much did she spend altogether?

C

Set out as in the examples.

1. 2684 + 1859
2. 3967 + 1375
3. 5874 + 2687
4. 9864 + 3582
5. 6497 + 1985
6. 8962 + 2479
7. 7659 + 2976
8. 7586 + 6278
9. 6594 + 5257
10. 7739 + 4608
11. There are 8552 ants in one anthill and 3949 ants in another. How many ants are there altogether?
12. After flying 4297 miles, a plane landed for refuelling. It flew a further 2635 miles to complete its journey. How far did the plane fly altogether?
13. Louis had £9674 in his bank account. He paid in a further £949. How much did he now have in his account?

I can use a written method for subtraction calculations.

COUNTING UP

```
 835          or      835
-267                 -267
  33 → 300              33 → 300
 500 → 800             535 → 835
  35 → 835             568
 568
```

DECOMPOSITION (TAKE AWAY METHOD)

```
 92 = 90 + 2 = 80 + 12        8 12
-38 = 30 + 8 = 30 +  8         92
               50 +  4 = 54   -38
                               54
```

A

Work out by counting up.

1. 351 − 183
2. 576 − 264
3. 283 − 56
4. 697 − 442
5. 734 − 197
6. 423 − 365
7. 345 − 89
8. 873 − 557
9. 541 − 194
10. 860 − 228
11. There are 827 trees in a forest. 236 trees are blown down in a gale. How many trees are left?
12. In January a large store sold 675 television sets. 348 fewer sets were sold in February. How many TVs were sold in February?

B

Use the decomposition method.

1. 83 − 37
2. 54 − 28
3. 71 − 25
4. 67 − 39
5. 95 − 26
6. 40 − 24
7. 82 − 55
8. 66 − 48
9. 94 − 57
10. 73 − 49
11. Daniel planned to cycle 91 miles in one day. He stopped for lunch after 43 miles. How much further did he have to go?
12. In ten minutes 86 cars were counted passing the school. 49 were going north. How many were going south?

C

Use the decomposition method.

1. 650 − 328
2. 314 − 174
3. 728 − 291
4. 284 − 135
5. 940 − 217
6. 582 − 265
7. 709 − 556
8. 518 − 379
9. 842 − 257
10. 675 − 568
11. Linda's balloon travelled 364 miles. Jake's travelled 197 miles. How much further did Linda's balloon travel?

A1 NUMBER PROBLEMS

I can use written methods to solve number problems and puzzles.

A

1. Find two numbers with:
   - **a)** a total of 100 and a difference of 30
   - **b)** a total of 200 and a difference of 84
   - **c)** a total of 500 and a difference of 146.

2. I think of a number.
   I add 86.
   I take 147.
   The answer is 215.
   What is my number?

3. I think of a number.
   I take 79.
   I add 54.
   The answer is 154.
   What is my number?

Copy and complete by writing the missing digits in the boxes.

4. 4□ + □3 = 109
5. □7 + 9□ = 130
6. □6 + 5□ = 138
7. 6□ + □4 = 143
8. 9□ − □6 = 36
9. □□7 − 8□ = 85
10. 19□ − □5 = 119
11. 11□ − □7 = 71

B

1. Find two numbers with:
   - **a)** a total of 1000 and a difference of 238
   - **b)** a total of 750 and a difference of 162.

2. I think of a number.
   I subtract 173.
   I add 369.
   The answer is 536.
   What is my number?

3. I think of a number.
   I add 215.
   I subtract 347.
   The answer is 295.
   What is my number?

Copy and complete.

4. 3□8 + □0□ = 563
5. □8□ + 1□8 = 761
6. □1□ − 2□3 = 63
7. 6□1 − □7□ = 413

C

1. Find two numbers with:
   - **a)** a total of 5000 and a difference of 1354
   - **b)** a total of 3800 and a difference of 478.

2. I think of a number.
   I add 2753.
   I subtract 3572.
   The answer is 4839.
   What is my number?

3. I think of a number.
   I subtract 562.
   I add 1716.
   The answer is 2348.
   What is my number?

Copy and complete.

4. □3□8 + 2□7□ = 4243
5. 3□7□ + □5□7 = 5070
6. 4□2□ − □6□9 = 2746
7. 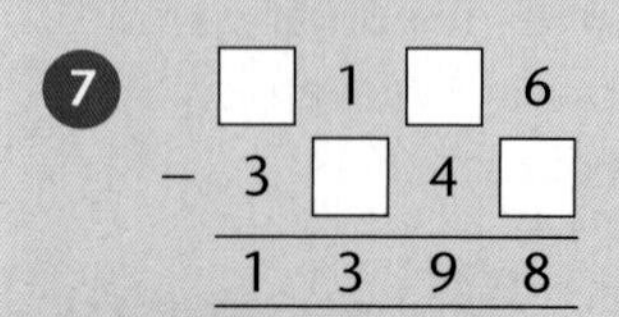
   □1□6 − 3□4□ = 1398

I can find all the factors of a two-digit number.

Factors are numbers that divide exactly into another number.
Factors can be shown by creating arrays.

Example
Two arrays can be created using 8 squares.

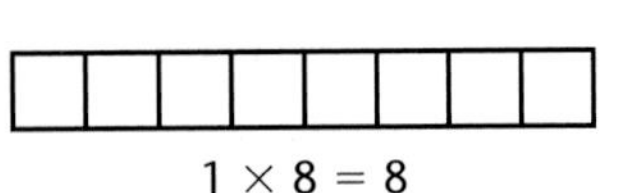

$1 \times 8 = 8$

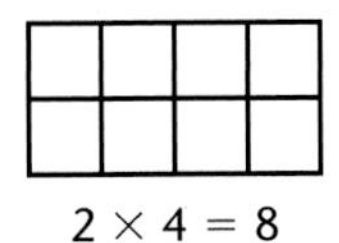

$2 \times 4 = 8$

The factors of 8 are 1, 2, 4, 8

A

1. What are the two factors of 6 shown in this array?

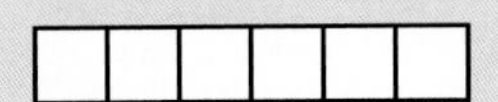

2. Draw a different array to show the other two factors of 6.
3. List the four factors of 6.
4. This array shows that 2 and 6 are factors of 12.

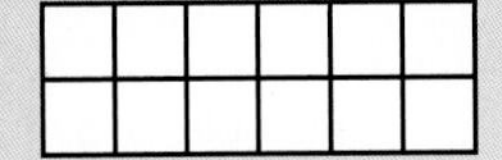

Draw two different arrays to show the other four factors of 12.

5. List the six factors of 12.
6. Draw two different arrays using 10 squares. List the four factors of 10.
7. Draw three different arrays using 18 squares. List the six factors of 18.

B

1. Copy and complete this table for all numbers from 11 to 20.

Number	Number of arrays	Factors
10	2	1, 2, 5, 10
11	1	1, 11
12	3	

2. Which of the numbers between 10 and 20 make a square array?
3. Can you explain why this number has a square array?
4. Numbers which have a square array are called square numbers. Give two more examples of square numbers by drawing their arrays.

List all the factors of these numbers. The number of factors is shown in the brackets.

5. 33(4)
6. 45(6)
7. 9(3)
8. 24(8)

C

1. The fourth square number is 16. List the first 10 square numbers.

Work out:

2. the 15th square number
3. the 20th square number
4. the 100th square number.

Find all the factors of the following numbers.

5. 20
6. 33
7. 64
8. 27
9. 80
10. 26
11. 66
12. 81
13. 45
14. 56
15. 78
16. 96

Fill in the box to complete each pair of factors.

17. $88 = 11 \times \square$
18. $360 = 90 \times \square$
19. $7200 = 80 \times \square$
20. $4000 = 800 \times \square$
21. $4800 = 160 \times \square$
22. $7500 = 150 \times \square$
23. $630 = 7 \times \square$
24. $320 = 40 \times \square$

I can classify numbers using Venn and Carroll diagrams.

Multiples are the numbers in a multiplication table.
The multiples of 2 are the numbers in the 2 times tables.

2, 4, 6, 8 …… 32, 34, 36, 38 … and so on

15 20 30 42 64 80 97 100

This Carroll diagram shows how the above numbers were sorted.

	under 50	not under 50
multiples of 10	20 30	80 100
not multiples of 10	15 42	64 97

6 16 20 30 50 64 75 80

This Venn diagram shows how the above numbers were sorted.

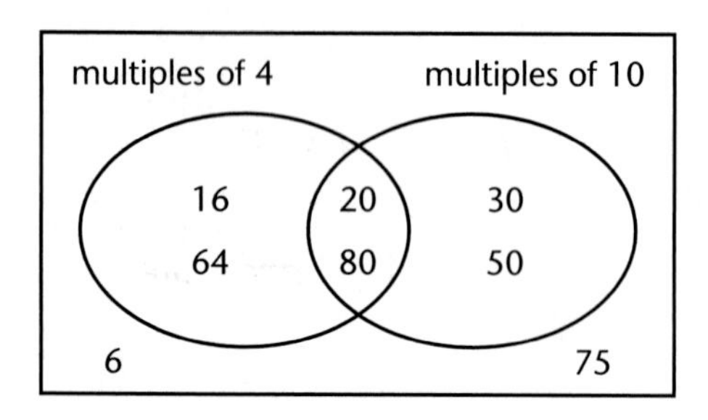

20 and 80 are common multiples of 4 and 10.

A

1 Copy the Carroll diagram and use it to sort the numbers.

	odd	not odd
over 50		
not over 50		

31 87 54 48 96 65
22 78 45 16 53 37

2 Copy the Venn diagram and sort these numbers by writing them in the right places.

16 20 32 35 38 40 42 50

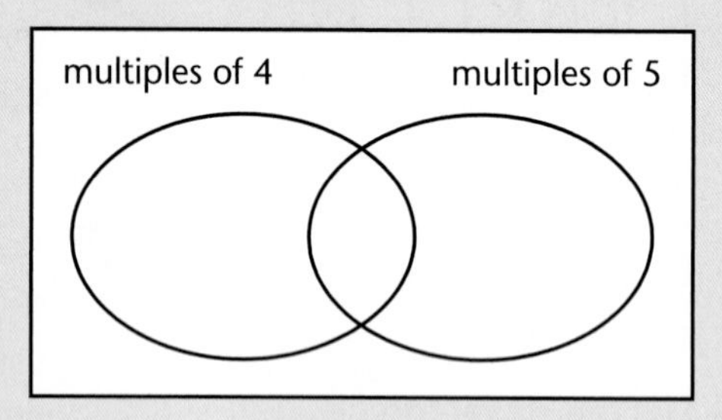

3 Use the numbers from 1 to 20.

a) List the multiples of 2.

b) List the multiples of 5.

c) Which numbers appear in both lists?

d) List all the numbers up to 100 which are multiples of both 2 and 5.

B

1. Copy the Carroll diagram and use it to sort these numbers.

   60 151 8 52 210 45
   5 87 70 195 38 306

	multiples of 5	not multiples of 5
2-digit numbers		
not 2-digit numbers		

2. Copy the Venn diagram and use it to sort the numbers 1 to 30.

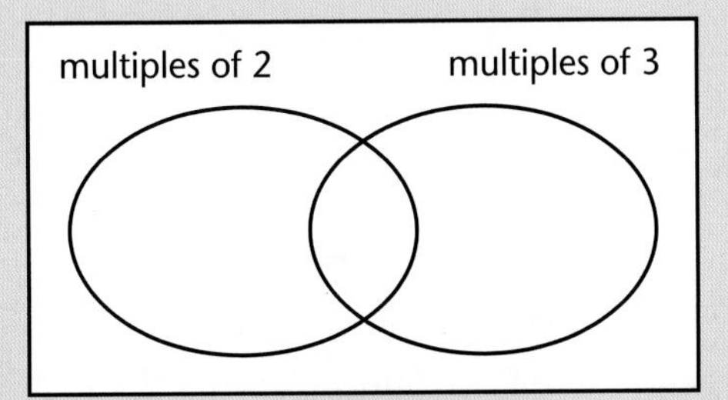

3. Which numbers in your diagram are common multiples of 2 and 3?

4. List the other two-digit numbers which are common multiples of 2 and 3.

5. Find three examples to match this statement.

   All common multiples of 3 and 4 are multiples of 12.

Find three numbers that are common multiples of:

6. 3 and 5
7. 5 and 10
8. 2 and 7
9. 4 and 5
10. 3 and 8.

C

1. Copy the Venn diagram and use it to sort the multiples of 3 under 50.

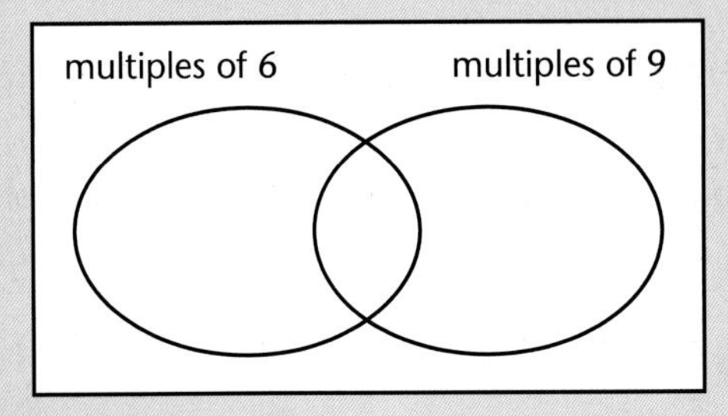

2. Copy the Carroll diagram and use it to sort all the even numbers to 36.

	multiples of 4	not multiples of 4
multiples of 6		
not multiples of 6		

3. Which of the numbers in your diagram are common multiples of 4 and 6?

4. List all the common multiples of 4 and 6 below 100.

5. Find three examples to match this statement.

   All common multiples of 2, 3 and 5 are multiples of 30.

Find three common multiples of:

6. 2, 3 and 7
7. 2, 5 and 9
8. 3, 4 and 5
9. 2, 7 and 9
10. 3, 5 and 8.

B1 MULTIPLICATION FACTS

I can quickly recall the multiplication and division facts to 10 × 10.

A

What is

1. 9 × 2
2. 4 × 9
3. 7 × 4
4. 6 × 7
5. 5 × 5
6. 7 × 6
7. 8 × 5
8. 6 × 9
9. 7 × 2
10. 4 × 6
11. 9 × 3
12. 7 × 8
13. 24 ÷ 3
14. 16 ÷ 8
15. 12 ÷ 2
16. 48 ÷ 6
17. 36 ÷ 4
18. 35 ÷ 7
19. 24 ÷ 4
20. 56 ÷ 7
21. 21 ÷ 3
22. 40 ÷ 8
23. 81 ÷ 9
24. 35 ÷ 5

B

Copy and complete.

1. □ × 6 = 72
2. □ × 2 = 16
3. □ × 7 = 28
4. □ × 9 = 45
5. □ × 5 = 45
6. □ × 8 = 64
7. □ ÷ 4 = 5
8. □ ÷ 7 = 3
9. □ ÷ 6 = 4
10. □ ÷ 3 = 8
11. □ ÷ 8 = 4
12. □ ÷ 9 = 7

Write the answer only.

13. 60 × 3
14. 90 × 8
15. 700 × 7
16. 800 × 4
17. 30 × 9
18. 500 × 6
19. 90 × 9
20. 800 × 5
21. 600 × 8
22. 30 × 6
23. 60 × 2
24. 500 × 7
25. 3000 ÷ 5
26. 630 ÷ 7
27. 7200 ÷ 9
28. 1800 ÷ 2
29. 420 ÷ 6
30. 2400 ÷ 8
31. 240 ÷ 60
32. 2700 ÷ 30
33. 540 ÷ 90
34. 420 ÷ 70
35. 3600 ÷ 40
36. 5600 ÷ 80

C

Copy and complete.

1. □ × 7 = 140
2. □ × 3 = 2100
3. □ × 6 = 5400
4. □ × 9 = 2700
5. □ × 5 = 350
6. □ × 8 = 3200
7. □ ÷ 6 = 500
8. □ ÷ 2 = 70
9. □ ÷ 7 = 80
10. □ ÷ 4 = 600
11. □ ÷ 8 = 500
12. □ ÷ 9 = 70

Write the answer only.

13. 0·6 × 6
14. 0·8 × 3
15. 0·9 × 8
16. 0·4 × 9
17. 0·8 × 2
18. 0·9 × 7
19. 4·8 ÷ 8
20. 2·4 ÷ 6
21. 3·2 ÷ 4
22. 4·5 ÷ 9
23. 4·9 ÷ 7
24. 4·5 ÷ 5
25. 2 × 0·9
26. 8 × 0·6
27. 7 × 0·4
28. 6 × 0·7
29. 3 × 0·8
30. 5 × 0·5
31. 0·28 ÷ 7
32. 0·42 ÷ 6
33. 0·18 ÷ 2
34. 0·64 ÷ 8
35. 0·18 ÷ 3
36. 0·72 ÷ 9

I can use rounding to estimate addition and subtraction calculations.

Always look at the column to the right of that to which you are rounding.

Examples

ROUNDING TO THE NEAREST:

10 362 → 360
100 8681 → 8700
1000 6546 → 7000
1 0·7 → 1 4·52 → 5

ESTIMATING CALCULATIONS

327 + 244
rounds to
330 + 240 = 570
Answer is about 570.

518 − 247
rounds to
520 − 250
Answer is about 270.

A

Round to the nearest 10.

1. 63
2. 31
3. 27
4. 49
5. 84
6. 96
7. 72
8. 18
9. 37
10. 65

Round to the nearest 100.

11. 836
12. 194
13. 505
14. 343
15. 299
16. 654
17. 461
18. 727
19. 283
20. 852

Estimate and then work out.

21. 294 + 135
22. 158 + 169
23. 371 + 218
24. 436 + 172

25. 68 − 37
26. 87 − 61
27. 94 − 46
28. 75 − 23

B

Choose the correct answer and then work out to check.

1. 923 − 289
   a) 624 c) 724
   b) 634 d) 734
2. 2988 + 1736
   a) 4524 c) 4724
   b) 4624 d) 4824

Copy and complete.

3. 8□14 − 369□ = 4818
4. 4□93 + 253□ = 7231
5. 297□ + 3□68 = 6242
6. 532□ − 1□53 = 3575

Estimate and then work out.

7. 436 + 323
8. 352 + 217
9. 269 + 352
10. 524 + 345

11. 361 − 138
12. 625 − 317
13. 753 − 394
14. 479 − 282

C

Choose the correct answer and then work out to check.

1. 40·65 + 35·47
   a) 75·12 c) 77·12
   b) 76·12
2. 38·05 − 23·78
   a) 14·27 c) 16·27
   b) 15·27

Copy and complete.

3. 494·□ + 3□7·5 = 862·3
4. 722·□ − 5□8·8 = 173·7
5. 8□·17 − 26·4□ = 56·68
6. 4□·36 + 20·5□ = 66·95

Estimate and then work out.

7. 536·5 + 124·8
8. 441·6 + 358·2
9. 21·54 + 17·39
10. 36·27 + 28·91

11. 321·5 − 149·4
12. 583·6 − 272·9
13. 76·21 − 35·87
14. 61·53 − 53·68

I can describe the properties of 3-D shapes.

A

Match each of the shapes A to L with one of the names of 3-D shapes.

cone	hemisphere	sphere
cube	hexagonal based prism	square based pyramid
cuboid	octagonal based prism	triangular based prism
cylinder	pentagonal based prism	triangular based pyramid

A 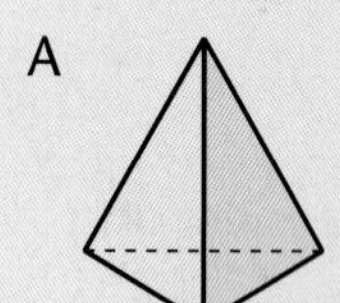
B 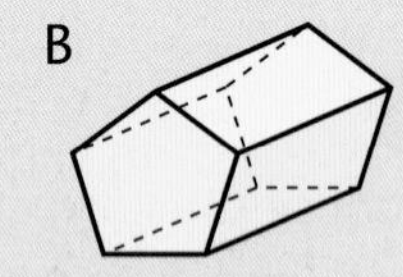
C 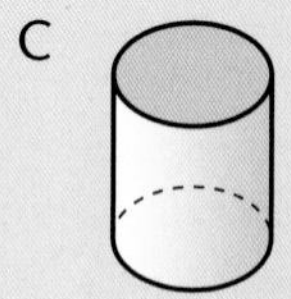
D 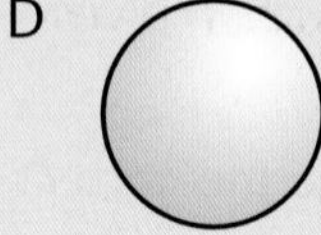
E 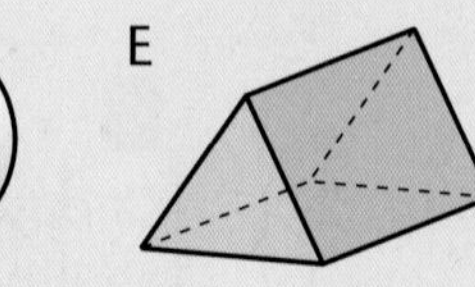
F  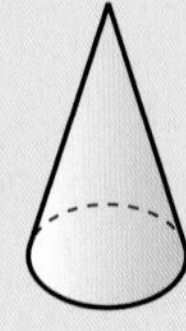

G 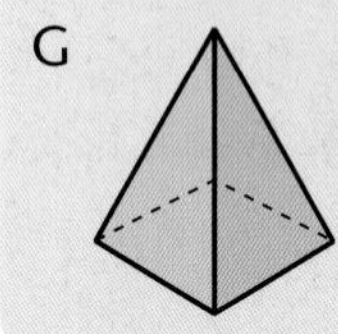
H 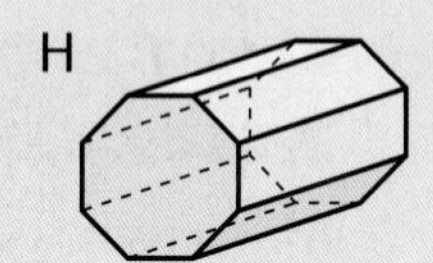
I 
J 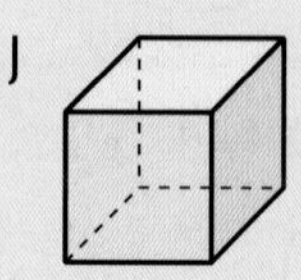
K 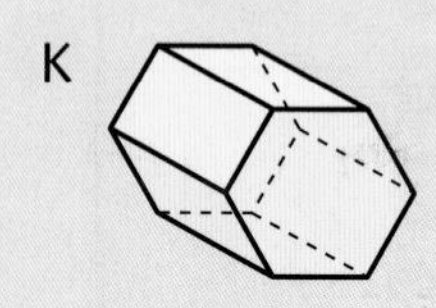
L 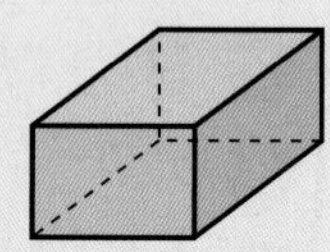

B

1 Write the names of:

a) 4 shapes with curved faces

b) 6 shapes which are prisms

c) 2 shapes with 5 faces

d) 2 shapes with 8 vertices

e) 2 shapes with an odd number of edges

f) 2 shapes each having identical faces.

2 Most of the above shapes with straight edges have the same number of edges meeting at each vertex.
Which shape is different?
Explain why.

3 Altogether there are eight different nets for an open cube.
Can you find the other seven?

C

1 Copy and complete this table showing the features of some 3-D shapes.

Name	Faces	Edges	Vertices
cube			
		15	
			4
		9	
	5		
			16
		12	
	8		

2 How many edges are there in:

a) a pentagonal pyramid

b) a decagonal (10 sided) prism?

3 How many faces are there in:

a) an heptagonal prism

b) an octagonal pyramid?

I can predict which quadrilaterals have diagonals that bisect each other or are of equal length.

DIAGONALS

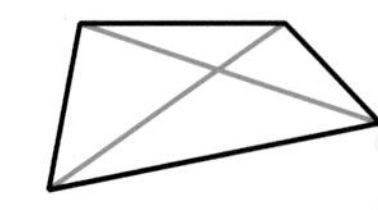

Diagonal lines go from one vertex of a shape to another.

LINES WHICH BISECT

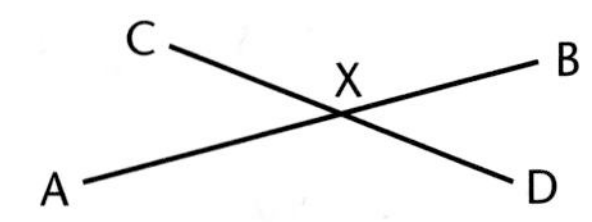

AX = BX
CX = DX

Bisect means cut in half. Lines which bisect cut each other in half.

PERPENDICULAR LINES

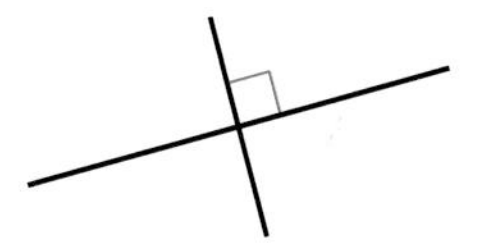

Perpendicular lines cross or meet at a right angle.

A

1. Use squared paper.
   Draw a square.
   Draw on the diagonals.

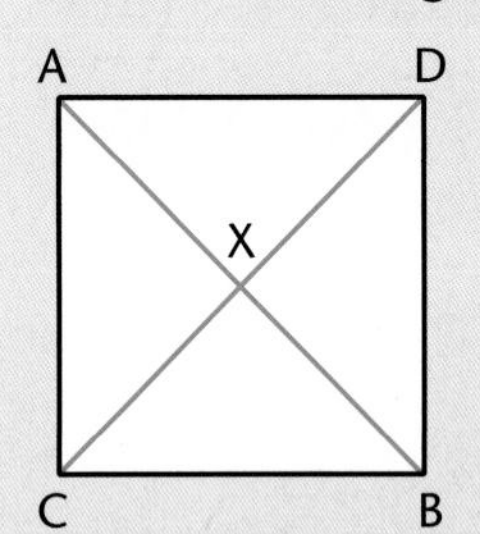

2. Measure the diagonals, AB and CD. Are they of equal length?
3. Measure AX and BX.
   Measure CX and DX.
   What do you find?
4. Use a set square.
   Do the diagonals cross at a right angle?
5. Draw a rectangle.
   Draw on the diagonals.
   - **a)** Are the diagonals of equal length?
   - **b)** Do the diagonals bisect each other?
   - **c)** Are the diagonals perpendicular?

B

For each of the quadrilaterals predict whether the diagonals:

a) are of equal length

b) bisect each other

c) are perpendicular.

1. 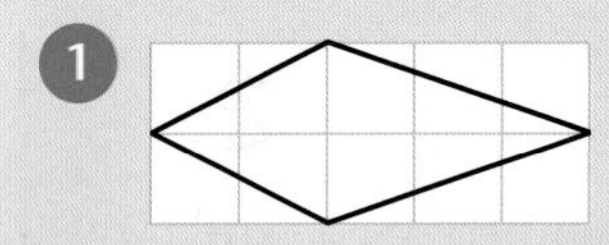
2. 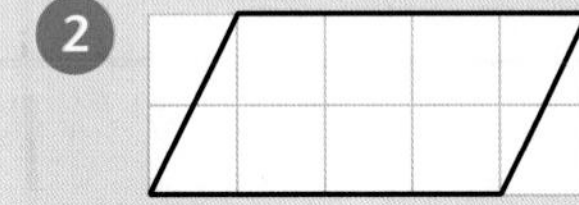
3. 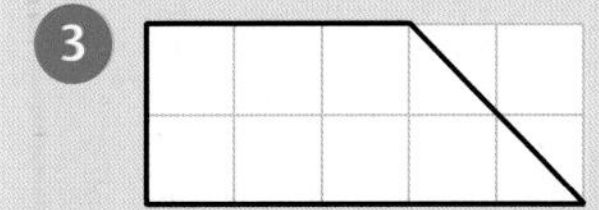
4. 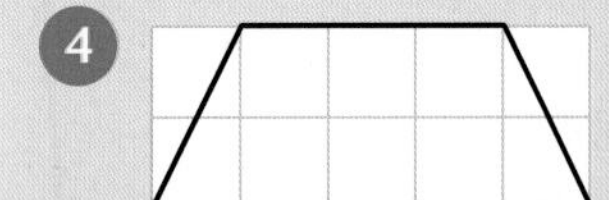
5. 
6. 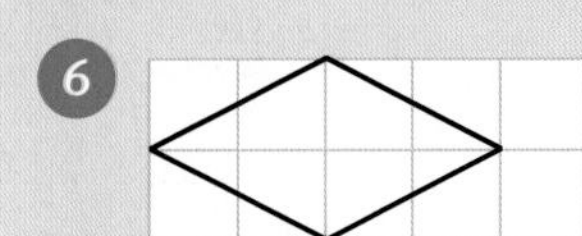
7. Copy the shapes onto squared paper. Draw on the diagonals.
   Check your predictions.

C

The following lines are the diagonals of quadrilaterals. For each pair of lines predict the properties of the shape. Are any pairs of lines equal, parallel or perpendicular? Are any angles equal? Is the shape symmetrical?
(Equal lines are shown with dashes. Right angles are marked.)

1 and 4

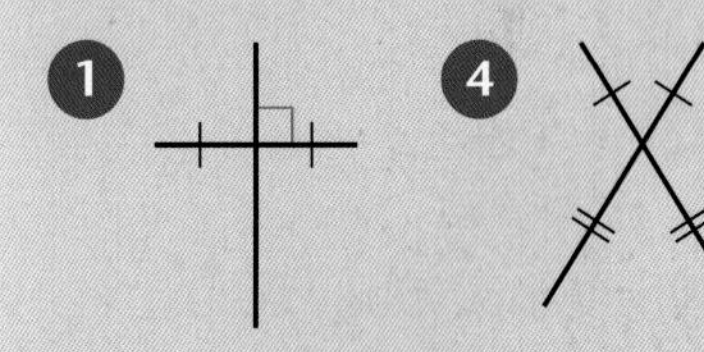

2 and 5

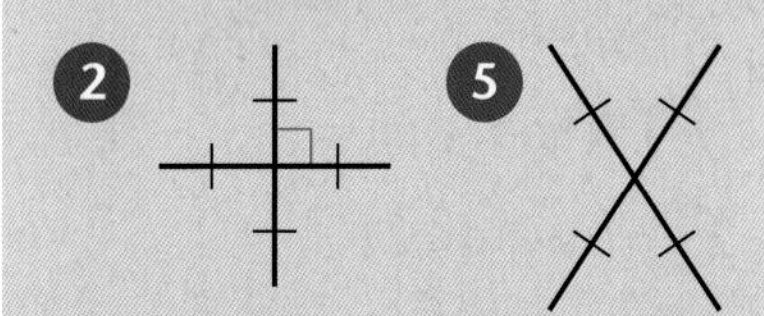

3 and 6

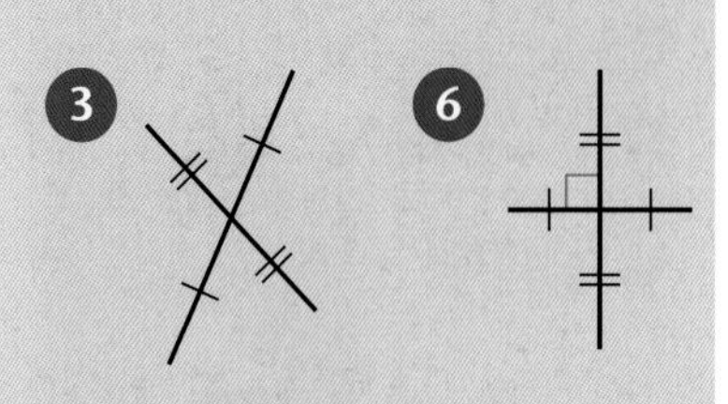

7. Construct the shapes.
   Check your predictions.

C1 METRIC UNITS OF WEIGHT

I can choose and use metric units to measure weight.

Examples

1000 g = 1 kg   3500 g = 3·5 kg   9120 g = 9·12 kg
6000 g = 6 kg   2600 g = 2·6 kg   4850 g = 4·85 kg

A

Copy and complete.

1. 3000 g = ☐ kg
2. 1000 g = ☐ kg
3. 6000 g = ☐ kg
4. 4 kg = ☐ g
5. 2 kg = ☐ g
6. 7 kg = ☐ g
7. 2500 g = ☐ kg
8. 3500 g = ☐ kg
9. 5500 g = ☐ kg
10. 6·5 kg = ☐ g
11. 1·5 kg = ☐ g
12. 4·5 kg = ☐ g

Which metric unit would you use to measure the weight of:

13. a light bulb
14. a wardrobe
15. a garden spade
16. a calculator
17. a spoon
18. a dog?

B

Copy and complete.

1. 8600 g = ☐ kg
2. 2400 g = ☐ kg
3. 800 g = ☐ kg
4. 3·1 kg = ☐ g
5. 1·2 kg = ☐ g
6. 9·7 kg = ☐ g
7. 5300 g = ☐ kg
8. 7100 g = ☐ kg
9. 6400 g = ☐ kg
10. 2·9 kg = ☐ g
11. 8·3 kg = ☐ g
12. 0·7 kg = ☐ g

Which metric unit would you use to measure the weight of:

13. a set of encyclopaedias
14. an egg
15. a piano
16. a telephone?

17. Think of three things with a weight of about:
    a) 1 g
    b) 100 g
    c) 1 kg.

C

Copy and complete.

1. 3160 g = ☐ kg
2. 390 g = ☐ kg
3. 4620 g = ☐ kg
4. 8·08 kg = ☐ g
5. 2·75 kg = ☐ g
6. 5·47 kg = ☐ g
7. 1940 g = ☐ kg
8. 6160 g = ☐ kg
9. 7530 g = ☐ kg
10. 0·22 kg = ☐ g
11. 2·31 kg = ☐ g
12. 9·85 kg = ☐ g

Copy and complete each sentence by choosing the best estimate.

13. At birth many babies have a mass of about (0·35 kg, 3·5 kg, 35 kg).
14. One pound coins have a mass of about (1 g, 10 g, 100 g).
15. Many footballers weigh about (70 kg, 700 kg, 7000 kg).
16. A tin of beans has a mass of about (0·004 kg), 0·04 kg, 0·4 kg).

I can organise a set of data into a table and find the mode.

Example

The marks in Class 4's weekly spelling test.

10 9 9 7 8 8 10 9
9 8 10 9 9 10 9 10
8 10 6 9 8 9 10 8
10 9 10 8 9 7 9 10

A tally chart showing the marks.

Marks	Tally	Total
6	|	1
7	||	2
8	卌 |	6
9	卌 卌 |||	13
10	卌 卌	10

The mode is the most common value.

Which mark is the mode?

Answer 9

A

The lengths in minutes of the tracks on a CD.

4 3 5 3 4
3 2 3 4 5
3 5 4 6 3
5 3 4 3 4

1. Copy and complete the frequency table for the above data.

Length (minutes)	Number of tracks

2. How many tracks are:
   a) 4 minutes long
   b) 6 minutes long?
3. How long is:
   a) the shortest track
   b) the longest track?
4. What is the most common length of track?

B

The ages of the girls in a Brownies pack.

9 8 10 8 9 8
10 8 9 7 8 9
8 10 8 9 8 10
8 7 9 8 11 9

1. Draw a tally chart to find the number of girls of each age.
2. Which age is the mode?
3. How many girls are in the pack?

The number of letters in the first names of Class 5.

6 4 7 3 6 5 7
8 5 6 5 7 6 4
7 9 6 4 8 5 6
4 7 8 6 5 3 7

4. Draw a frequency table to show the total for each name length.
5. How many letters is the mode?
6. How many names are longer than 7 letters?

C

The highest daily temperatures recorded in November.

11 10 8 12 7 13
12 9 10 11 12 8
13 6 12 8 13 10
7 12 8 10 9 13
10 8 13 7 12 11

1. Draw a frequency table or tally chart to find the number of days each temperature was recorded.
2. On how many days was the temperature:
   a) more than 10°C
   b) less than 10°C?
3. Which temperature was the mode?
4. What was the range (the difference between the highest and the lowest value) of the temperatures?
5. Find the range for each set of data in Sections A and B.

I can organise data using tables and tallies and present results in bar charts and pictograms.

Examples

A tally chart showing the numbers of bunches of bananas sold by a greengrocer each day.

Day	Tally	Total
Tuesday	卌 卌 ||	12
Wednesday	卌 ||||	9
Thursday	卌 卌 |||	13
Friday	卌 卌 卌 |	16
Saturday	卌 卌 卌 ||||	19

The data in the tally chart can be shown in a pictogram.

Tuesday

Wednesday

Thursday

Friday

Saturday

represents 2 bunches of bananas.

The data can also be shown in a bar chart.

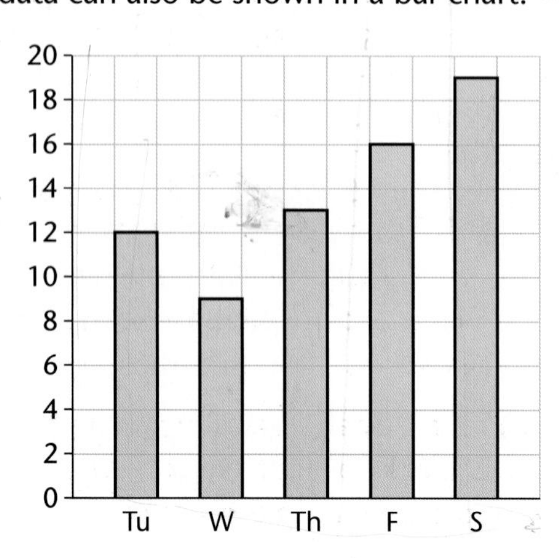

The children in Class 5 chose their favourite fruit. These were the results.

Fruit	Votes
apples	8
bananas	14
grapes	7
melon	6
oranges	11

1. Draw a bar chart to show the information.
2. Draw a pictogram to show the information.
3. Which way shows the information most clearly? Give a reason for your answer.

This frequency table shows the number of grapefruit sold each day by a greengrocer.

Day	Grapefruit
Monday	35
Tuesday	40
Wednesday	25
Thursday	60
Friday	75
Saturday	90

4. Draw a bar chart to show the information. You will need to use a different scale to the one which you used in Question 1.

Janice kept a record of how many portions of fruit and vegetables she ate each day for 4 weeks. These are the results.

3	4	0	3	4	2	3
1	3	5	2	4	3	4
3	2	4	5	1	3	2
3	4	6	3	4	2	3

1. Present the results as:
   - **a)** a frequency table
   - **b)** a pictogram
   - **c)** a bar chart.

2. For each of the three methods of presenting the data, write down:
   - **a)** one way in which it shows the information more clearly than the other two methods
   - **b)** one way in which it is less clear than the other two methods.

3. All the children in Class 5 kept a record of the number of portions of fruit and vegetables they ate each day for one week. This information was collected to provide the following class data.

Daily Portions of Fruit and Vegetables	Frequency
1	10
2	15
3	40
4	55
5	65
6	10
7	5

Present the above data in a bar chart or pictogram.

The weights in grams of the 30 apples brought to school by Class 5

165	150	180	135	120	155
125	115	145	185	150	140
160	130	165	155	145	175
140	150	160	110	150	130
155	190	135	160	170	145

1. Copy and complete the tally showing the grouped weights.

Weight (g)	Tally	Total
101–120	|||	3
121–140		
141–160		
161–180		
181–200		

2. Display the data in a bar chart.

3. This table shows the numbers of different desserts chosen each day for one week in the school canteen.

Desserts	M	Tu	W	Th	F
Cake	35	80	70	25	50
Fruit	60	35	55	50	30
Ice Cream	75	45	35	80	55
Yoghurt	45	50	75	55	75

   - **a)** Draw a pictogram to show the number of ice creams chosen each day.
   - **b)** Draw a bar chart to show the total number of each type of dessert chosen during the week.

D1 CONVERTING UNITS OF LENGTH

I can multiply and divide whole numbers by 10, 100 and 1000 and use this to convert units of length.

		Examples	
×/÷ by 10	units move 1 place to left/right	57 × 10 = 570	300 ÷ 10 = 30
×/÷ by 100	units move 2 places to left/right	8 × 100 = 800	5000 ÷ 100 = 50
×/÷ by 1000	units move 3 places to left/right	4 × 1000 = 4000	3000 ÷ 1000 = 3

A

×10

1. 42
2. 80
3. 136
4. 57

÷10

5. 200
6. 920
7. 3000
8. 780

×100

9. 24
10. 60
11. 7
12. 91

÷100

13. 600
14. 4100
15. 8000
16. 1500

×1000

17. 3
18. 12
19. 5
20. 40

÷1000

21. 29 000
22. 70 000
23. 9000
24. 46 000

Copy and complete.

25. ☐ × 10 = 370
26. ☐ × 100 = 2000
27. ☐ × 1000 = 7000
28. ☐ ÷ 10 = 640
29. ☐ ÷ 100 = 19
30. ☐ ÷ 1000 = 8

B

Copy and complete.

1. ☐ × 100 = 46 000
2. 27 × ☐ = 27 000
3. ☐ ÷ 10 = 1670
4. 9000 ÷ ☐ = 90
5. ☐ × 10 = 3140
6. 18 × ☐ = 1800
7. ☐ ÷ 1000 = 65
8. 16 700 ÷ ☐ = 1670

Copy and complete.

9. 7 cm = ☐ mm
10. 2 cm = ☐ mm
11. 60 mm = ☐ cm
12. 100 mm = ☐ cm
13. 3 m = ☐ cm
14. 12 m = ☐ cm
15. 900 cm = ☐ m
16. 2400 cm = ☐ m
17. 5 km = ☐ m
18. 42 km = ☐ m
19. 8000 m = ☐ km
20. 10 000 m = ☐ km

C

Copy and complete.

1. 70 000 × ☐ = 700 000
2. ☐ × 100 = 300 000
3. 260 × ☐ = 260 000
4. ☐ × 10 = 62 000
5. 157 000 ÷ ☐ = 1570
6. ☐ ÷ 1000 = 347
7. 493 000 ÷ ☐ = 49 300
8. ☐ ÷ 100 = 286

Copy and complete.

9. 3·9 cm = ☐ mm
10. 0·6 cm = ☐ mm
11. 117 mm = ☐ cm
12. 58 mm = ☐ cm
13. 1·8 m = ☐ cm
14. 0·57 m = ☐ cm
15. 243 cm = ☐ m
16. 9 cm = ☐ m
17. 2·7 km = ☐ m
18. 0·8 km = ☐ m
19. 1500 m = ☐ km
20. 4360 m = ☐ km

I can solve problems involving length.

A

1. One shelf is 65 cm long. Another shelf is 78 cm long. What is their total length in metres?
2. Lisa is 1·50 m tall. Shaun is 35 cm shorter. How tall is Shaun in metres?
3. Gary needs 10 pieces of ribbon. Each piece must be 50 cm long. How many metres of ribbon does he need to buy?
4. A machine makes a staple from 20 mm of wire. How many staples will it make from 50 cm of wire?
5. Grace walks 80 m in one minute. How far does she walk in one hour in kilometres?
6. Ethan's middle finger is 10·6 cm long. His ring finger is 9 mm shorter. How long is his ring finger in centimetres?
7. A square field has a perimeter of 1·2 km. How long is one side of the field in metres?

B

1. A cyclist travels 2 km in eight minutes. How far in metres does she cycle in one minute?
2. Jacob jumps 1·95 m. The winning jump is 17 cm higher. What is the height of the winning jump?
3. A golf hole is 0·43 km long. A golfer drives the ball 264 m. How much further does he have to play?
4. There are 24 tiles in a stack. Each tile is 8 mm thick. How high is the stack in centimetres?
5. Each paper tissue is 20 cm long. How many metres of paper are needed to fill a box with 150 tissues?
6. Stuart is 1·28 m tall. His father is 38 cm taller. How tall is Stuart's father?
7. The top shelf is 96 cm long. The two lower shelves are both 64 cm long. What is the combined length of the shelves in metres?

C

1. Samantha saws four strips of 52 cm from a 3 m length of wood. How long is the wood that is left?
2. A table has a perimeter of 5 m. It is 68 cm wide. What is its length?
3. A set of encyclopaedias takes up 96 cm of shelving. Each volume is 32 mm wide. How many encyclopaedias are there in the set?
4. An athlete trains by running 300 m eight times and 200 m six times. How far does he run in kilometres?

5. A mineshaft is 0·78 km long. A further 367 m is drilled. How long is the mineshaft in metres?
6. A candle is 12 cm tall. 36 mm is used. How long is the candle that is left in centimetres?

I can estimate and measure lengths and work out the perimeter of a regular or an irregular polygon.

Examples

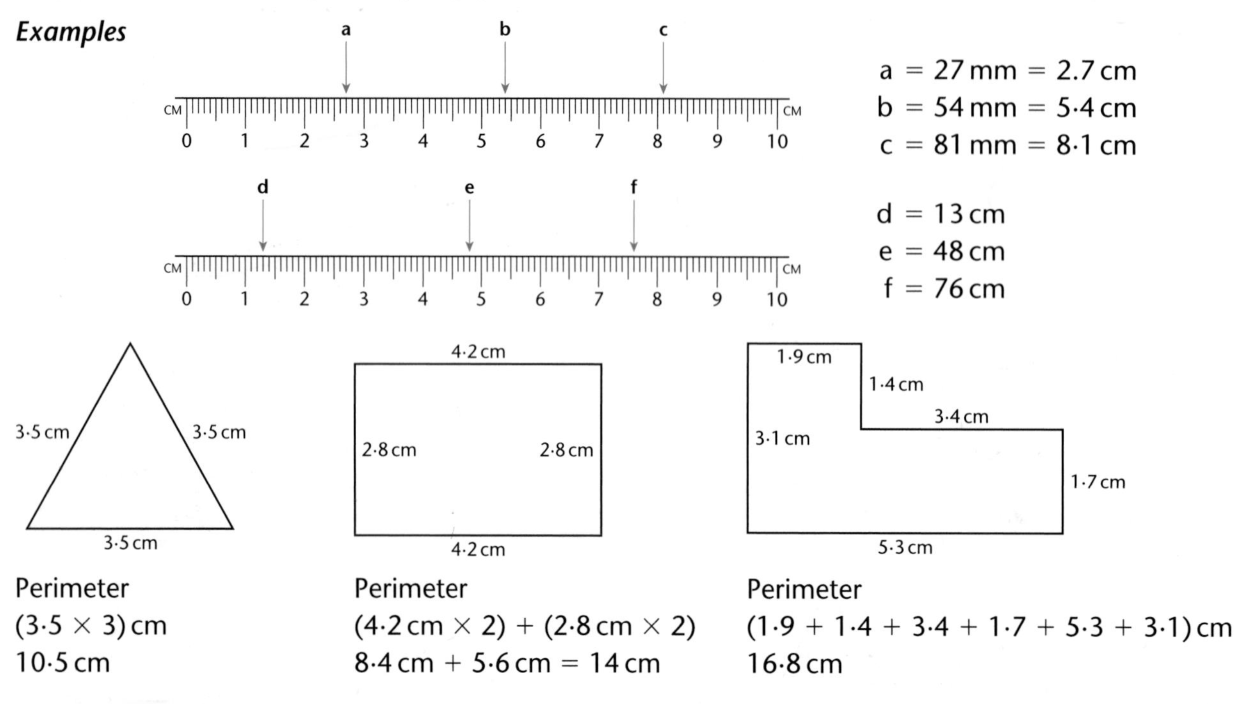

Perimeter
(3·5 × 3) cm
10·5 cm

Perimeter
(4·2 cm × 2) + (2·8 cm × 2)
8·4 cm + 5·6 cm = 14 cm

Perimeter
(1·9 + 1·4 + 3·4 + 1·7 + 5·3 + 3·1) cm
16·8 cm

A

Read the measurements shown on each scale.

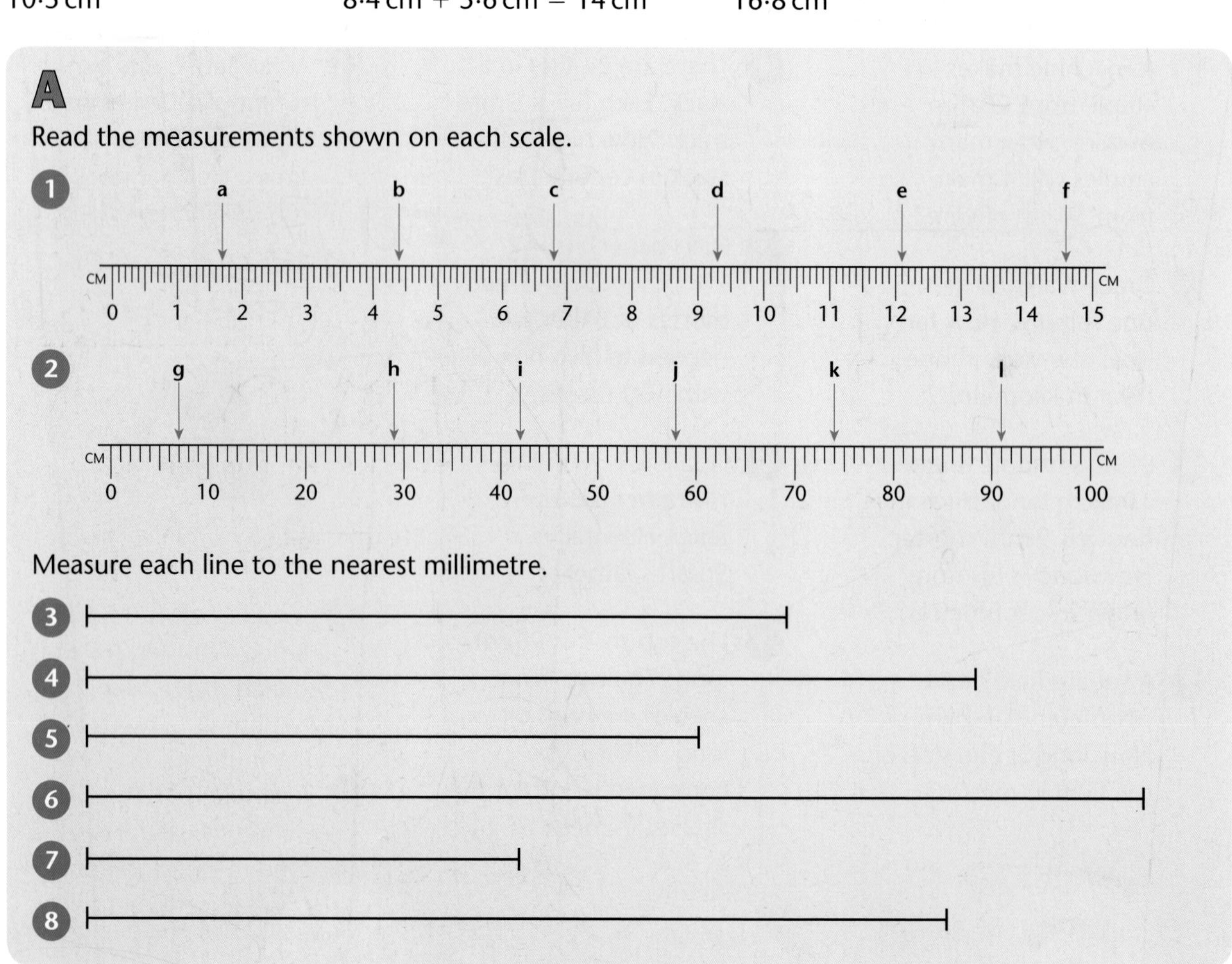

B

1. For each shape:
   a) measure the sides to the nearest mm
   b) work out the perimeter.

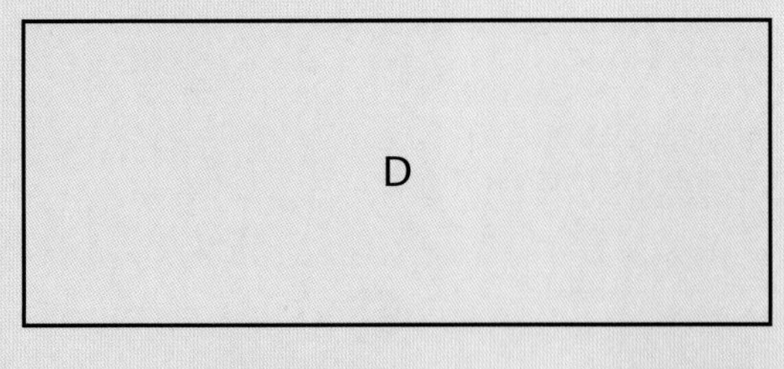

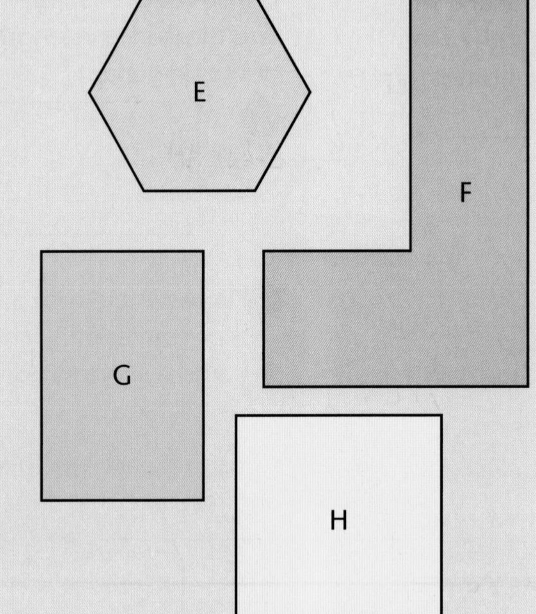

For each of the following lengths:

a) estimate the measurement

b) measure

c) work out the difference between your estimate and the actual length.

2. the width of a book
3. the length of a finger nail
4. the height of a chair
5. the length of a display board
6. the length of a drawing pin
7. the length of a radiator
8. the thickness of a shelf
9. the length of a corridor

C

1. For each shape:
   a) measure the sides to the nearest mm
   b) work out the perimeter.

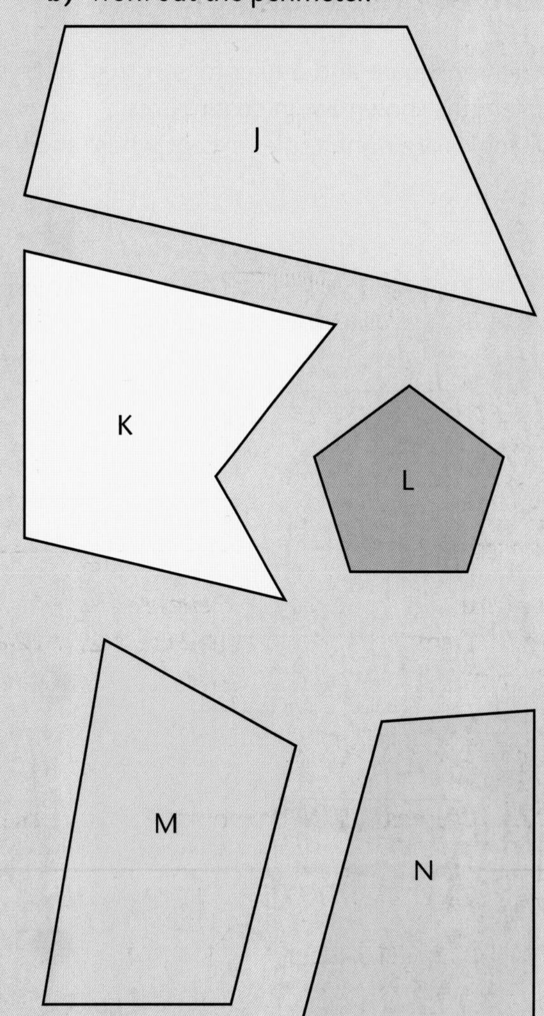

For each of the following objects:

a) estimate the perimeter

b) measure the sides and work out the perimeter

c) work out the difference.

2. a table
3. a book
4. a mat
5. a door
6. a sheet of A4 paper
7. a stamp or sticker
8. a set square
9. the playground

I can use a set square and a ruler to construct squares, rectangles and right angled triangles.

Use a set square and a ruler to construct each shape.
All lengths shown are in centimetres.
All angles are right angles except where shown with an arc as in this example.

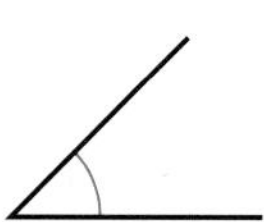

A

Construct each shape and check that the opposite sides are equal.

1

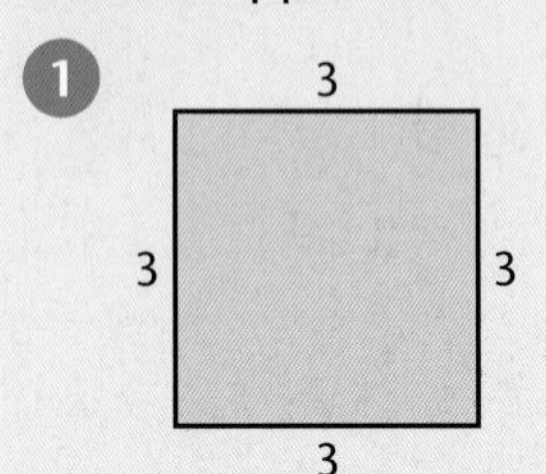

2

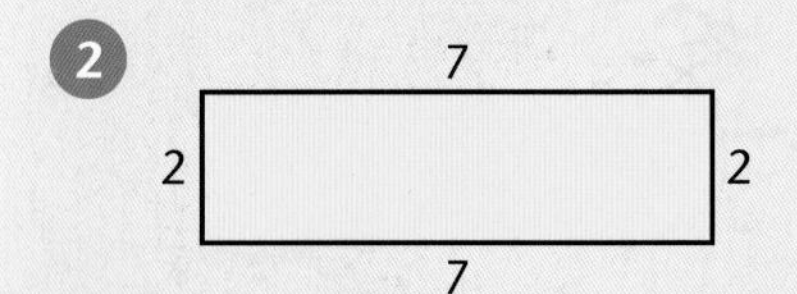

3

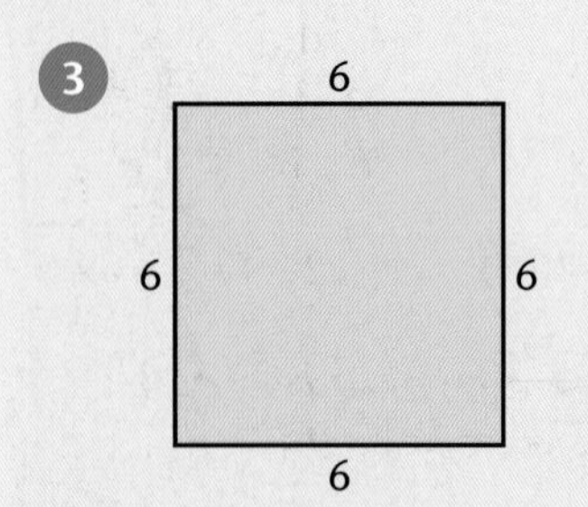

4

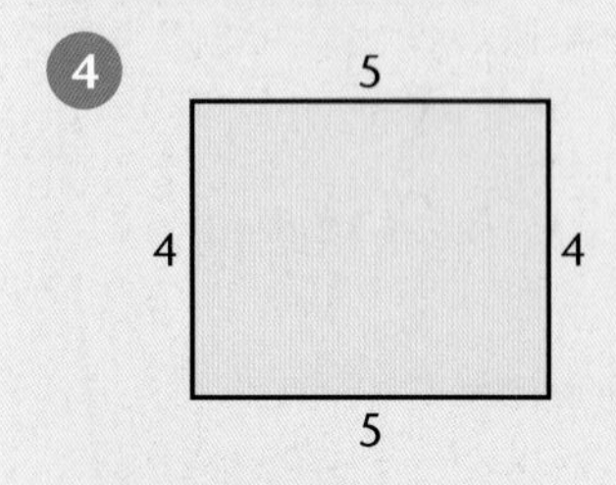

5. Construct a square with a perimeter of 16 cm.
6. Construct a rectangle with a perimeter of 18 cm and a longest side of 6 cm.
7. Construct a rectangle with a perimeter of 20 cm and a shortest side of 2 cm.

B

Construct each shape and measure the length of the diagonal to the nearest mm.

1

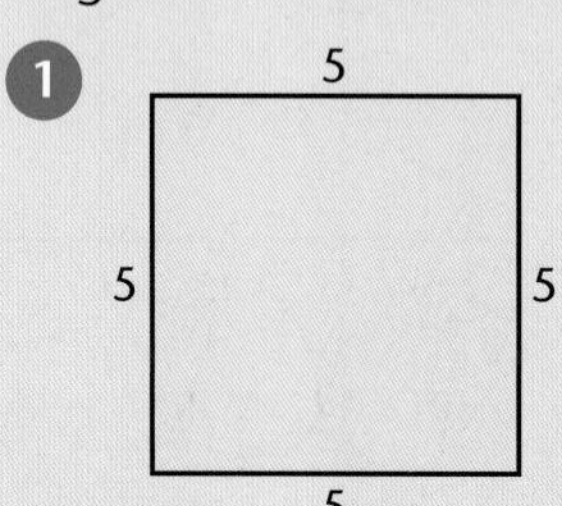

2

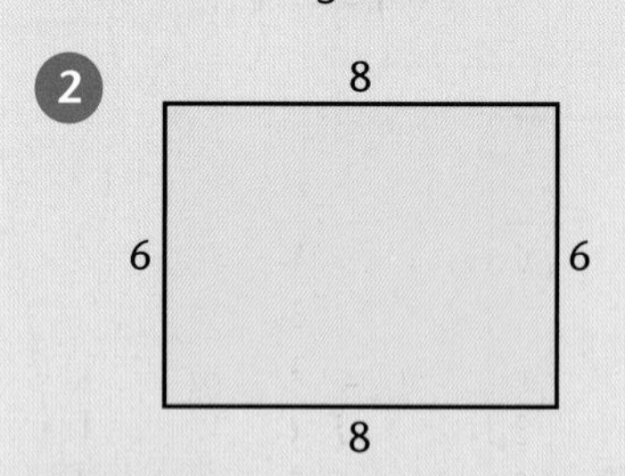

3. a square with a perimeter of 14 cm.
4. a rectangle with a perimeter of 17 cm and a longest side of 4·5 cm.

Construct each triangle and measure the length of the longest side to the nearest mm.

5

6

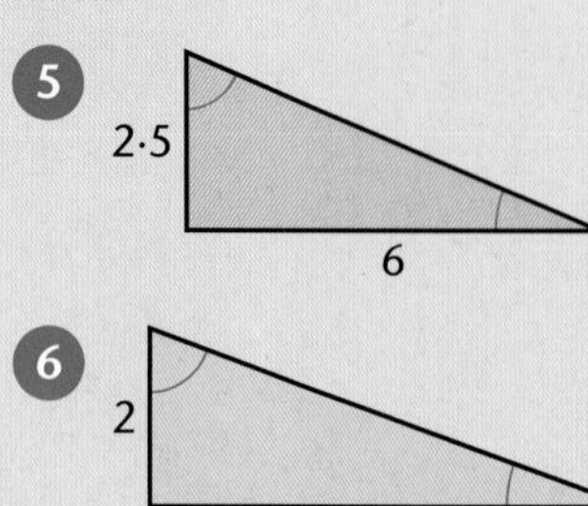

C

Construct each shape and measure the length of the diagonal.

1

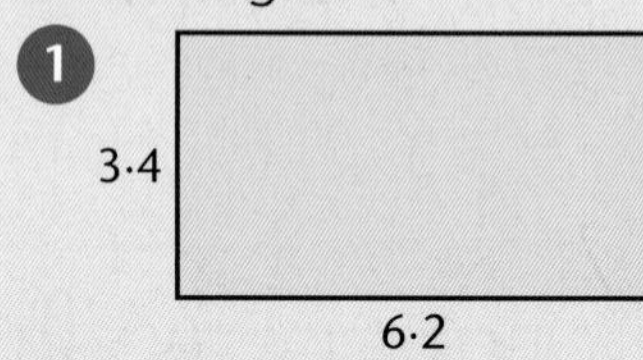

2. a rectangle with a perimeter of 30 cm and a shortest side of 4·7 cm.

Construct each triangle and measure the longest side.

3

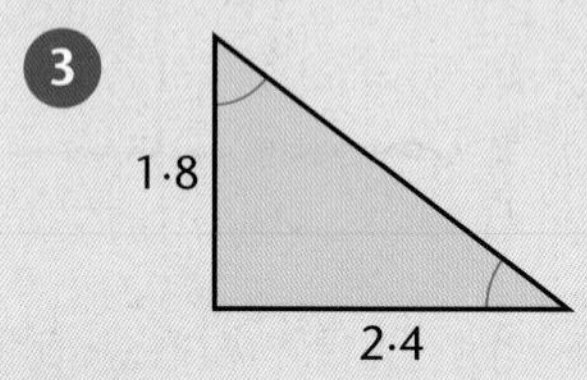

4

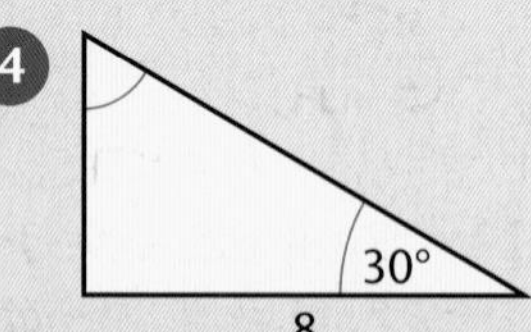

5. Construct the irregular pentagon. Find the height of the shape.

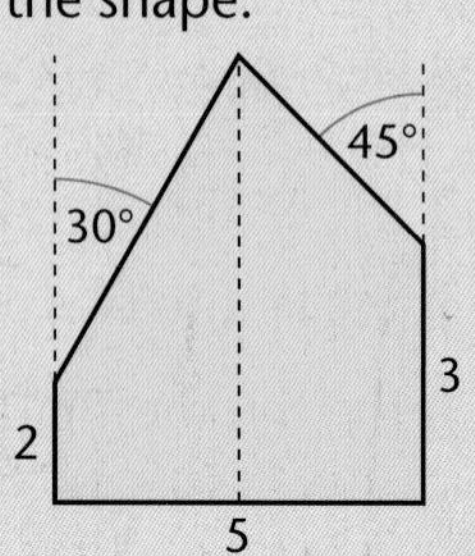

D1 CALENDARS

I can use a calendar to find the day of the week for a particular date and to find how long it is between two dates.

30 days has September,
April, June and November.
All the rest have 31,
Save for February alone,
Which has but 28 days clear
And 29 in each leap year.

Leap years occur every four years. The years which are leap years are easy to remember because they are multiples of four: 2004, 2008, 2012, etc.

How many days are there in:

1. March
2. April
3. May and June
4. July and August?

FEBRUARY						
Su	**M**	**Tu**	**W**	**Th**	**F**	**Sa**
	1	2	3	4	5	6
7	8	9	10	11	12	13
14	15	16	17	18	19	20
21	22	23	24	25	26	27
28						

5. Look at the calendar. Is this a leap year? How do you know?
6. On what day will these children have their birthday?
   a) Gavin – 4th February
   b) Kate – 23rd February
   c) Davina – 6th March
   d) Amy – 31st January
7. Jack's birthday is on the first Saturday of February. Rose's birthday is one week later. When is Rose's birthday?
8. Half term starts on Friday 23rd October. It lasts one week. What is the date of the first Monday back at school?

B

What will be the date two weeks after:

1. 22nd April
2. 18th September
3. 25th December
4. 19th October?

MARCH 2011						
Su	**M**	**Tu**	**W**	**Th**	**F**	**Sa**
		1	2	3	4	5
6	7	8	9	10	11	12
13	14	15	16	17	18	19
20	21	22	23	24	25	26
27	28	29	30	31		

Use the above calendar. On what day of the week do these birthdays fall?

5. Leon – March 13th
6. Meera – March 23rd
7. Marc – February 25th
8. Judy – April 10th
9. Write out the calendar for April 2011.
10. Christmas Day is a Tuesday. What day of the week is New Year's Eve?

C

What will be the date five weeks after:

1. 10th October
2. 8th June
3. 28th November
4. 26th March?

JANUARY 2015						
Su	**M**	**Tu**	**W**	**Th**	**F**	**Sa**
				1	2	3
4	5	6	7	8	9	10
11	12	13	14	15	16	17
18	19	20	21	22	23	24
25	26	27	28	29	30	31

On which day will these Saint's Days fall?

5. St. Stephen's Day December 26th 2014
6. St. David's Day March 1st 2015
7. St. Andrew's Day November 30th 2014
8. How many complete weeks and days left over are there in a non-leap year?

On what day will fall:

9. January 1st 2014
10. January 1st 2016?

I can use am and pm for 12-hour clock times and convert these to 24-hour clock times.

Examples

Analogue clocks have faces.
Read the minutes as:
past before 30 minutes
to after 30 minutes.

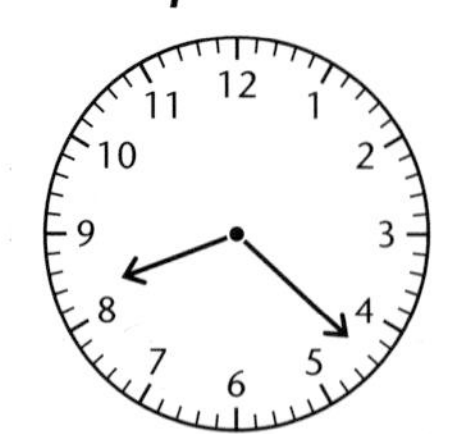

Digital clocks have figures only.
The minutes are always shown
as minutes past the hour.

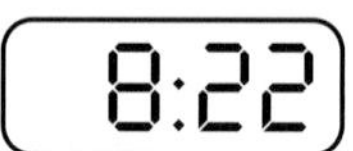

6:48

12-hour clock time uses am and pm.
am means before 12 noon.
pm means after 12 noon.

morning	evening
8:22 am	6:48 pm

24-hour clocks always have four
digits on display. Midnight is 00:00.

08:22   18:48

A

Write each time shown to the nearest minute:

a) in words   **b)** in 12-hour clock time using am and pm.

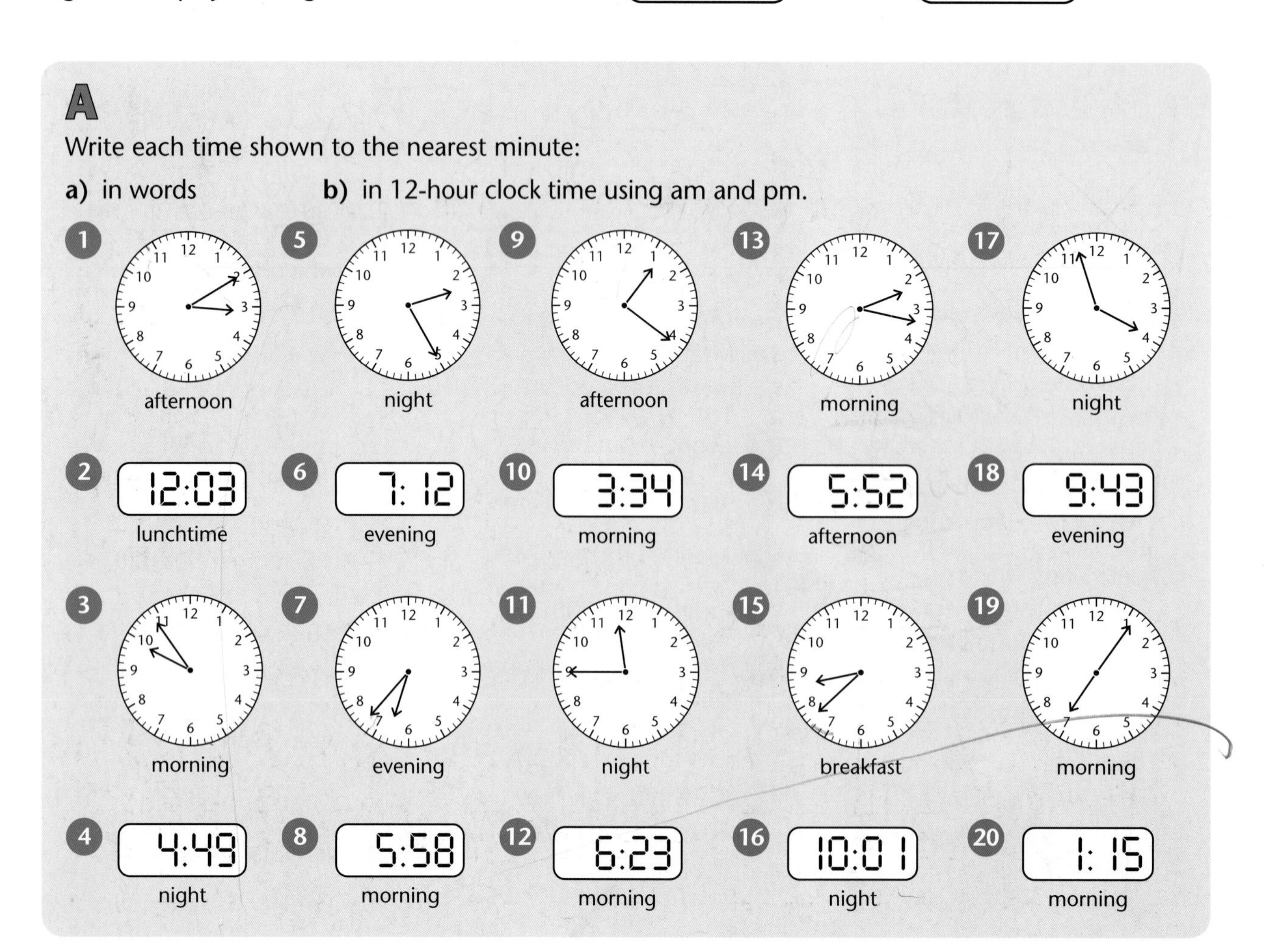

B

1 Copy and complete the table.

TIME IN WORDS	12-HOUR CLOCK	24-HOUR CLOCK
quarter to eight in the morning	7:45 am	07:45
		20:30
		10:35
		03:52
		14:24
	4:08 am	
	10:19 pm	
	9:37 am	
	6:16 pm	
28 minutes past 11 in the morning		
7 minutes to 7 in the evening		
4 minutes past 1 at night		
12 minutes to 4 in the afternoon		

2 For each of the above times work out how many minutes there are to the next hour.

C

Write each time shown to the nearest minute:

a) in words **b)** in 12-hour clock time **c)** in 24-hour clock time.

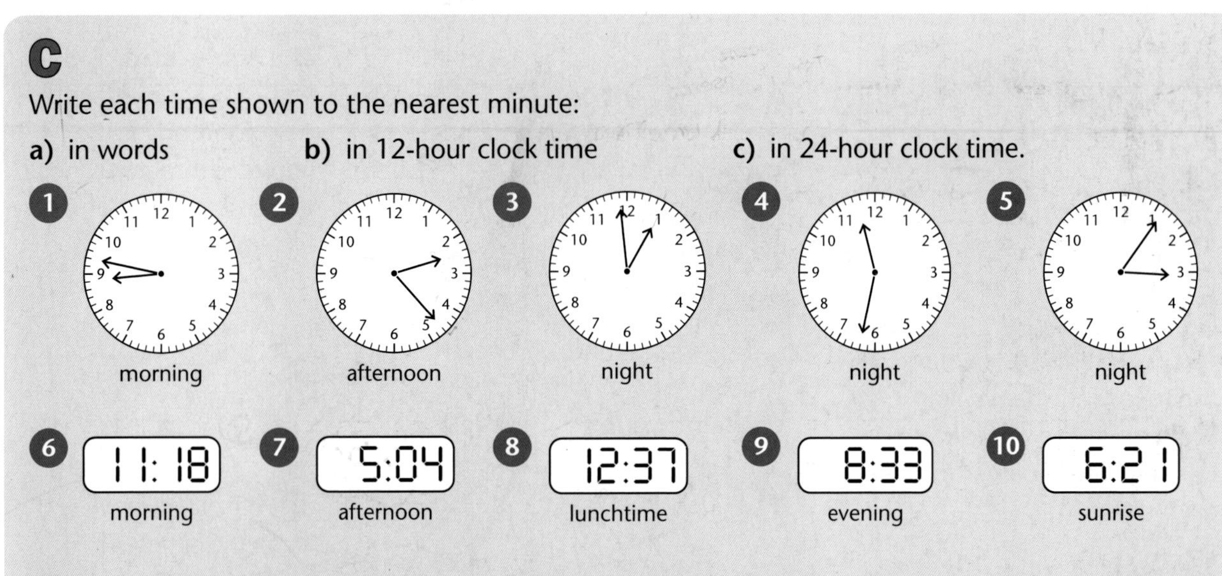

11 For each of the above times work out how many hours and minutes there are to midnight.

12 Copy and complete the table, changing 12-hour clock times to 24-hour clock times.

	Jan. 2nd	March 6th	May 1st	July 3rd	Sept. 4th	Nov. 6th
Sunrise	8:06 am	6:36 am	5:34 am	4:49 am	6:17 am	7:02 am
Sunset	4:03 pm	5:49 pm	8:23 pm	9:20 pm	7:41 pm	4:26 pm
Daylight length	7 h 57 mins.					

I can read and plot co-ordinates and find the missing points of shapes.

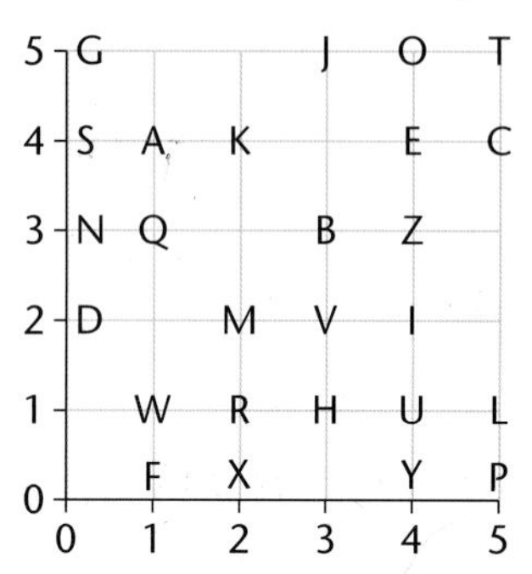

The position of a point on a grid is given by its x and y co-ordinates.

Examples

Point A is (1, 4).
Point U is (4, 1).
Point D is (0, 2).

Remember:
The x co-ordinate always comes first.

A

Use the above grid.
Which letter is at point:

1. (5, 1)
2. (1, 3)
3. (4, 5)
4. (2, 0)
5. (3, 5)
6. (0, 4)
7. (2, 1)
8. (5, 0)

Give the position of:

9. N
10. H
11. F
12. C
13. Z
14. G
15. K
16. V

Draw a 5 × 5 grid.
Plot the points for each of the following shapes. Join them up in the order given. Use a different colour for each shape.

17. (2, 1) (3, 4) (4, 1) (2, 1)
18. (0, 3) (0, 5) (2, 5) (2, 3) (0, 3)
19. (0, 0) (0, 2) (5, 0) (0, 0)
20. (5, 2) (5, 4) (1, 4) (1, 2) (5, 2)

B

Use the above grid to write the name of:

1. your teacher
2. your favourite colour
3. a pop group
4. a football team.
5. A(2, 6) B D C(7, 2)

   Write the co-ordinates of points B and D.
6. (5, 9) (10, 9) and (5, 4) are three vertices of a square. What is the fourth vertex?
7. 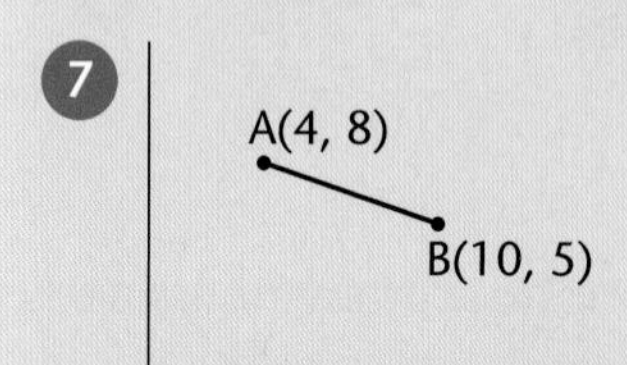

   AB is one side of the right-angled triangle ABC. Give the co-ordinates of point C. How many solutions can you find?

C

1. (1, 3) (3, 5) and (4, 0) are three vertices of a rectangle. What is the fourth vertex?
2. 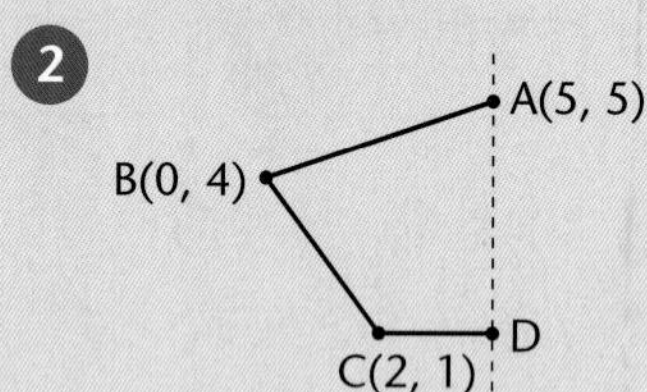

   The above shape is one half of a symmetrical pentagon. AD is the line of symmetry. Find the co-ordinates of the two missing vertices.
3. 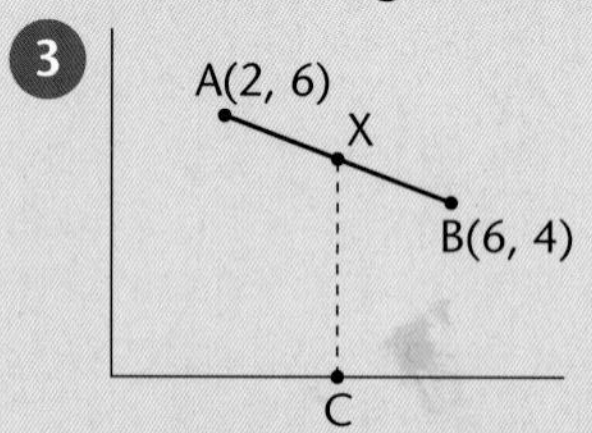

   a) Point X is the mid-point of line AB. Give the co-ordinates of X.
   b) Line XC is parallel to the y axis. Give the co-ordinates of C.
   c) D is the fourth vertex of square ABCD. Give the co-ordinates of D.

E1 MULTIPLICATION FACTS

I can use multiplication facts to multiply and divide multiples of 10 and 100.

A

What is

1. 3 × 9
2. 7 × 2
3. 6 × 8
4. 9 × 6
5. 8 × 5
6. 2 × 7
7. 6 × 3
8. 5 × 6
9. 7 × 9
10. 9 × 4
11. 8 × 7
12. 4 × 8
13. 36 ÷ 6
14. 21 ÷ 3
15. 18 ÷ 9
16. 64 ÷ 8
17. 30 ÷ 5
18. 28 ÷ 7
19. 16 ÷ 2
20. 81 ÷ 9
21. 18 ÷ 6
22. 42 ÷ 7
23. 32 ÷ 4
24. 40 ÷ 8

B

Copy and complete.

1. ☐ × 5 = 45
2. ☐ × 9 = 36
3. ☐ × 4 = 28
4. ☐ × 7 = 35
5. ☐ × 8 = 72
6. ☐ × 6 = 48
7. ☐ ÷ 2 = 9
8. ☐ ÷ 7 = 7
9. ☐ ÷ 9 = 6
10. ☐ ÷ 3 = 9
11. ☐ ÷ 6 = 2
12. ☐ ÷ 8 = 3

Write the answer only.

13. 60 × 4
14. 70 × 60
15. 800 × 3
16. 5 × 90
17. 700 × 80
18. 3 × 700
19. 60 × 200
20. 80 × 90
21. 2 × 80
22. 700 × 50
23. 900 × 7
24. 40 × 60
25. 3200 ÷ 8
26. 180 ÷ 2
27. 5600 ÷ 70
28. 28 000 ÷ 400
29. 300 ÷ 60
30. 6300 ÷ 90
31. 4000 ÷ 500
32. 14 000 ÷ 70
33. 5400 ÷ 6
34. 210 ÷ 3
35. 2700 ÷ 90
36. 48 000 ÷ 800

C

Copy and complete.

1. ☐ × 7 = 210
2. ☐ × 20 = 1400
3. ☐ × 900 = 54 000
4. ☐ × 60 = 24 000
5. ☐ × 50 = 300
6. ☐ × 8 = 5600
7. ☐ ÷ 90 = 20
8. ☐ ÷ 400 = 80
9. ☐ ÷ 7 = 60
10. ☐ ÷ 600 = 6
11. ☐ ÷ 30 = 90
12. ☐ ÷ 80 = 500

Write the answer only.

13. 6 × 0·4
14. 9 × 0·7
15. 8 × 0·2
16. 9 × 0·8
17. 8 × 0·9
18. 3 × 0·6
19. 0·9 × 5
20. 0·2 × 8
21. 0·5 × 9
22. 0·4 × 7
23. 0·8 × 3
24. 0·7 × 6
25. 8·1 ÷ 9
26. 3·5 ÷ 5
27. 6·4 ÷ 8
28. 3·0 ÷ 6
29. 3·6 ÷ 4
30. 4·9 ÷ 7
31. 1·2 ÷ 2
32. 3·6 ÷ 9
33. 4·8 ÷ 6
34. 1·8 ÷ 3
35. 2·4 ÷ 8
36. 4 ÷ 5

I can multiply and divide TU by U by using partitioning or by using factors and I can suggest linked division calculations with the same answer.

Examples

BY PARTITIONING

53×6 | $78 \div 6$
$(50 + 3) \times 6$ | $(60 + 18) \div 6$
$300 + 18$ | $10 + 3$
318 | 13

USING FACTORS

15×6 | $90 \div 6$
$15 \times 2 \times 3$ | $(90 \div 3) \div 2$
30×3 | $30 \div 2$
90 | 15

LINKED CALCULATIONS

$112 \div 16 = 7$ | $1120 \div 16 = 70$
$56 \div 8 = 7$ | $560 \div 8 = 70$
$28 \div 4 = 7$ | $280 \div 4 = 70$
$14 \div 2 = 7$ | $140 \div 2 = 70$

A

Use partitioning to work out.

1. 13×3
2. 18×3
3. 24×3
4. 12×4
5. 19×4
6. 23×4
7. $34 \div 2$
8. $60 \div 5$
9. $39 \div 3$
10. $56 \div 4$
11. $46 \div 2$
12. $75 \div 5$

Copy and complete to work out.

13. $7 \times 6 = (7 \times 3) \times 2$
14. $9 \times 8 = (9 \times 4) \times 2$
15. $9 \times 6 = (9 \times 3) \times 2$
16. $60 \div 4 = (60 \div 2) \div 2$
17. $84 \div 6 = (84 \div 2) \div 3$
18. $108 \div 12 = (108 \div 2) \div 6$

Use a calculator.
Copy and complete.

19. $128 \div \square = 8$
20. $64 \div \square = 8$
21. $32 \div \square = 8$
22. $16 \div \square = 8$
23. Find similar linked calculations.

B

Use partitioning

1. 34×4
2. 57×5
3. 42×6
4. 24×7
5. 28×8
6. 32×9
7. $84 \div 6$
8. $76 \div 4$
9. $78 \div 3$
10. $94 \div 2$
11. $87 \div 3$
12. $92 \div 4$

Use factors to work out

13. 15×6
14. 12×8
15. 13×12
16. 9×14
17. 17×9
18. 6×18
19. $128 \div 8$
20. $180 \div 12$
21. $126 \div 6$
22. $120 \div 15$
23. $210 \div 14$
24. $252 \div 18$

Use a calculator.
Copy and complete.

25. $1200 \div \square = 50$
26. $600 \div \square = 50$
27. $300 \div \square = 50$
28. $150 \div \square = 50$
29. Find similar linked calculations.

C

Copy and complete.

1. $\square \times 6 = 372$
2. $\square \times 7 = 119$
3. $\square \times 8 = 344$
4. $\square \times 9 = 207$
5. $\square \times 6 = 264$
6. $\square \times 8 = 208$

Use factors to work out

7. 3×16
8. 12×25
9. 17×21
10. 13×24
11. 9×27
12. 25×18
13. $189 \div 21$
14. $288 \div 16$
15. $306 \div 18$
16. $240 \div 16$
17. $270 \div 15$
18. $780 \div 26$

Use a calculator.
Copy and complete.

19. $2160 \div \square = 60$
20. $1080 \div \square = 60$
21. $540 \div \square = 60$
22. $180 \div \square = 60$
23. Find similar linked calculations.

I can use mental methods to solve problems involving multiplication and division.

A

4 5 6 9

Look at the above numbers.

1. Which numbers are factors of:
   - **a)** 30 **c)** 45
   - **b)** 18 **d)** 48?
2. What is the product of:
   - **a)** the two largest numbers
   - **b)** the three smallest numbers?
3. Make two square numbers using the above digits only.

Write Yes or No

4. Is 78 a multiple of 2?
5. Is 42 a multiple of 3?
6. Is 54 a multiple of 4?
7. Is 72 a multiple of 6?

Complete these factor pairs of 90.

8. ☐ and 2
9. ☐ and 15
10. Find all nine factors of 36.
11. Find all six factors of 92.
12. Find a number that is a multiple of both 3 and 7.

B

3 5 7 8

Use the above digits.

1. Which numbers are factors of:
   - **a)** 75 **c)** 84
   - **b)** 56 **d)** 120?
2. What is the product of:
   - **a)** the three largest numbers
   - **b)** the three smallest numbers?
3. Use the above digits to make 2 two-digit multiples of:
   - **a)** 19 **b)** 29.
4. Find two common multiples of:
   - **a)** 4 and 9
   - **b)** 5 and 13.
5. Find all the factors of:
   - **a)** 48 **b)** 76.
6. What is the smallest number with exactly:
   - **a)** 3 factors
   - **b)** 4 factors
   - **c)** 6 factors
   - **d)** 5 factors.
7. What is the largest two-digit number with:
   - **a)** only 2 factors
   - **b)** only 3 factors
   - **c)** only 4 factors.

C

1. What is the smallest number that is a common multiple of:
   - **a)** 2 and 9
   - **b)** 4 and 6
   - **c)** 10 and 8
   - **d)** 9 and 12?
2. Find the highest factor shared by:
   - **a)** 28 and 42
   - **b)** 48 and 64
   - **c)** 36 and 60
   - **d)** 54 and 90.
3. Find a two-digit number with exactly:
   - **a)** 8 factors
   - **b)** 10 factors
   - **c)** 7 factors
   - **d)** 9 factors.
4. What is the largest two-digit number with exactly:
   - **a)** 10 factors
   - **b)** 6 factors
   - **c)** 8 factors
   - **d)** 5 factors?

1 2 5 7 9

5. Use the above digits. Make as many two-digit numbers as you can that are multiples of:
   - **a)** 6 **b)** 4 **c)** 3.

I can multiply HTU by U and TU by TU.

Examples

273		273
× 8		× 8
1600	200 × 8	2184
560	70 × 8	5 2
24	3 × 8	
2184		
1		

46		46	
× 28		× 28	
800	40 × 20	920	46 × 20
120	6 × 20	368	46 × 8
320	40 × 8	1288	
48	6 × 8	1	
1288			
1			

See page 95 for grid method for TU × TU.

A

Work out

1. 39 × 3
2. 58 × 2
3. 17 × 6
4. 36 × 4
5. 14 × 8
6. 28 × 5
7. 23 × 6
8. 45 × 7
9. 16 × 13
10. 29 × 12
11. 24 × 14
12. 18 × 15
13. 27 × 14
14. 35 × 18
15. 29 × 13
16. 46 × 15
17. 3 7 5
    - **a)** Use each of the above digits once only. Find the six different ways you can complete this calculation.

      □□ × □

    - **b)** Which calculation gives you the largest product?
    - **c)** Which gives you the smallest product?

B

Work out

1. 243 × 6
2. 375 × 7
3. 168 × 9
4. 249 × 8
5. 368 × 5
6. 547 × 4
7. 258 × 7
8. 165 × 6
9. 34 × 23
10. 28 × 25
11. 42 × 27
12. 56 × 24
13. 68 × 32
14. 43 × 38
15. 57 × 45
16. 75 × 26
17. Find the largest two-digit number which, multiplied by itself, gives an answer of less than 500.
18. 

    - **a)** Use each digit once only. Find all the ways to complete this calculation.

    - **b)** Which calculation gives you the largest product?
    - **c)** Which gives you the smallest product?

C

Work out

1. 1847 × 2
2. 2792 × 4
3. 2537 × 5
4. 4861 × 3
5. 1936 × 7
6. 2648 × 9
7. 1349 × 6
8. 2759 × 8
9. 128 × 19
10. 247 × 26
11. 171 × 34
12. 365 × 38
13. 192 × 45
14. 436 × 18
15. 259 × 52
16. 378 × 27
17. Find the smallest two-digit number which, multiplied by itself, gives an answer of more than 5000.
18. What is the largest product you can make using:
    - **a)** 2 two-digit numbers
    - **b)** 2 different two-digit numbers?
19. Find two consecutive numbers which give a product of:
    - **a)** 306
    - **b)** 1122
    - **c)** 3192
    - **d)** 8556.

I can find other fractions that are equivalent to a given fraction.

A

Write the equivalent fractions shown in each pair of diagrams.

Example $\frac{2}{5} = \frac{4}{10}$

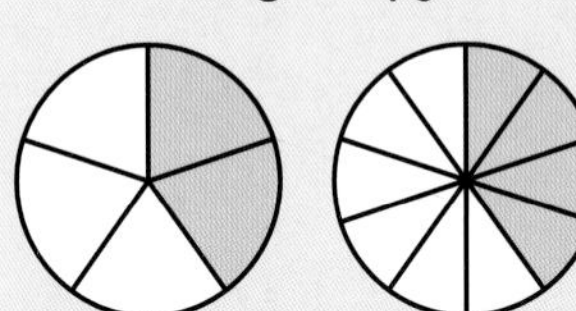

1 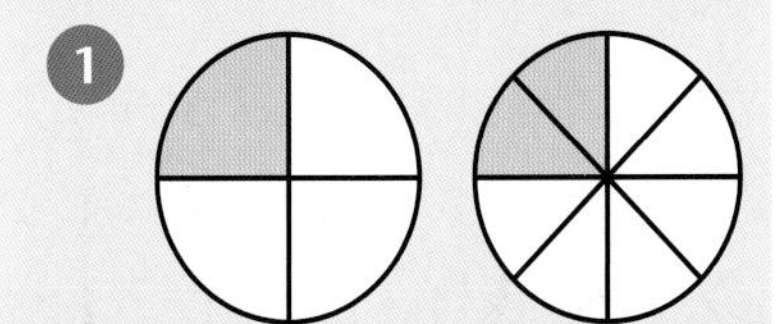

2 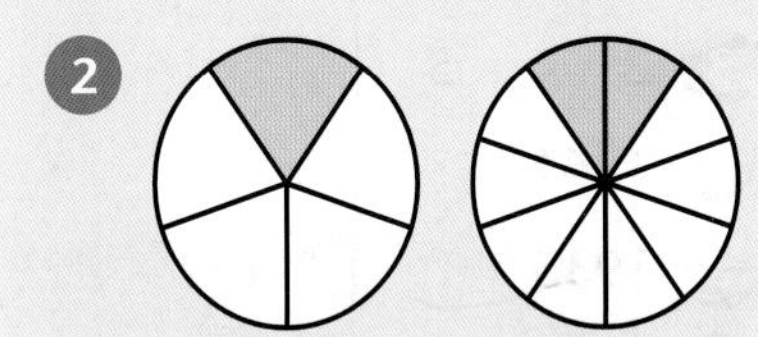

3 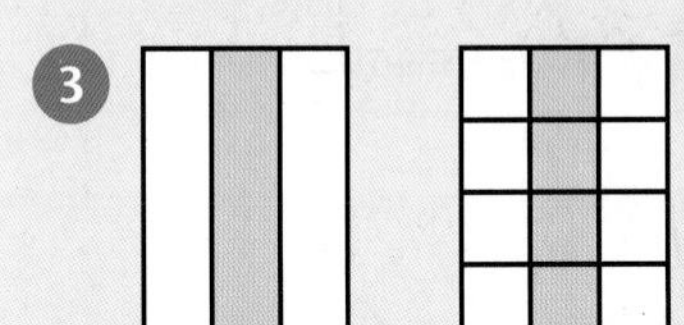

4 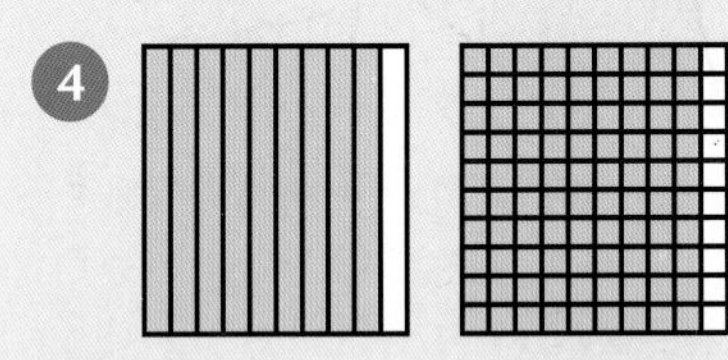

5 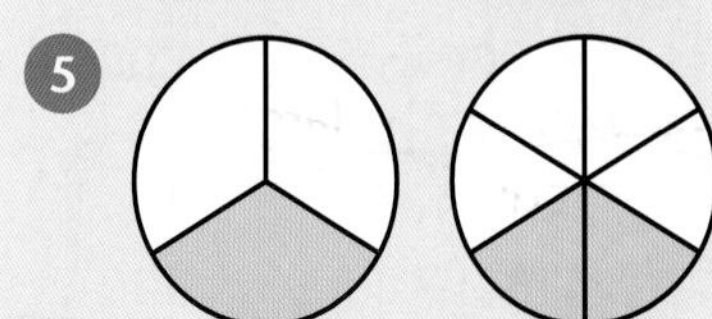

6 

7 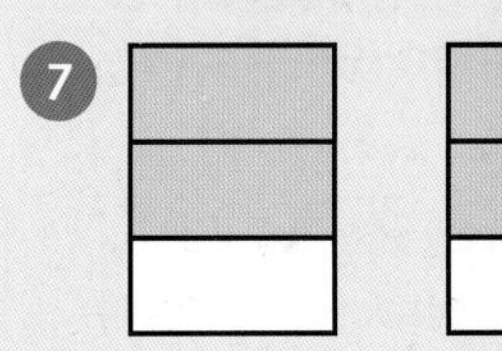

B

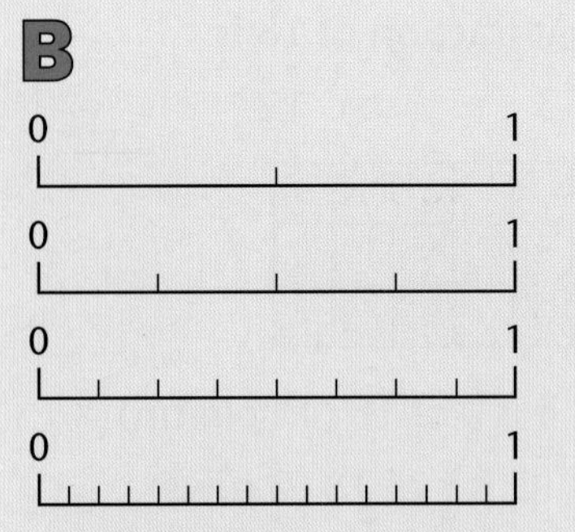

Use the number lines above.
Copy and complete the equivalent fractions.

1. $\frac{1}{4} = \frac{\square}{16}$
2. $\frac{1}{2} = \frac{\square}{8}$
3. $\frac{1}{8} = \frac{\square}{16}$
4. $\frac{3}{4} = \frac{\square}{8}$
5. $\frac{5}{8} = \frac{\square}{16}$
6. $\frac{1}{2} = \frac{\square}{16}$
7. $\frac{2}{4} = \frac{\square}{16}$
8. $\frac{3}{8} = \frac{\square}{16}$
9. $\frac{1}{2} = \frac{\square}{4}$
10. $\frac{1}{4} = \frac{\square}{8}$
11. $\frac{7}{8} = \frac{\square}{16}$
12. $\frac{3}{4} = \frac{\square}{16}$

Use the number lines.
Copy and complete.

13. $\frac{2}{3} = \frac{\square}{9}$
14. $\frac{5}{6} = \frac{\square}{12}$
15. $\frac{1}{3} = \frac{\square}{6}$
16. $\frac{6}{9} = \frac{\square}{12}$
17. $\frac{2}{3} = \frac{\square}{6}$
18. $\frac{4}{6} = \frac{\square}{9}$
19. $\frac{3}{9} = \frac{\square}{3}$
20. $\frac{4}{12} = \frac{\square}{9}$
21. $\frac{2}{12} = \frac{\square}{6}$
22. $\frac{8}{12} = \frac{\square}{3}$
23. $\frac{3}{9} = \frac{\square}{6}$
24. $\frac{4}{12} = \frac{\square}{3}$

C

Copy and complete the equivalent fractions.

1. $\frac{2}{5} = \frac{\square}{10}$
2. $\frac{3}{4} = \frac{\square}{16}$
3. $\frac{7}{10} = \frac{\square}{100}$
4. $\frac{1}{6} = \frac{\square}{18}$
5. $\frac{19}{25} = \frac{\square}{100}$
6. $\frac{5}{7} = \frac{\square}{14}$
7. $\frac{10}{15} = \frac{\square}{3}$
8. $\frac{12}{20} = \frac{\square}{5}$
9. $\frac{8}{16} = \frac{\square}{2}$
10. $\frac{20}{100} = \frac{\square}{20}$
11. $\frac{6}{18} = \frac{\square}{3}$
12. $\frac{15}{20} = \frac{\square}{4}$

Continue these fraction chains for four further terms.

13. $\frac{3}{4} = \frac{6}{8} = \frac{9}{12}$
14. $\frac{1}{6} = \frac{2}{12} = \frac{3}{18}$
15. $\frac{2}{5} = \frac{4}{10} = \frac{6}{15}$
16. $\frac{1}{8} = \frac{2}{16} = \frac{3}{24}$
17. $\frac{2}{3} = \frac{4}{6} = \frac{6}{9}$
18. $\frac{9}{10} = \frac{18}{20} = \frac{27}{30}$

Write three more fractions equivalent to:

19. $\frac{5}{13}$
20. $\frac{8}{36}$
21. $\frac{10}{24}$
22. $\frac{18}{33}$
23. $\frac{9}{16}$
24. $\frac{35}{40}$
25. $\frac{28}{60}$
26. $\frac{42}{150}$

I can write a number as a fraction of a larger number.

Examples

What fraction of 8 is 2?

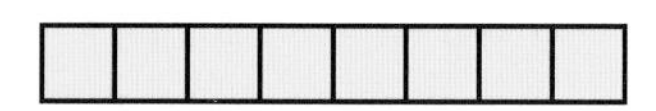

$8 = 4 \times 2$
2 is $\frac{1}{4}$ of 8

What fraction of 18 is:

a) 3 **b)** 12?

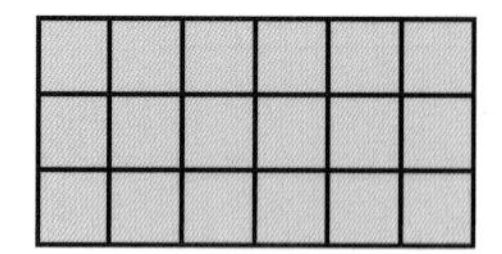

a) 3 is $\frac{1}{6}$ of 18 (1 column)
b) 12 is $\frac{2}{3}$ of 18 (2 rows)

What fraction of £1 is:

a) 5p **b)** 15p?

a) $£1 = 20 \times 5p$
5p is $\frac{1}{20}$ of £1.

b) $15p = 3 \times 5p$
15p is $\frac{3}{20}$ of £1

A

For each diagram copy and complete the number sentences.

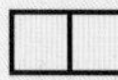

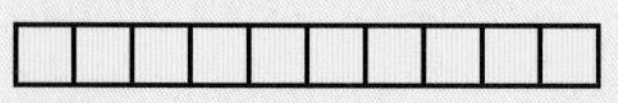

1. 10 = ☐ × 2
2. 2 is ☐ of 10

3. 9 = ☐ × 3
4. 3 is ☐ of 9

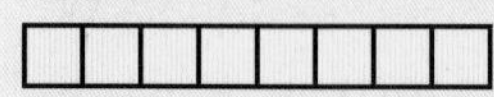

5. 8 = ☐ × 4
6. 4 is ☐ of 8

7. 6 = ☐ × 2
8. 2 is ☐ of 6

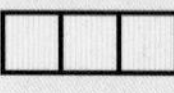

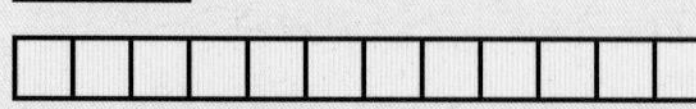

9. 12 = ☐ × 3
10. 3 is ☐ of 12

B

1. 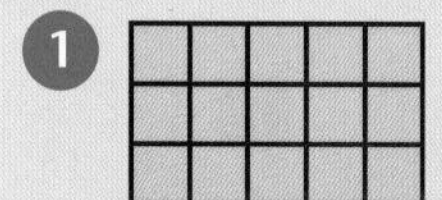

   What fraction of 15 is:

   a) 3 **b)** 5 **c)** 6 **d)** 10?

2. What fraction of 32 is:

   a) 8 **b)** 24 **c)** 4 **d)** 12?

3. What fraction of £1 is:

   a) 10p **b)** 25p **c)** 35p **d)** 80p?

4. What fraction of 1 km is:

   a) 50 m **b)** 200 m **c)** 250 m **d)** 750 m?

5. What fraction of 1 day is

   a) 1 hour
   b) 4 hours
   c) 6 hours
   d) 8 hours?

C

1. What fraction of 50 is:

   a) 5 **b)** 10 **c)** 30 **d)** 45?

2. What fraction of 60 is:

   a) 10 **b)** 5 **c)** 25 **d)** 12?

3. What fraction of 48 is:

   a) 8 **b)** 12 **c)** 36 **d)** 30?

4. What fraction of £1 is:

   a) 2p **b)** 45p **c)** 99p **d)** 12p?

5. What fraction of 1 km is:

   a) 20 m **b)** 125 m **c)** 800 m **d)** 50 m?

6. Simon is driving 400 miles. In the first hour he drives 50 miles. What fraction of the journey has he completed? What fraction is left?

7. A bag of flour holds 2 kg. 250 g is used. What fraction is left?

I can find fractions of amounts.

Examples

$\frac{1}{3}$ of 18 = 18 ÷ 3
= 6

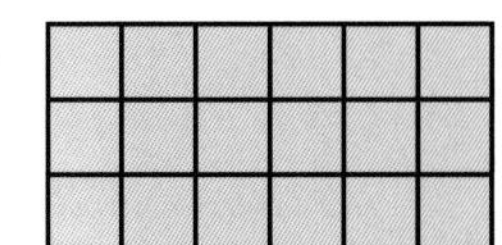

$\frac{2}{3}$ of 18 = (18 ÷ 3) × 2
= 6 × 2
= 12

$\frac{3}{5}$ of 90 = (90 ÷ 5) × 3
= 18 × 3
= 54

A

Use the array to help you find the answer.

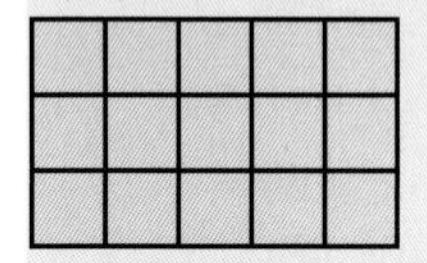

1. $\frac{1}{3}$ of 15
2. $\frac{1}{5}$ of 15

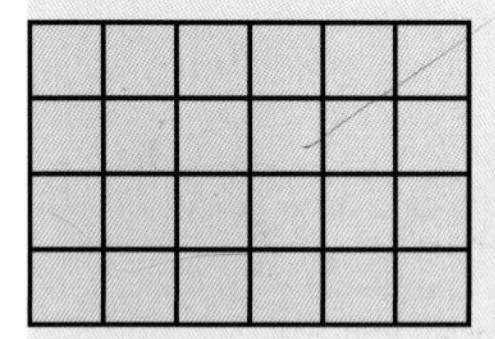

3. $\frac{1}{4}$ of 24
4. $\frac{1}{6}$ of 24

Find $\frac{1}{10}$ of:

5. 30
6. 80
7. 20p
8. 50p

Find $\frac{1}{5}$ of:

9. 10
10. 30
11. 25 cm
12. 45 cm

Find $\frac{1}{3}$ of:

13. 9
14. 27
15. £30
16. £12

Find $\frac{1}{4}$ of:

17. 8
18. 32
19. 20 m
20. 36 m

B

Find

1. $\frac{1}{10}$ of 60
2. $\frac{3}{10}$ of 60
3. $\frac{1}{4}$ of 16
4. $\frac{3}{4}$ of 16
5. $\frac{1}{5}$ of 50
6. $\frac{4}{5}$ of 50
7. $\frac{1}{3}$ of 21
8. $\frac{2}{3}$ of 21
9. $\frac{5}{6}$ of 12
10. $\frac{2}{5}$ of 35
11. $\frac{4}{9}$ of 27
12. $\frac{7}{10}$ of 90
13. $\frac{2}{7}$ of 70p
14. $\frac{3}{4}$ of 28p
15. $\frac{5}{8}$ of £16
16. $\frac{2}{3}$ of £24
17. $\frac{5}{6}$ of 30 cm
18. $\frac{7}{9}$ of 18 cm
19. $\frac{3}{8}$ of 40 m
20. $\frac{4}{7}$ of 21 m

C

Find

1. $\frac{21}{100}$ of 4 m
2. $\frac{5}{7}$ of £42
3. $\frac{2}{9}$ of 63 litres
4. $\frac{9}{20}$ of 1 metre
5. $\frac{5}{6}$ of £5·40
6. $\frac{7}{8}$ of 48
7. $\frac{3}{5}$ of 400 g
8. $\frac{421}{1000}$ of 2 km
9. A cake weighs 640 g. It is cut into eight equal slices. Five slices are eaten. What is the weight of the cake that is left?
10. There are 72 children in Year 5. Four ninths are girls. How many boys are there?
11. A bucket holds 2·5 litres of water. Three tenths spills out. How much water is left?
12. A TV programme is 2 hours long. Two fifteenths of the programme is adverts. How long do the adverts last?

E1 FRACTION PROBLEMS

I can solve problems involving fractions using a calculator if needed.

Example

There are 352 people on a plane flying from London to Sydney. $\frac{9}{16}$ of the passengers are Australian. How many passengers are Australian?

$352 \div 16 = 22$

$22 \times 9 = 198$

Answer *198 passengers are Australian.*

A

1. A ribbon is 40 cm long. One fifth is cut off. How long are the two pieces of ribbon?
2. There are 20 biscuits in a packet. One quarter are eaten. How many biscuits are left?
3. A baker makes 48 cakes. One sixth are not sold. How many are sold?
4. There are 30 children in a class. One tenth are absent. How many are present?
5. A class of 24 children vote for their favourite pet. One third choose hamsters. One quarter choose dogs. How many children vote for:
   a) hamsters
   b) dogs
   c) other pets?

B

1. There are 36 safety pins in a packet. Three quarters are used. How many are left?
2. Kelly drinks seven tenths of a 1 litre bottle of water. How much is left?
3. A piece of wood is 35 cm long. Harry saws off two fifths. How long are the two pieces?
4. Penny's mother weighs 60 kg. Penny weighs two thirds of her mother's weight? How much does Penny weigh?
5. A long distance footpath is 312 miles in length. Mike walks five eighths in two weeks. How much further does he have to go?
6. One mile is 1760 yards. What is eight elevenths of a mile?
7. There are 448 people at a panto. Four sevenths are children. How many adults are in the audience?

C

1. A can of cherries weighs 480 g. Five twelfths of this is the weight of the juice. What do the cherries weigh?
2. A crowd of 48 357 watch a football match. Two ninths of the spectators support Arsenal. How many people in the crowd are Arsenal supporters?
3. Three eighths of a 5 kg bag of potatoes has been eaten. How much is left?
4. Hamid has a 750 ml bottle of juice. He pours two fifths into a jug and one sixth into a glass. How much is left in the bottle?
5. Helen's book has 285 pages. She has read four fifteenths. How many pages has she read?
6. What is two thirds of three fifths of one metre?

A2 PARTITIONING DECIMALS

I can partition decimals using both fractions and decimals.

Examples

	$2{\cdot}8 = 2\frac{8}{10}$	$2{\cdot}85 = 2\frac{85}{100}$	$2{\cdot}856 = 2\frac{856}{1000}$
Partitioned using decimals	$2 + 0{\cdot}8$	$2 + 0{\cdot}8 + 0{\cdot}05$	$2 + 0{\cdot}8 + 0{\cdot}05 + 0{\cdot}006$
Partitioned using fractions	$2 + \frac{8}{10}$	$2 + \frac{8}{10} + \frac{5}{100}$	$2 + \frac{8}{10} + \frac{5}{100} + \frac{6}{1000}$

A

Write as a decimal.

1. $2\frac{7}{10}$
2. $5\frac{4}{10}$
3. $1\frac{3}{10}$
4. $\frac{8}{10}$
5. $9\frac{1}{10}$
6. $4\frac{6}{10}$
7. $7\frac{9}{10}$
8. $\frac{7}{10}$
9. $3\frac{2}{10}$
10. $6\frac{5}{10}$
11. $8\frac{8}{10}$
12. $\frac{3}{10}$

Write as a fraction.

13. 2·1
14. 0·6
15. 1·2
16. 5·9
17. 0·5
18. 2·8
19. 7·3
20. 3·7
21. 0·1
22. 9·5
23. 6·4
24. 0·2

Copy and complete.

25. 0·4 + □ = 0·7
26. 1·5 + □ = 1·7
27. 3·7 + □ = 3·8
28. 0·2 + □ = 0·8
29. 2·3 + □ = 2·7
30. 5·2 − □ = 5·0
31. 1·6 − □ = 1·1
32. 5·4 − □ = 5·2
33. 2·9 − □ = 2·3
34. 3·5 − □ = 3·1

B

Partition using decimals.

1. $8\frac{47}{100}$
2. $2\frac{23}{100}$
3. $\frac{91}{100}$
4. $1\frac{7}{100}$
5. $5\frac{73}{100}$
6. $4\frac{38}{100}$
7. $7\frac{82}{100}$
8. $3\frac{46}{100}$
9. $20\frac{8}{100}$
10. $9\frac{94}{100}$
11. $5\frac{29}{100}$
12. $\frac{65}{100}$

Partition using fractions.

13. 4·63
14. 7·45
15. 0·12
16. 3·77
17. 5·09
18. 0·21
19. 7·06
20. 11·43
21. 4·04
22. 23·62
23. 0·58
24. 6·95

Copy and complete.

25. 3·23 + □ = 3·26
26. 1·37 + □ = 1·87
27. 0·65 + □ = 0·67
28. 4·12 + □ = 4·72
29. 6·73 + □ = 6·8
30. 0·51 − □ = 0·31
31. 2·76 − □ = 2·71
32. 8·93 − □ = 8·33
33. 1·82 − □ = 1·52
34. 0·68 − □ = 0·64

C

Write as decimals.

1. $2 + \frac{7}{10} + \frac{6}{100} + \frac{1}{1000}$
2. $5 + \frac{2}{10} + \frac{3}{100} + \frac{9}{1000}$
3. $8 + \frac{1}{100} + \frac{4}{1000}$
4. $\frac{6}{10} + \frac{8}{1000}$
5. $7 + \frac{3}{10} + \frac{5}{100} + \frac{6}{1000}$
6. $4 + \frac{9}{10} + \frac{1}{1000}$

Partition using fractions.

7. 2·475
8. 5·821
9. 3·083
10. 0·146
11. 1·904
12. 8·512
13. 3·639
14. 0·207
15. 5·061
16. 0·496
17. 4·358
18. 6·702

Copy and complete.

19. 0·531 + □ = 0·536
20. 2·908 + □ = 2·938
21. 4·072 + □ = 4·08
22. 1·653 + □ = 1·853
23. 5·824 + □ = 5·884
24. 0·642 − □ = 0·442
25. 1·719 − □ = 1·714
26. 6·256 − □ = 6·246
27. 3·983 − □ = 3·083
28. 2·407 − □ = 2·4

A2 DECIMAL FRACTIONS

I can express a fraction as a decimal and say what any digit in a decimal is worth.

Examples

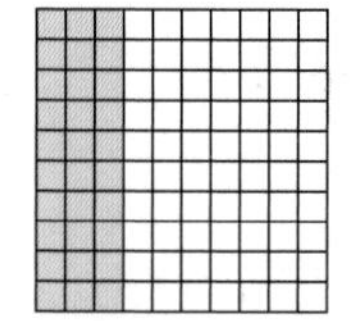

three tenths

$\frac{3}{10} = 0{\cdot}3$

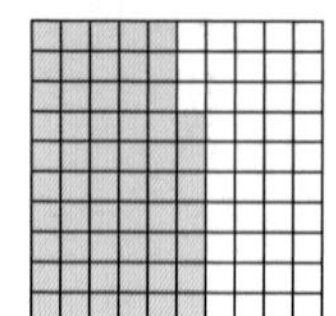

fifty-seven hundredths

$\frac{5}{10} + \frac{7}{100} = \frac{57}{100} = 0{\cdot}57$

The value of a digit depends upon its position in a number.

Each digit in a number is 10 times higher than the digit to the right. This applies to decimal fractions as well as to whole numbers.

	T	U	·	$\frac{1}{10}$	$\frac{1}{100}$	$\frac{1}{1000}$
30 =	3	0	·	0		
3 =		3	·	0		
$\frac{3}{10}$ =		0	·	3		
$\frac{3}{100}$ =		0	·	0	3	
$\frac{3}{1000}$ =		0	·	0	0	3

	T	U	·	$\frac{1}{10}$	$\frac{1}{100}$	$\frac{1}{1000}$
24 =	2	4	·	0		
$2\frac{4}{10}$ =		2	·	4		
$\frac{24}{100}$ =		0	·	2	4	
$\frac{24}{1000}$ =		0	·	0	2	4

A

What part of each shape is shaded?
Write your answer as a fraction and as a decimal fraction.

1
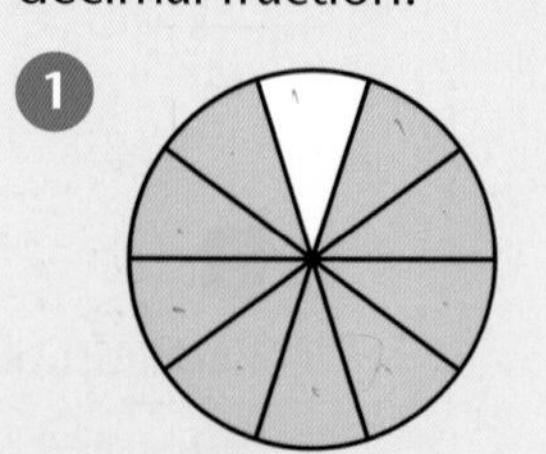

5

2
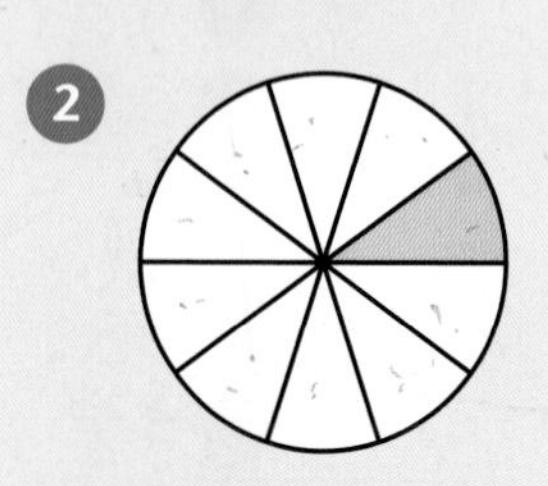

6
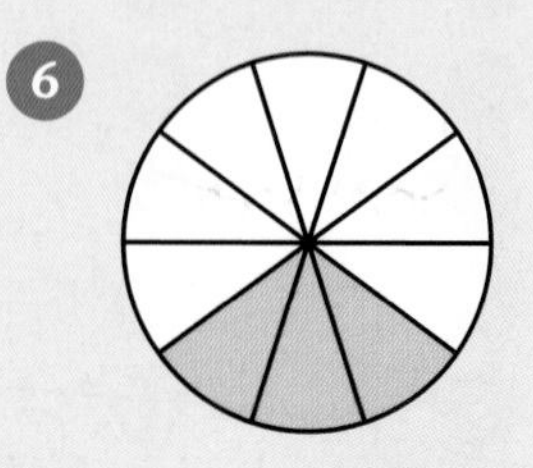

3
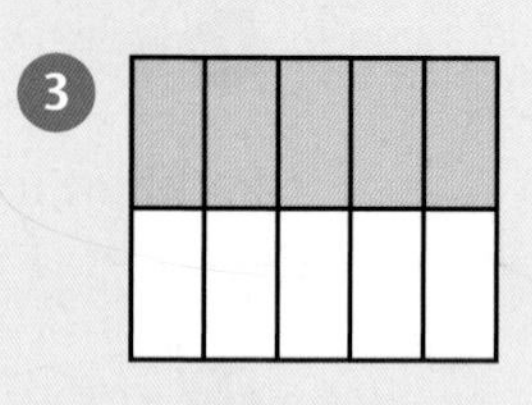

7
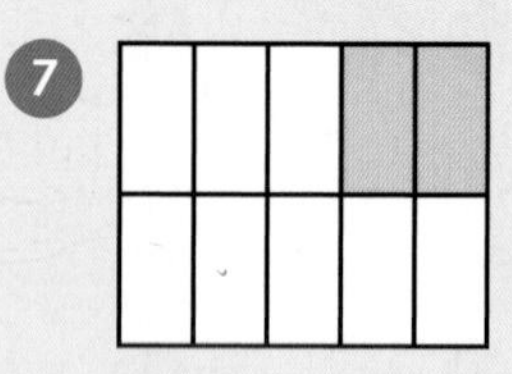

4
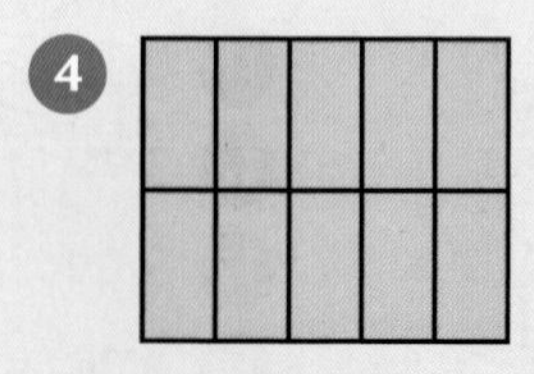

8
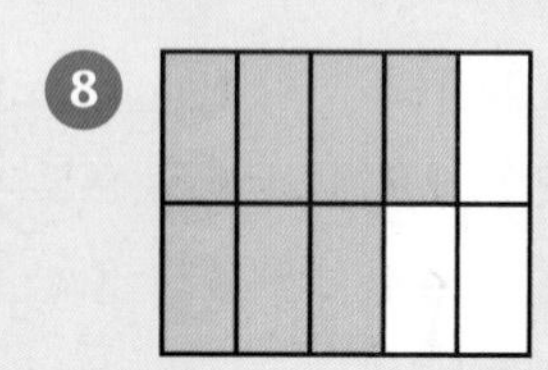

9 Write each number shown by the arrows as a decimal fraction.

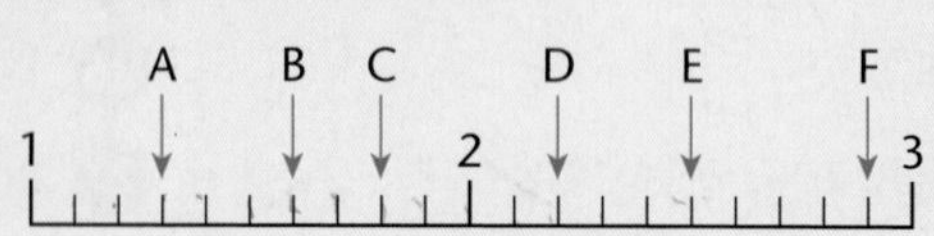

Write each of these numbers as a decimal fraction.

10 $\frac{4}{10}$

11 $1\frac{7}{10}$

12 $3\frac{3}{10}$

13 $2\frac{9}{10}$

14 $6\frac{8}{10}$

15 $\frac{6}{10}$

16 $10\frac{5}{10}$

17 $17\frac{2}{10}$

18 $4\frac{1}{10}$

B

Express the shaded part of each diagram as a fraction and as a decimal fraction.

1
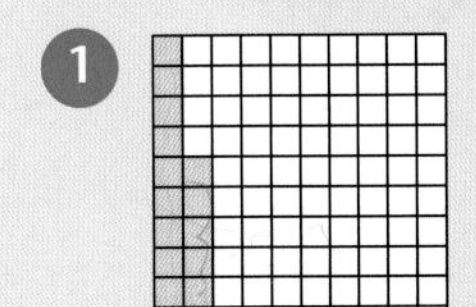

3
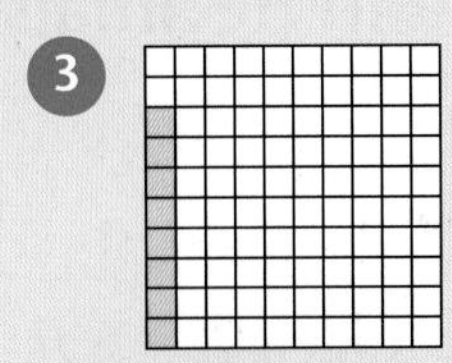

2
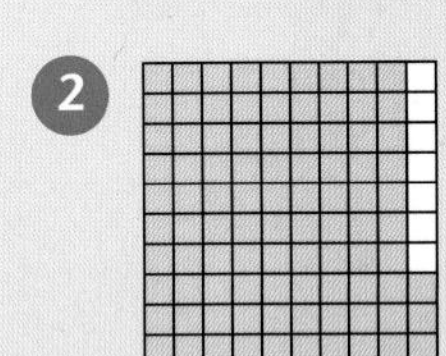

4
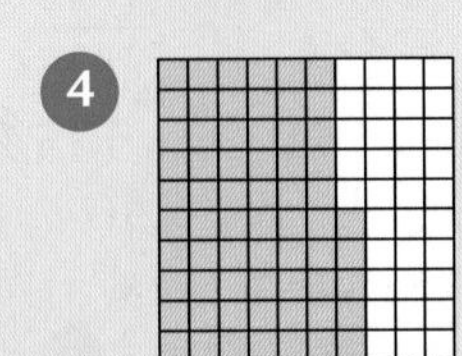

Write each number shown by the arrows as a decimal fraction.

5
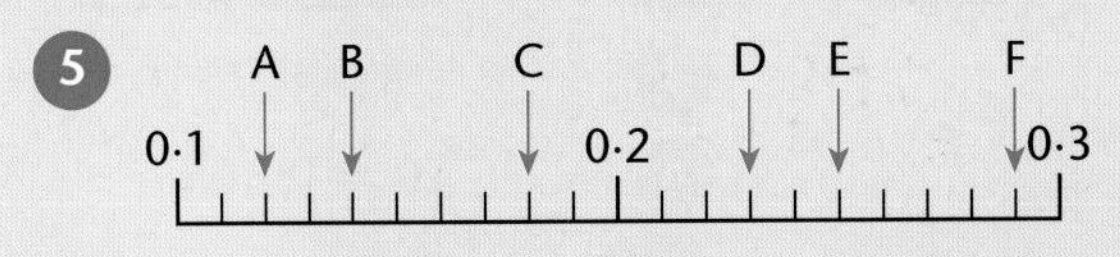

6
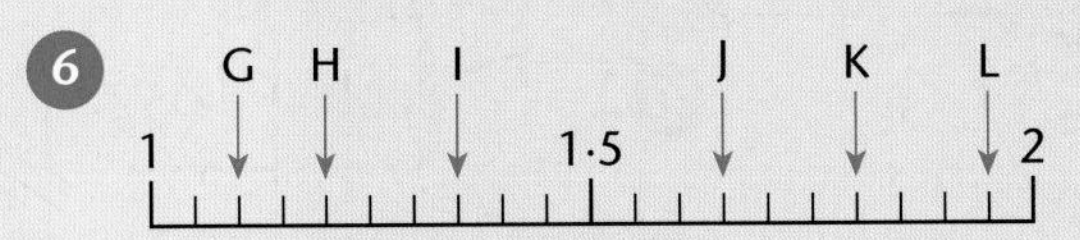

Give the value of the underlined figure in each of these numbers.

7. $2{\cdot}\underline{5}8$
8. $1\underline{8}{\cdot}67$
9. $\underline{4}5{\cdot}76$
10. $1\underline{6}{\cdot}53$
11. $13{\cdot}3\underline{2}$
12. $36{\cdot}\underline{9}$
13. $20{\cdot}\underline{1}3$
14. $7{\cdot}9\underline{2}$
15. $12{\cdot}\underline{4}1$
16. $2{\cdot}8\underline{5}$
17. $1{\cdot}6\underline{1}$
18. $13{\cdot}\underline{2}4$

Give the next five terms in each of these sequences.

19. 0·01, 0·02, 0·03, 0·04, 0·05
20. 1·0, 1·02, 1·04, 1·06, 1·08
21. 1·92, 1·93, 1·94, 1·95, 1·96
22. 0·91, 0·93, 0·95, 0·97, 0·99
23. 0·6, 0·65, 0·7, 0·75, 0·8
24. 4·07, 4·06, 4·05, 4·04, 4·03

C

Example

$4 + \frac{6}{10} + \frac{3}{100} + \frac{5}{1000}$

$4\frac{635}{1000}$

4·635

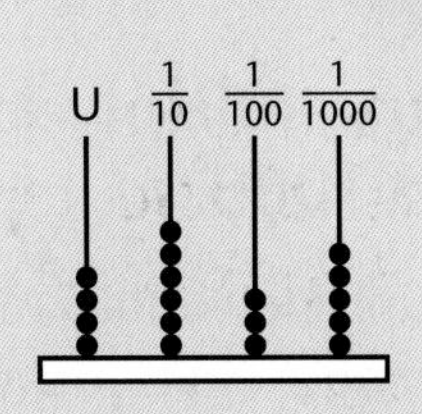

Write the decimal fraction shown on each abacus.

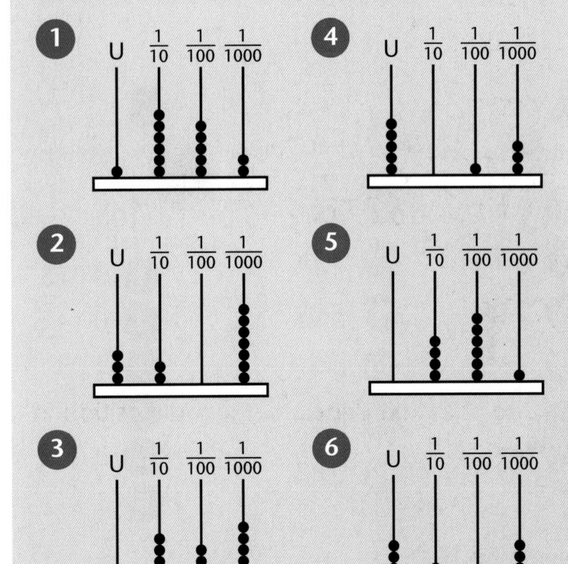

Copy and complete.

7. $1 + \square + \frac{1}{100} + \frac{7}{1000} = 1{\cdot}417$
8. $\frac{3}{10} + \frac{2}{100} + \frac{8}{1000} = \square$
9. $\frac{9}{10} + \square = 0{\cdot}906$
10. $5 + \square + \frac{2}{1000} = 5{\cdot}032$

Write these numbers as decimal fractions.

11. $\frac{3}{100}$
12. $\frac{263}{1000}$
13. $1\frac{18}{100}$
14. $5\frac{169}{1000}$
15. $\frac{72}{1000}$
16. $\frac{451}{1000}$
17. $2\frac{96}{1000}$
18. $6\frac{9}{100}$
19. $1\frac{316}{1000}$

Give the value of the underlined figure in each of these numbers.

20. $4{\cdot}\underline{6}2$
21. $16{\cdot}\underline{7}91$
22. $18{\cdot}13\underline{5}$
23. $\underline{6}{\cdot}472$
24. $11{\cdot}\underline{1}09$
25. $33{\cdot}3\underline{3}$
26. $41{\cdot}61\underline{8}$
27. $1\underline{9}{\cdot}72$
28. $3{\cdot}0\underline{6}5$

I can multiply and divide whole numbers and decimals by 10, 100 and 1000.

Multiplying – digits move left
Dividing – digits move right
×/÷ by 10 – digits move 1 place
×/÷ by 100 – digits move 2 places
×/÷ by 1000 – digits move 3 places

Examples

0·36 × 10 = 3·6
0·36 × 100 = 36
0·36 × 1000 = 360

125 ÷ 10 = 12·5
125 ÷ 100 = 1·25
125 ÷ 1000 = 0·125

A

Multiply by 10.

1. 0·5
2. 2·4
3. 0·05
4. 1·72
5. 0·3
6. 0·91
7. 3·6
8. 2·18
9. 5·09
10. 0·2
11. 6·8
12. 0·43

Divide by 10.

13. 32
14. 6
15. 1·5
16. 0·4
17. 76
18. 2·5
19. 0·8
20. 8
21. 4·1
22. 0·3
23. 99
24. 5

Copy and complete.

25. □ × 10 = 7
26. □ × 10 = 1·6
27. □ × 10 = 40·9
28. □ × 10 = 52
29. □ ÷ 10 = 0·8
30. □ ÷ 10 = 0·03
31. □ ÷ 10 = 1·5
32. □ ÷ 10 = 0·29

B

Multiply by

100

1. 0·015
2. 0·14
3. 2·03
4. 0·2
5. 0·06
6. 5·8

1000

7. 0·339
8. 0·07
9. 1·4
10. 0·002
11. 6·17
12. 0·5

Divide by

100

13. 9
14. 472
15. 0·3
16. 1850
17. 63
18. 4·1

1000

19. 7
20. 45 300
21. 16
22. 20
23. 1306
24. 158

Copy and complete.

25. □ × 10 = 26·9
26. □ ÷ 100 = 74
27. □ × 100 = 610
28. □ ÷ 1000 = 3·58
29. 0·7 × □ = 700
30. 0·8 ÷ □ = 0·08
31. 9·01 × □ = 90·1
32. 10 ÷ □ = 0·01

C

Copy and complete.

1. □ × 10 = 85
2. □ ÷ 100 = 0·09
3. □ × 1000 = 7110
4. □ ÷ 10 = 0·305
5. □ × 100 = 46
6. □ ÷ 1000 = 0·052
7. 6·3 × □ = 630
8. 2·8 ÷ □ = 0·28
9. 0·57 × □ = 570
10. 4·6 ÷ □ = 0·046
11. 0·04 × □ = 0·4
12. 30 ÷ □ = 0·03

Work out and write each answer as a decimal.

13. one tenth of two tenths
14. one hundredth of a half
15. one thousandth of 100

What number is:

16. 10 times larger than nine hundredths
17. 100 times larger than a quarter
18. 1000 times larger than one half?

I can use a written method for addition calculations including numbers with one or two decimal places.

Examples

$$\begin{array}{r} 8{\cdot}7 \\ +\ 3{\cdot}4 \\ \hline 12{\cdot}1 \\ \hline {\scriptstyle 1} \end{array} \qquad \begin{array}{r} 8{\cdot}7 \\ +\ 3{\cdot}45 \\ \hline 12{\cdot}15 \\ \hline {\scriptstyle 1} \end{array} \qquad \begin{array}{r} 8{\cdot}79 \\ +\ 3{\cdot}45 \\ \hline 12{\cdot}24 \\ \hline {\scriptstyle 1\ 1} \end{array}$$

$1{\cdot}6 + 0{\cdot}63$

$$\begin{array}{r} 1{\cdot}6 \\ +\ 0{\cdot}63 \\ \hline 2{\cdot}23 \\ \hline {\scriptstyle 1} \end{array}$$

Line up the decimal points.

Copy and complete.

1. $4{\cdot}6 + 3{\cdot}8$
2. $7{\cdot}2 + 5{\cdot}7$
3. $5{\cdot}8 + 4{\cdot}5$
4. $19{\cdot}0 + 7{\cdot}6$
5. $43{\cdot}7 + 9{\cdot}2$
6. $52{\cdot}3 + 8{\cdot}9$
7. $41{\cdot}7 + 6{\cdot}5$
8. $13{\cdot}4 + 2{\cdot}7$
9. $38{\cdot}6 + 9{\cdot}4$
10. $37{\cdot}8 + 16{\cdot}7$
11. Norma walks 11·6 km in the morning and 8·7 km in the afternoon. How far has she walked altogether?
12. A bath is filled with 39·4 litres of hot water and 17·8 litres of cold. How much water is in the bath?

B

Copy and complete.

1. $67{\cdot}4 + 14{\cdot}8$
2. $4{\cdot}93 + 2{\cdot}39$
3. $8{\cdot}48 + 6{\cdot}7$
4. $9{\cdot}8 + 2{\cdot}75$
5. $78{\cdot}4 + 29{\cdot}3$
6. $5{\cdot}07 + 1{\cdot}94$
7. $12{\cdot}5 + 7{\cdot}83$
8. $3{\cdot}89 + 0{\cdot}71$
9. $34{\cdot}62 + 1{\cdot}8$
10. $90{\cdot}9 + 14{\cdot}5$
11. Jarvis weighs 36·4 kg. His father weighs 25·65 kg more. What does Jarvis' father weigh?
12. Tania buys a present for £8·79 and a card for £1·25. How much does she spend?
13. Kerry throws the javelin 48·5 metres. The winning throw is 6·33 metres longer. What is the winning throw?

C

Set out as in the examples.

1. $48{\cdot}5 + 18{\cdot}9$
2. $6{\cdot}87 + 2{\cdot}96$
3. $70{\cdot}94 + 28{\cdot}4$
4. $5{\cdot}76 + 9{\cdot}75$
5. $14{\cdot}3 + 3{\cdot}82$
6. $5{\cdot}92 + 43{\cdot}6$
7. $670{\cdot}5 + 1{\cdot}83$
8. $1{\cdot}57 + 0{\cdot}64$
9. $13{\cdot}68 + 9{\cdot}56$
10. $45{\cdot}4 + 3{\cdot}79$
11. There is 12·9 litres of petrol in a fuel tank. 17·83 litres is added. How much petrol is in the tank now?
12. An athlete runs 48·7 km in one week and 16·45 km further in the next week. How far does he run in the second week?

I can use a written method to subtract three-digit numbers and decimals.

Examples

COUNTING UP

```
 472          47·2
−169         −16·9
  31 → 200     3·1 → 20·0
 272 → 472    27·2 → 47·2
 303          30·3
 1            1
```

DECOMPOSITION (TAKE AWAY METHOD)

472 − 169

```
 400 + 70 + 2 = 400 + 60 + 12      6 12
−100 + 60 + 9 = 100 + 60 +  9      4/7/2
                                  −169
                300 +  0 +  3 = 303   303
```

A

Work out

1. 361 − 223
2. 508 − 472
3. 715 − 306
4. 473 − 249
5. 814 − 291
6. 864 − 647
7. 725 − 309
8. 380 − 241
9. 539 − 175
10. 657 − 383
11. The Taylor family bought a new computer in a sale. The price of £832 was reduced by £175. How much did the Taylors pay?

B

Work out

1. 60·7 − 43·1
2. 59·4 − 26·8
3. 32·8 − 19·7
4. 45·2 − 36·1
5. 78·3 − 13·9
6. 5·29 − 1·58
7. 3·61 − 2·07
8. 8·74 − 4·36
9. 5·77 − 2·91
10. 4·56 − 3·84
11. A sack of coal contains 46·4 kg. 18·5 kg is removed. How much coal is left?
12. Jessica has £7·35. Tom has £2·69 less. How much does Tom have?
13. Karim jumps 2·16 metres. Ollie jumps 1·38 metres. How much further does Karim jump?

C

Set out as in the examples.

1. 52·74 − 28·23
2. 86·09 − 14·56
3. 75·83 − 21·74
4. 4·357 − 3·294
5. 618·4 − 463·7
6. 90·69 − 54·99
7. 6·495 − 3·927
8. 28·07 − 15·38
9. 8·026 − 4·946
10. 537·1 − 353·7
11. 95·09 − 28·24
12. 7·842 − 5·756
13. Rayan runs the 200 metres in 23·24 seconds. The winner runs 0·57 seconds faster. What is the winning time?
14. Carmen has £83·27. She spends £25·93. How much does she have left?

I can use the multiplication facts up to 10 × 10 to ×/÷ multiples of 10 and 100.

A

What is

1. 6×2
2. 8×4
3. 4×6
4. 9×5
5. 5×7
6. 7×8
7. 8×6
8. 7×4
9. 6×7
10. 9×3
11. 4×9
12. 8×5
13. $18 \div 3$
14. $25 \div 5$
15. $72 \div 9$
16. $28 \div 7$
17. $18 \div 2$
18. $24 \div 8$
19. $30 \div 6$
20. $14 \div 2$
21. $20 \div 4$
22. $48 \div 8$
23. $24 \div 3$
24. $54 \div 9$

B

Copy and complete.

1. $\square \times 5 = 35$
2. $\square \times 7 = 56$
3. $\square \times 4 = 36$
4. $\square \times 8 = 40$
5. $\square \times 6 = 18$
6. $\square \times 9 = 63$
7. $\square \div 2 = 8$
8. $\square \div 6 = 6$
9. $\square \div 9 = 5$
10. $\square \div 7 = 9$
11. $\square \div 8 = 4$
12. $\square \div 3 = 7$

Write the answer only.

13. 30×9
14. 600×2
15. 900×8
16. 70×7
17. 50×3
18. 700×6
19. 3×900
20. 6×50
21. 9×70
22. 8×600
23. 5×800
24. 7×90
25. $210 \div 7$
26. $3000 \div 5$
27. $540 \div 6$
28. $8100 \div 9$
29. $2400 \div 4$
30. $640 \div 8$
31. $4000 \div 80$
32. $280 \div 40$
33. $1400 \div 70$
34. $360 \div 60$
35. $3600 \div 90$
36. $1800 \div 20$

C

Copy and complete.

1. $\square \times 6 = 480$
2. $\square \times 4 = 160$
3. $\square \times 9 = 5400$
4. $\square \times 70 = 3500$
5. $\square \times 20 = 140$
6. $\square \times 80 = 5600$
7. $\square \div 7 = 80$
8. $\square \div 3 = 600$
9. $\square \div 6 = 70$
10. $\square \div 80 = 40$
11. $\square \div 50 = 9$
12. $\square \div 90 = 50$

Write the answer only.

13. $0{\cdot}9 \times 8$
14. $0{\cdot}8 \times 4$
15. $0{\cdot}3 \times 7$
16. $0{\cdot}4 \times 6$
17. $0{\cdot}8 \times 2$
18. $0{\cdot}7 \times 9$
19. $4{\cdot}8 \div 8$
20. $5{\cdot}4 \div 6$
21. $2{\cdot}1 \div 3$
22. $4{\cdot}2 \div 7$
23. $7{\cdot}2 \div 9$
24. $3{\cdot}5 \div 5$
25. $7 \times 0{\cdot}7$
26. $8 \times 0{\cdot}3$
27. $3 \times 0{\cdot}6$
28. $6 \times 0{\cdot}5$
29. $8 \times 0{\cdot}8$
30. $3 \times 0{\cdot}9$
31. $6.3 \div 7$
32. $1{\cdot}2 \div 2$
33. $8{\cdot}1 \div 9$
34. $3{\cdot}2 \div 4$
35. $3{\cdot}6 \div 6$
36. $2{\cdot}4 \div 8$

I can multiply a two-digit numbers by a one-digit number.

Example 46×7

$$46 \times 7 = (40 \times 7) + (6 \times 7)$$
$$= 280 + 42$$
$$= 322$$

$$\begin{array}{r|r} & 40 + 6 \\ \times & 7 \\ \hline & 280 \\ & 42 \\ \hline & 322 \end{array}$$

$$\begin{array}{rrl} & 40 + 6 & \\ \times & 7 & \\ \hline & 280 & (40 \times 7) \\ & 42 & (6 \times 7) \\ \hline & 322 & \end{array}$$

$$\begin{array}{rr} & 46 \\ \times & 7 \\ \hline & 280 \\ & 42 \\ \hline & 322 \\ & {}_{1} \end{array}$$

A

Work out

1. 25×5
2. 16×2
3. 33×4
4. 57×3
5. 32×7
6. 15×8
7. 29×4
8. 58×2
9. There are 18 slices of bread in one loaf. How many are there in four loaves?
10. There are three classes in Year 5. Each class has 27 children. How many children are in Year 5?
11. Peter cycles 34 miles every day. How far does he cycle in 5 days?

B

Work out

1. 75×4
2. 49×7
3. 62×8
4. 58×6
5. 46×5
6. 74×9
7. 39×3
8. 96×6
9. 87×2
10. 93×5
11. 74×6
12. 35×7
13. 59×9
14. 36×6
15. 45×8
16. 68×7
17. There are 48 eggs in one tray. How many eggs are there in six trays?
18. One bag of crisps weighs 34 g. What is the weight of a pack of nine bags?
19. Maisie has read one third of her book. She has finished page 86. How many pages are there in her book?
20. One ice cream costs 95p. What do five cost?

C

Work out

1. 129×2
2. 236×3
3. 431×4
4. 273×5
5. 137×6
6. 168×4
7. 345×3
8. 168×5
9. 184×7
10. 236×8
11. 227×9
12. 384×6
13. 257×7
14. 193×9
15. 185×8
16. 265×6
17. One ticket to fly to India costs £359. What do eight tickets cost?

18. One can of sardines weighs 126 g. What do six cans weigh?
19. Lalita earns £457 every week. How much does she earn in four weeks?

A2 WRITTEN METHOD FOR DIVISION

I can divide a two-digit number by a one-digit number.

Examples

$86 \div 5$

Estimate first.

$5 \times 10 = 50$

$5 \times 20 = 100$

$50 < 86 < 100$

$10 < \text{Answer} < 20$

$$
\begin{aligned}
86 \div 5 &= (50 \div 5) + (36 \div 5) \\
&= 10 + 7\text{r}1 \\
&= 17\text{r}1
\end{aligned}
$$

$$
\begin{array}{rl}
86 & \\
-\underline{50} & (5 \times 10) \\
36 & \\
-\underline{35} & (5 \times 7) \\
1 &
\end{array}
$$

Answer 17r1

$186 \div 5$

$$
\begin{array}{rl}
186 & \\
-\underline{150} & (5 \times 30) \\
36 & \\
\underline{35} & (5 \times 7) \\
1 &
\end{array}
$$

Answer 37r1

A

Work out

1. $27 \div 2$
2. $44 \div 3$
3. $78 \div 5$
4. $50 \div 4$
5. $36 \div 2$
6. $89 \div 5$
7. $68 \div 6$
8. $96 \div 8$
9. $31 \div 2$
10. $100 \div 9$
11. $87 \div 6$
12. $66 \div 5$
13. $75 \div 4$
14. $91 \div 7$
15. $52 \div 3$
16. $70 \div 6$
17. There are 57 children in Year 5. They are split into groups of three. How many groups are there?
18. Two friends share a prize of £35. How much do they each get?
19. Hamid has read one fifth of his 80 page book. How many pages does he have left?
20. What is one quarter of 65 metres?

B

Work out

1. $69 \div 4$
2. $98 \div 6$
3. $74 \div 3$
4. $119 \div 7$
5. $97 \div 5$
6. $134 \div 8$
7. $49 \div 2$
8. $162 \div 9$
9. $95 \div 4$
10. $130 \div 7$
11. $94 \div 3$
12. $118 \div 6$
13. $123 \div 5$
14. $151 \div 9$
15. $85 \div 2$
16. $140 \div 8$
17. How many weeks are there in 126 days?
18. A school buys eight footballs for £98. How much does each football cost?
19. Janice has driven one sixth of her 150 mile journey. How much further does she have to go?
20. What is one fifth of £172?

C

Work out

1. $138 \div 6$
2. $256 \div 8$
3. $177 \div 7$
4. $164 \div 3$
5. $284 \div 9$
6. $263 \div 4$
7. $292 \div 6$
8. $185 \div 8$
9. $252 \div 7$
10. $287 \div 5$
11. $252 \div 9$
12. $376 \div 8$
13. $213 \div 6$
14. $296 \div 4$
15. $345 \div 7$
16. $512 \div 9$
17. One third of the 204 children had school dinners. How many children did not have school dinners?
18. Four friends share the £111 cost of a meal. How much should they each pay?
19. There are 512 seats in a theatre. One eighth are empty. How many seats are occupied?
20. How many complete weeks are there in 500 days?

I can find all the factor pairs of two-digit numbers.

Factors are numbers that divide exactly into another number. It is often useful to think of factors as pairs of numbers whose product is the target number.

Examples

Find all the factors of 12
Factor pairs of 12
$1 \times 12 \quad 2 \times 6 \quad 3 \times 4$
Factors of 12: 1, 2, 3, 4, 6, 12

Using factors for calculations

$23 \times 6 = 23 \times 3 \times 2$
$= 69 \times 2$
$= 138$

$80 \div 16 = 80 \div 2 \div 8$
$= 40 \div 8$
$= 5$

A

Complete the factor pairs.

1. The factor pairs of 6.
   1 and ☐ 2 and ☐
2. The factor pairs of 8.
   ☐ and 4 ☐ and 8
3. The factor pairs of 14.
   14 and ☐ ☐ and 2
4. The factor pairs of 15.
   5 and ☐ ☐ and ☐
5. The factor pairs of 27.
   ☐ and ☐ ☐ and ☐
6. The factor pairs of 30.
   ☐ and 1 2 and ☐
   3 and ☐ ☐ and ☐

Find pairs of factors for each target number.

7. 20 (3 pairs)
8. 12 (3 pairs)
9. 16 (3 pairs)
10. 40 (4 pairs)

B

Find all the factors of each target number. The number of factors is shown in brackets.

1. 21 (4)
2. 18 (6)
3. 36 (9)
4. 54 (8)
5. 28 (6)
6. 48 (10)
7. 77 (4)
8. 80 (10)

Break down the second number into factors to help work out each problem.

9. 24×6
10. 15×8
11. 16×12
12. 21×14
13. $60 \div 4$
14. $84 \div 14$
15. $90 \div 15$
16. $72 \div 18$

Fill in the box to complete the pair of factors of the target number.

17. 350 → ☐ and 50
18. 120 → 3 and ☐
19. 180 → 20 and ☐
20. 240 → ☐ and 6
21. 240 → 80 and ☐
22. 450 → 5 and ☐

C

Find all the factors of:

1. 64
2. 100
3. 120
4. 132
5. 102
6. 200
7. 108
8. 160
9. 125
10. 198

Break the second number down into factors to help work out each problem.

11. 18×18
12. 32×24
13. 46×25
14. 41×36
15. $210 \div 15$
16. $192 \div 12$
17. $154 \div 22$
18. $312 \div 24$

Find the highest factor shared by both:

19. 8 and 12
20. 12 and 15
21. 20 and 30
22. 15 and 25
23. 12 and 18
24. 24 and 40
25. 21 and 35
26. 18 and 24
27. 36 and 54
28. 36 and 48

I can find common multiples of two numbers.

Multiples are the numbers in a multiplication table.

Examples

The multiples of 2 are the numbers in the 2 times table.

2, 4, 6, 8, 10, 12, ... 34, 36, 38, 40, ... 122, 124, 126, 128 and so on.

A

Write down the first five multiples of:

1. 4
2. 5
3. 10
4. 6
5. 9
6. 20.

Write Yes or No.

7. Is 56 a multiple of 2?
8. Is 32 a multiple of 3?
9. Is 85 a multiple of 5?
10. Is 26 a multiple of 4?
11. Is 82 a multiple of 8?
12. Is 150 a multiple of 10?
13. Is 60 a multiple of 3?
14. Is 65 a multiple of 1?
15. Is 54 a multiple of 9?
16. Is 47 a multiple of 7?
17. Is 42 a multiple of 6?
18. Is 84 a multiple of 4?
19. Is 54 a multiple of 5?
20. Is 75 a multiple of 15?
21. Is 89 a multiple of 11?
22. Is 24 a multiple of 8?
23. Is 300 a multiple of 50?
24. Is 210 a multiple of 20?

B

Which number should not be in the box?

1. Multiples of 5
   106, 80, 75, 135
2. Multiples of 8
   48, 72, 54, 32
3. Multiples of 6
   42, 36, 46, 54
4. Multiples of 9
   81, 54, 69, 99

Find two numbers that are common multiples of:

5. 2 and 7
6. 3 and 4
7. 3 and 5
8. 4 and 5
9. 3 and 10
10. 4 and 6
11. 5 and 7
12. 2 and 11.

What is the smallest whole number divisible by:

13. 2 and 3
14. 3 and 8
15. 6 and 4
16. 4 and 10
17. 5 and 3
18. 6 and 8
19. 10 and 6
20. 2 and 9?

C

Find three numbers that are multiples of both:

1. 2 and 9
2. 3 and 8
3. 8 and 10
4. 4 and 7
5. 5 and 6
6. 8 and 6
7. 14 and 21
8. 5 and 9.

Find the lowest common multiple of:

9. 2 and 11
10. 3 and 13
11. 6 and 12
12. 4 and 18
13. 5 and 12
14. 10 and 12
15. 8 and 12
16. 9 and 15.

Use these digits for 17 to 24.

5 3 1 8 6 2

Make as many 2-digit numbers as you can that are multiples of:

17. 2
18. 3
19. 5
20. 8
21. 7
22. 9
23. 4
24. 6

25. The ages of both Len and his grandfather are multiples of 9. Next year both ages will be multiples of 7. How old are they both?

I can solve inverse operation and word problems.

Example

David has 66 books.
Lindsey has 35 more.
How many do they have altogether?

66 + 35 = 101
101 + 66 = 167
They have 167 books altogether.

A

Copy and complete.

1. 8·4 + ☐ = 10
2. ☐ − 5 = 1·3
3. 480 ÷ ☐ = 80
4. ☐ × 9 = 108
5. Mark is 18. His father is 38 years older. How old is Mark's father?
6. Two thirds of the 27 passengers on a bus are adults. How many of the passengers are children?
7. A video shop has three racks with 80 videos and four racks with 120 videos. How many videos are there on the racks?
8. Calvin buys a burger for £3·69 and a drink for £1·45. He pays with a £10 note. How much change does he receive?

B

Copy and complete.

1. £1·74 + ☐ = £5·00
2. 7·2 ÷ ☐ = 0·8
3. 25 × ☐ = 400
4. 10 − ☐ = 3·78
5. ☐ × 7 = 3·5
6. ☐ + 96 = 263
7. ☐ − 0·15 = 0·9
8. ☐ ÷ 6 = 5·3
9. This year there will be 190 school days. How many days will not be school days?
10. A car travels 9 miles per litre of petrol. How many litres of petrol will be used in travelling 144 miles?
11. Paul has read 45 pages of his book. He needs to read 26 more to reach half way. How many pages does Paul's book have?
12. Kirsty and Pru have £17·40 between them. Kirsty has £2·60 more than Pru. How much money do they have each?

C

Copy and complete.

1. 6·3 − ☐ = 5·55
2. 4 × ☐ = 18
3. 2·58 + ☐ = 5·19
4. 12 ÷ ☐ = 0·6
5. ☐ × 17 = 289
6. ☐ − 1·27 = 4·1
7. ☐ + 0·325 = 0·5
8. ☐ ÷ 24 = 3·6
9. Bradley swims 50 lengths of a pool every day. How many lengths would he swim in April?
10. During the day 257 books are returned to a library and 149 are borrowed. At the end of the day there are 2 415 books. How many books were there in the library at the start of the day?
11. The garden centre had eight trays with 24 potted plants in each. Another six trays had 30 plants in each. 143 plants were sold. How many plants were left?
12. A stall at a fete sells cakes for 85p each. The stall raises £113·90. How many cakes are sold?

I can find the sums and differences and the doubles and halves of numbers with up to two decimal places.

Examples

46 + 39 = 85	65 − 37 = 28	58 × 2 = 116	358 ÷ 2 = 179
4·6 + 3·9 = 8·5	6·5 − 3·7 = 2·8	5·8 × 2 = 11·6	35·8 ÷ 2 = 17·9
0·46 + 0·39 = 0·85	0·65 − 0·37 = 0·28	0·58 × 2 = 1·16	3·58 ÷ 2 = 1·79
460 + 390 = 850	6500 − 3700 = 2800	580 × 2 = 1160	3580 ÷ 2 = 1790

A

63 − 37 = 26

Use the above fact to work out these linked calculations.

1. 63 − 26
2. 26 + 37
3. 37 + 26
4. 630 − 370
5. 6·3 − 3·7
6. 370 + 260
7. 0·63 − 0·37
8. 2·6 + 3·7

Double these numbers.

9. 17
10. 1·7
11. 35
12. 350
13. 29
14. 0·29
15. 46
16. 4600

Halve these numbers.

17. 32
18. 3·2
19. 46
20. 460
21. 74
22. 0·74
23. 52
24. 5200

B

Write the answers only.

1. 4·6 + 3·7
2. 0·63 − 0·29
3. 390 + 230
4. 8500 − 4300
5. 0·65 + 0·58
6. 7·5 − 3·8
7. 3600 + 4800
8. 940 − 670
9. 7·3 + 2·9
10. 0·81 − 0·34

Double these numbers.

11. 5·2
12. 670
13. 0·59
14. 6500
15. 840
16. 0·76
17. 3700
18. 0·93

Halve these numbers.

19. 920
20. 8·4
21. 1·48
22. 16 200
23. 0·56
24. 1580
25. 12·8
26. 19 600

C

Copy and complete.

1. □ + 0·46 = 0·72
2. □ − 3·2 = 5·9
3. 3300 + □ = 7500
4. 970 − □ = 530
5. □ + 4·7 = 11·3
6. □ − 0·41 = 0·39
7. 160 + □ = 8400
8. 6200 − □ = 3800
9. □ + 0·17 = 0·76
10. □ − 0·25 = 0·82
11. □ × 2 = 14·6
12. □ × 2 = 1940
13. □ × 2 = 1·38
14. □ × 2 = 15 200
15. □ × 2 = 11·4
16. □ ÷ 2 = 550
17. □ ÷ 2 = 0·66
18. □ ÷ 2 = 9·7
19. □ ÷ 2 = 8300
20. □ ÷ 2 = 0·99

B2 MULTIPLICATION FACTS

I can use the multiplication facts up to 10 × 10 to ×/÷ multiples of 10 and 100.

A

What is

1. 8 × 2
2. 7 × 4
3. 4 × 7
4. 6 × 5
5. 9 × 6
6. 5 × 9
7. 9 × 9
8. 8 × 5
9. 3 × 7
10. 4 × 8
11. 9 × 4
12. 6 × 3
13. 27 ÷ 3
14. 48 ÷ 8
15. 32 ÷ 4
16. 49 ÷ 7
17. 24 ÷ 6
18. 12 ÷ 2
19. 30 ÷ 6
20. 14 ÷ 2
21. 64 ÷ 8
22. 45 ÷ 5
23. 63 ÷ 9
24. 15 ÷ 3

B

Copy and complete.

1. ☐ × 4 = 24
2. ☐ × 7 = 63
3. ☐ × 5 = 35
4. ☐ × 9 = 36
5. ☐ × 6 = 36
6. ☐ × 8 = 56
7. ☐ ÷ 3 = 8
8. ☐ ÷ 9 = 6
9. ☐ ÷ 7 = 8
10. ☐ ÷ 8 = 5
11. ☐ ÷ 2 = 9
12. ☐ ÷ 6 = 7

Write the answer only

13. 300 × 8
14. 90 × 50
15. 50 × 7
16. 800 × 9
17. 300 × 90
18. 800 × 6
19. 60 × 20
20. 800 × 70
21. 1800 ÷ 6
22. 280 ÷ 4
23. 4200 ÷ 70
24. 7200 ÷ 8
25. 320 ÷ 80
26. 2100 ÷ 30
27. 540 ÷ 6
28. 4500 ÷ 9
29. Use the given multiplication fact to develop a family of linked facts.

    7 × 4 = 28

C

Copy and complete.

1. ☐ × 7 = 280
2. ☐ × 3 = 2700
3. ☐ × 60 = 4200
4. ☐ × 80 = 400
5. ☐ × 900 = 8100
6. ☐ × 5 = 300
7. ☐ ÷ 60 = 80
8. ☐ ÷ 2 = 90
9. ☐ ÷ 7 = 700
10. ☐ ÷ 90 = 500
11. ☐ ÷ 40 = 90
12. ☐ ÷ 800 = 60

Write the answer only

13. 0·8 × 7
14. 0·5 × 5
15. 0·7 × 9
16. 0·4 × 6
17. 0·06 × 9
18. 0·07 × 2
19. 0·05 × 6
20. 0·07 × 8
21. 1·8 ÷ 3
22. 7·2 ÷ 8
23. 4·2 ÷ 7
24. 7·2 ÷ 9
25. 0·63 ÷ 7
26. 0·24 ÷ 4
27. 0·64 ÷ 8
28. 0·36 ÷ 6
29. Use the given division fact to develop a family of linked facts.

    0·35 ÷ 7 = 0·05

I can investigate a statement and explain why it is true or false.

Factors are numbers that divide exactly into another number. Factors can be shown by creating arrays.

Example

Two arrays can be made using 6 squares.

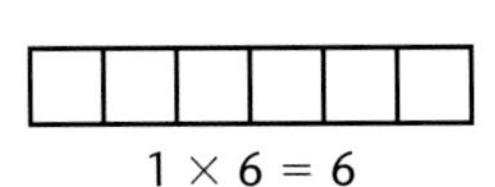

$1 \times 6 = 6$

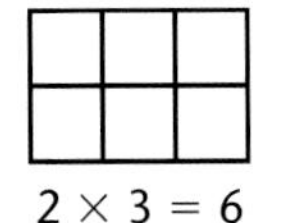

$2 \times 3 = 6$

The factors of 6 are 1, 2, 3, 6

A

1. Draw two different arrays using 8 squares.
2. List the four factors of 8.
3. Draw two different arrays using 15 squares.
4. List the four factors of 15.
5. Draw two different arrays using 4 squares.
6. List the three factors of 4.
7. Draw three different arrays using 20 squares.
8. List the six factors of 20.

Find as many pairs of numbers as you can with a product of:

9. 14
10. 18
11. 22
12. 27
13. 28
14. 32
15. 40
16. 54.

A multiple of 4 is also a multiple of 2.

17. Find three examples of the above statement.
18. Explain why the statement is true.

B

Find all the factors of:

1. 34
2. 52
3. 25
4. 59
5. 70
6. 63
7. 55
8. 84.

Fill in the box to complete each pair of factors.

9. $\square \times 6 = 4200$
10. $\square \times 5 = 200$
11. $80 \times \square = 720$
12. $600 \times \square = 2400$

Find as many pairs of numbers as you can with a product of:

13. 36
14. 44
15. 80
16. 48.

The product of an odd number and an even number is always even.

17. Give four examples of the above statement.
18. Explain why the statement is true.

A multiple of 8 is always twice a multiple of 4.

19. Give four examples of the above statement.
20. Explain why the statement is true.

C

Find the highest factor shared by:

1. 45 and 60
2. 39 and 65
3. 72 and 40
4. 84 and 63.

Fill in the box to complete each pair of factors.

5. $\square \times 70 = 6300$
6. $\square \times 3 = 2400$
7. $800 \times \square = 5600$
8. $9 \times \square = 8100$

Find as many pairs of numbers as you can with a product of:

9. 2200
10. 600
11. 320
12. 4900.

The product of any two consecutive numbers is always even.

13. Give four examples of the above statement.
14. Explain why the statement is true.

A factor of 20 is also a factor of 100.

15. Give four examples of the above statement.
16. Explain why the statement is true.

I can find examples to match a general statement.

Example

The product of any whole number and 10 will end in a zero.

e.g. 34 × 10 = 340
127 × 10 = 1270
9 × 10 = 90

The statement is true because all multiples of 10 end in zero.

A

Find three examples for each statement.

1. A multiple of 4 is also a multiple of 2.
2. A multiple of 10 is always twice a multiple of 5.
3. A number is not a multiple of 5 if it does not end in a 5 or a 0.
4. If you add two different numbers the other way round the answer is the same.

B

For each statement:

a) find three examples
b) explain why it is true.

1. If you multiply different numbers the other way round the answer is the same.
2. A multiple of 6 is also a multiple of 3.
3. A number is a multiple of 4 if its last two digits are divisible by 4.
4. The product of an odd number and an even number is always even.

C

For each statement:

a) find three examples
b) explain why it is true.

1. A multiple of 6 is also a multiple of 3.
2. Dividing a number by 100 moves every digit two places to the right.
3. The product of any three consecutive numbers is always even.
4. The product of any two odd numbers is always odd.

I can make up number stories to match statements.

Example

5·4 ÷ 4 = 1·35

Four milkshakes cost £5·40.
One milkshake costs £1·35.

A

Make up a story to match each number sentence.

1. 48 + 37 = 85
2. 97 − 42 = 55
3. 19 × 4 = 76
4. 450 ÷ 3 = 150
5. 326 + 64 = 390
6. 200 − 120 = 80
7. 60 × 5 = 300
8. 58 ÷ 2 = 29

B

Make up a story to match each number sentence.

1. 3·4 + 1·7 = 5·1
2. 6 − 4·2 = 1·8
3. 248 × 7 = 1736
4. 232 ÷ 8 = 29
5. 463 + 179 = 642
6. 435 − 78 = 357
7. 16·5 × 26 = 429
8. 28·8 ÷ 9 = 3·2

C

Make up a story to match each number sentence.

1. 159·6 + 63·75 = 223·35
2. 42·9 − 28·65 = 14·25
3. 5·36 × 24 = 128·64
4. 49·6 ÷ 8 = 6·2
5. 0·05 + 0·03 = 0·08
6. 19·2 − 3·64 = 15·56
7. 27 × 36 = 972
8. 144 ÷ 40 = 3·6

Do not write in this book

I can solve word problems.

A boat sailed 428 miles in the first week of its voyage and 136 miles further in the second week. How far has it sailed altogether?

428 + 136 = 564
428 + 564 = 992
The boat has sailed 992 miles altogether.

A

1. There are 74 apples on a tree. 19 are picked. How many apples are there on the tree now?
2. There are 12 biscuits in each packet. How many biscuits are there in 6 packets?
3. Cards cost 65p each. Lorette buys a pack of 10 cards for £4·80. How much has she saved?
4. Gill has 800 g of flour. She uses 250 g for pastry and 325 g for a cake. How much flour is left?
5. The 60 children in Year 5 were asked what pets they owned. One quarter of the children had no pets at all, 12 had cats and 17 had dogs. How many children had other sorts of pets?

B

1. There are 80 tea bags in a box. How many boxes will 400 tea bags fill?
2. 134 parents watched the afternoon performance of the School Concert. 97 more came that evening. How many parents saw the evening performance?
3. 303 children in a school go on a trip. Five coaches each carry 51 children. The rest travel by minibus, each of which can carry 13 children. How many minibuses are there?
4. Max has 175 photos. He keeps 79 photos in one album. The rest are equally divided between three more identical albums. How many photos are there in each of Max's identical albums?
5. Four lengths of 1·6 m and three of 0·75 m are cut from a 10 metre rope. How much rope is left?
6. Saurav buys two games and a toy. Each game costs £1·29. He pays with a £10 note and receives £4·17 change. How much does the toy cost?

C

1. 62 386 people watched Manchester United's match on Wednesday. How many saw the next match when there were 649 fewer spectators?
2. There are 260 people watching a film. Two fifths of the audience are adults. How many children are watching the film?
3. How many seconds are there in five hours?
4. There are 120 sugar cubes in a packet. How many packets could 3000 sugar cubes fill?
5. One can of soup costs 46p. Jed buys sixteen cans. How much change will he have from a £20 note?
6. Each bottle of wine holds 0·75 litres. There are 64 guests at a wedding. How many bottles are needed to fill a 0·2 litre wine glass for each guest?

B2 SYMMETRICAL PATTERNS

I can complete patterns with two lines of symmetry.

Use squared paper. Copy the patterns. Shade in as many squares as necessary to complete the symmetrical pattern.

1. 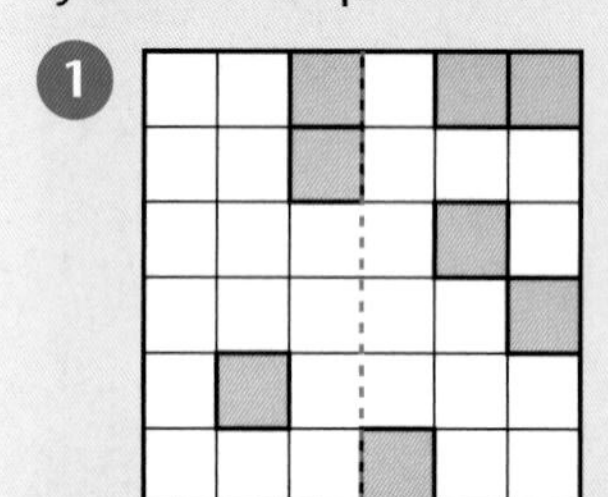

2. 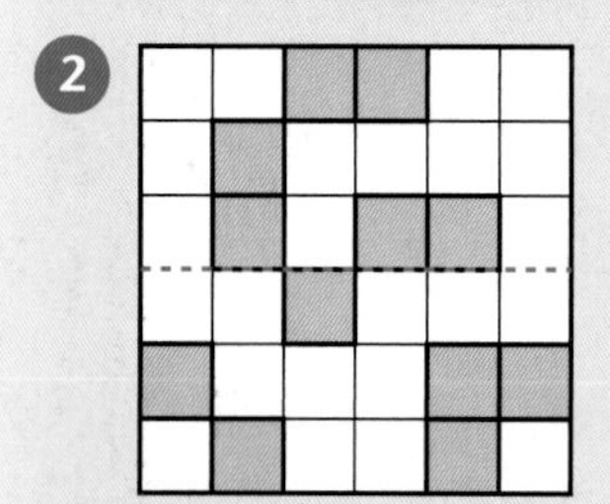

3. These symmetrical shapes have been made by placing 5 squares together.

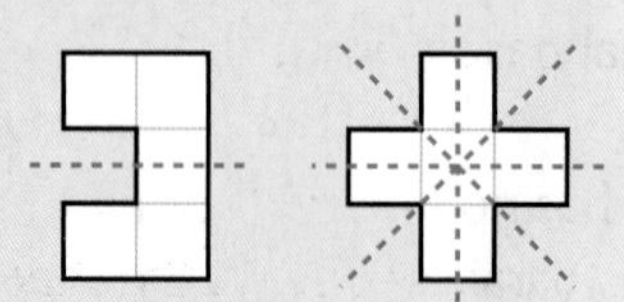

Investigate making symmetrical shapes by placing 6 squares together.

4. Copy the equilateral triangle and the square.

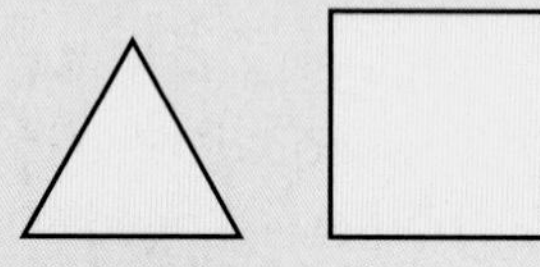

Draw the lines of symmetry in each shape.

B

Use squared paper.
Copy and complete the symmetrical patterns.

1. 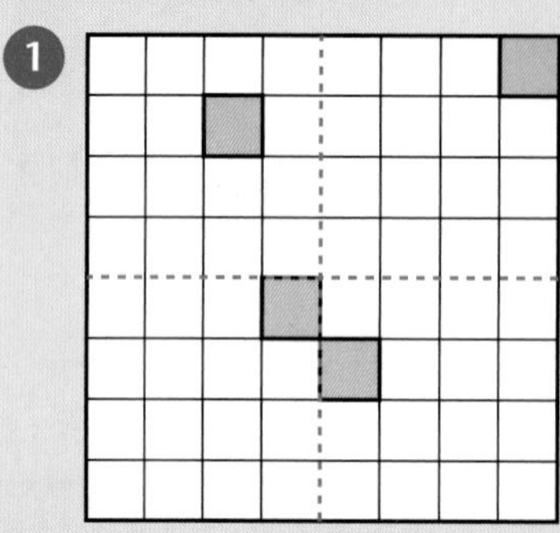

2. 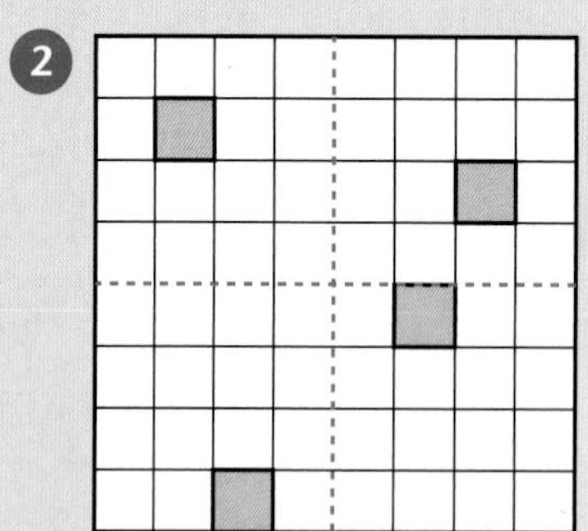

3. Investigate the symmetrical patterns that can be made by placing 8 squares together.

4. Copy the regular pentagon and the regular hexagon.

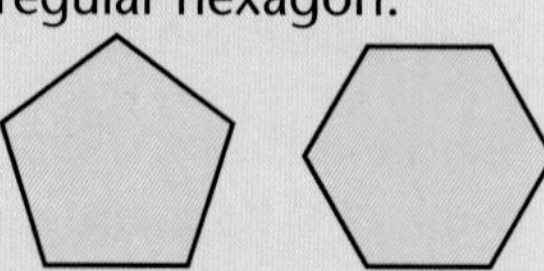

Draw the lines of symmetry in each shape.

5. Make a general statement about the number of lines of symmetry in a regular polygon.

C

Use squared paper.
Copy and complete the symmetrical pattern.

1. 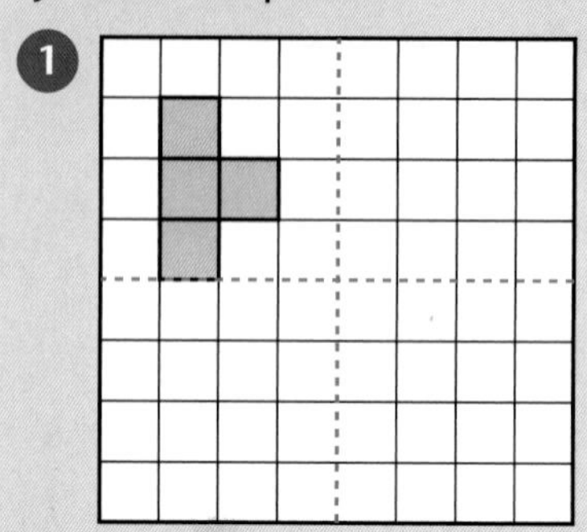

2. 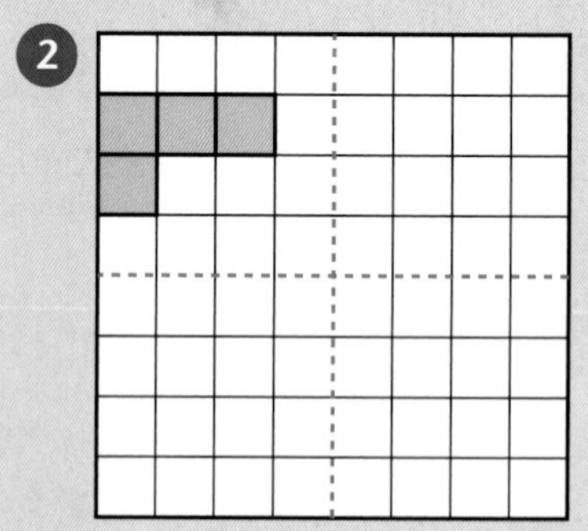

3. 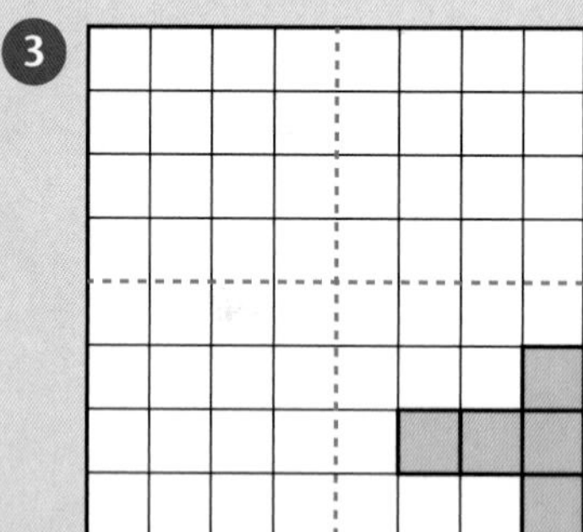

4. Investigate the symmetrical patterns that can be made by placing 9 squares together.

5. Investigate the angle between the lines of symmetry at the centre of a regular polygon. What do you notice?

I can identify 3-D shapes that have pairs of parallel or perpendicular edges.

Match each of the shapes A to L with one of the names of 3-D shapes.

cone	hemisphere	pentagonal based prism
cube	hexagonal based prism	square based pyramid
cuboid	octagonal based prism	tetrahedron
cylinder	octahedron	triangular based pyramid

A 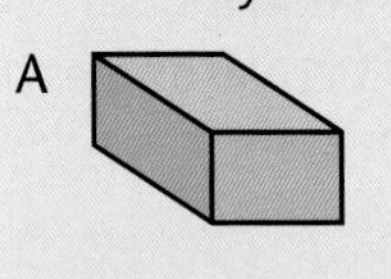
B 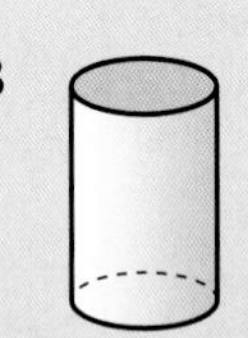
C 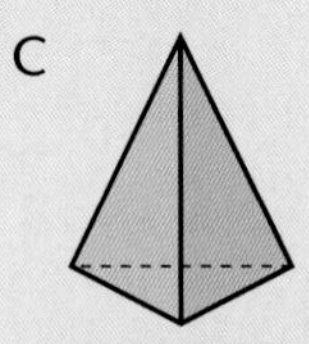
D 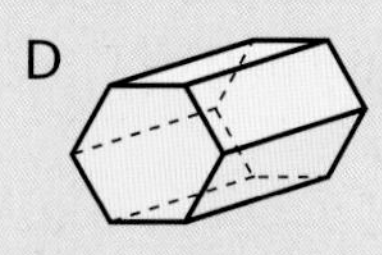
E 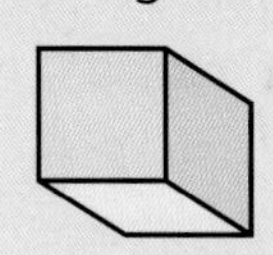
F 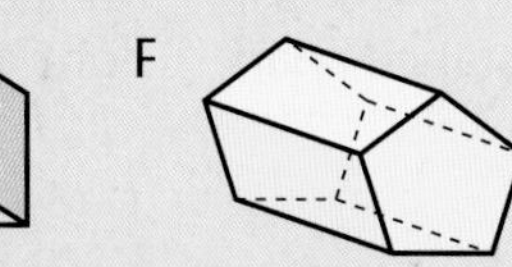

G 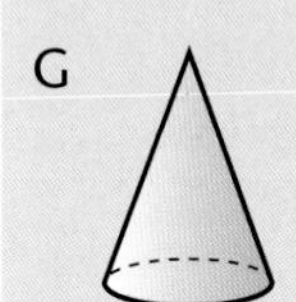
H 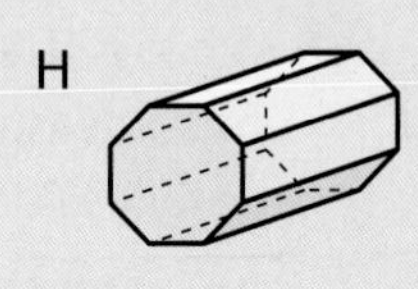
I 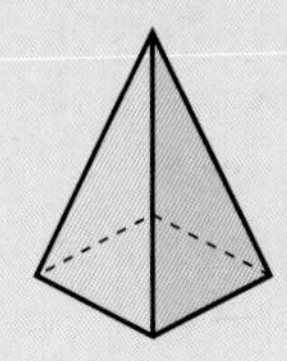
J 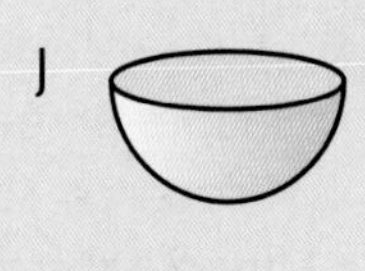
K 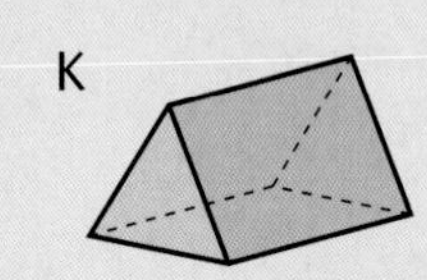
L 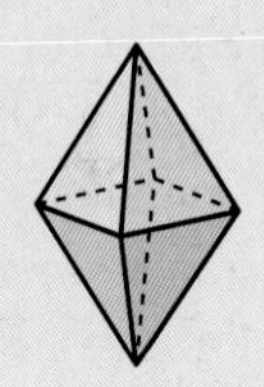

Look at the above shapes with straight edges. Which of the shapes have pairs of parallel edges in:

1. all their faces
2. more than one half of their faces
3. one face only
4. none of their faces?

Which faces have pairs of perpendicular edges in:

5. a cube
6. a square based pyramid
7. a triangular based prism
8. a cuboid?
9. Which shape with straight edges has no perpendicular edges?
10. Which shape has perpendicular edges in the shape but not in any face?

C

How many faces have pairs of parallel edges in:

1. an hexagonal pyramid
2. a decagonal (10-sided) based prism
3. an heptagonal based prism?
4. Which shape has no face with parallel edges but has parallel edges in the shape?

How many faces have perpendicular edges in:

5. a pentagonal pyramid
6. an hexagonal pyramid
7. an heptagonal based prism
8. a decagonal based prism?
9. How many edges are there on the end faces of a prism with:
   a) 9 faces with perpendicular edges
   b) 14 faces with perpendicular edges?

I can identify pairs of parallel or perpendicular lines in 2-D shapes and I can recognise and draw different types of triangles.

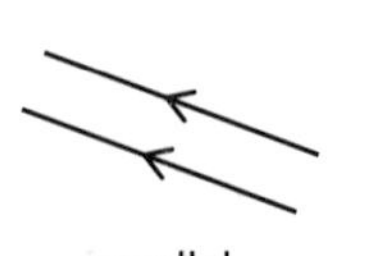

parallel lines

the same distance apart

perpendicular lines

meet at right angles

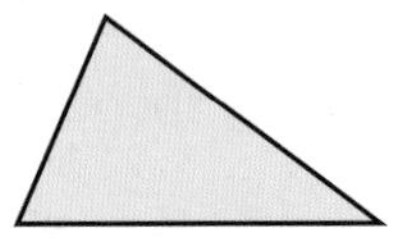

scalene triangle

no equal sides
no equal angles

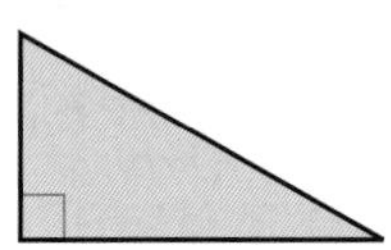

right-angled triangle

one 90° angle

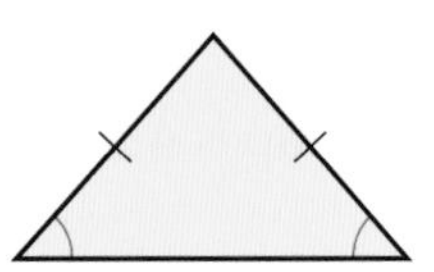

isosceles triangle

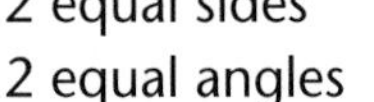

2 equal sides
2 equal angles

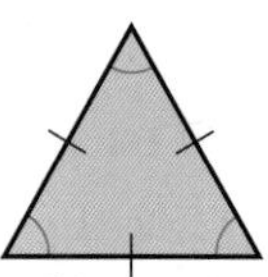

equilateral triangle

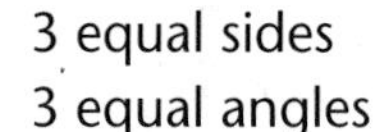

3 equal sides
3 equal angles

1 Copy the 2-D shapes below. Show all the parallel sides with arrow heads (see above). Show all the perpendicular sides by marking right angles (see above).

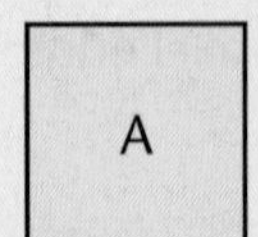

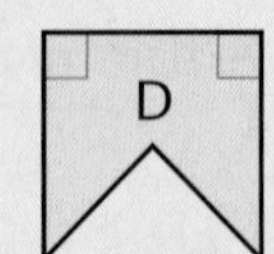

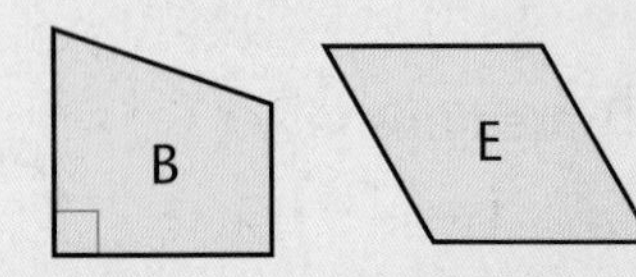

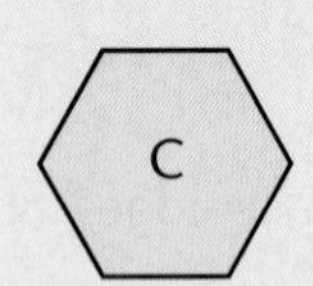

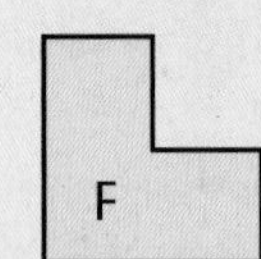

2 Use square paper. Draw and label:

a) 2 different right-angled triangles

b) 2 different isosceles triangles

c) 2 different scalene triangles.

1 Draw and label different shapes on grids of 4 squares. Show all the parallel sides and perpendicular sides.

Examples

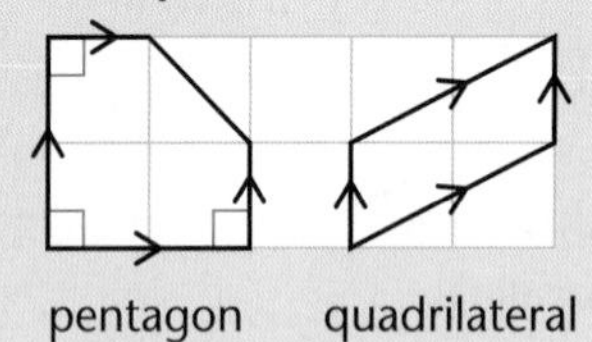

pentagon quadrilateral

2 Copy the octagon or draw round a template.

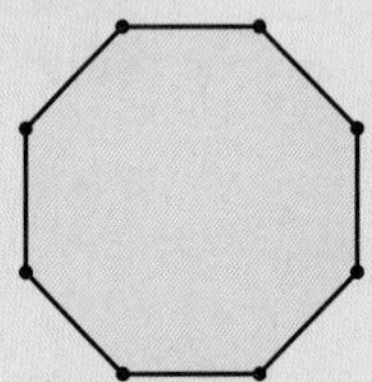

Join three dots to make:

a) a right-angled triangle

b) a scalene triangle

c) 3 different isosceles triangles.

3 Use a set square and ruler. Draw a right-angled isosceles triangle with shorter sides of 3·5 cm.

1 What is the largest possible number of parallel sides in:

a) a pentagon

b) a hexagon?

2 What is the largest possible number of perpendicular sides in:

a) a pentagon

b) a hexagon?

3 Investigate the largest possible number of:

a) parallel sides in polygons

b) perpendicular sides in polygons.

Describe any patterns you find.

4 Use a ruler and a protractor. Draw:

a) a right angled triangle with an angle of 55° and a shortest side of 3 cm

b) an isosceles triangle with two angles of 65° and a shortest side of 2·5 cm.

C2 METRIC UNITS OF CAPACITY

I can choose and use metric units of capacity.

Examples

1000 ml = 1 litre
4000 ml = 4 litres

2500 ml = 2·5 litres
1900 ml = 1·9 litres

3170 ml = 3·17 ℓ
2680 ml = 2·68 ℓ

A

Copy and complete.

1. 2000 ml = ☐ litres
2. 5000 ml = ☐ litres
3. 1000 ml = ☐ litre
4. 3 litres = ☐ ml
5. 4 litres = ☐ ml
6. 8 litres = ☐ ml
7. 6500 ml = ☐ litres
8. 500 ml = ☐ litres
9. 7500 ml = ☐ litres
10. 3·5 litres = ☐ ml
11. 1·5 litres = ☐ ml
12. 9·5 litres = ☐ ml

Which metric unit would you use to measure the capacity of:

13. a washing machine
14. a spoonful of medicine
15. an eyebath
16. a paddling pool
17. a stream
18. a bottle of nail varnish?

B

Copy and complete.

1. 4300 ml = ☐ litres
2. 1700 ml = ☐ litres
3. 900 ml = ☐ litres
4. 7·1 litres = ☐ ml
5. 2·6 litres = ☐ ml
6. 5·3 litres = ☐ ml
7. 9200 ml = ☐ litres
8. 6700 ml = ☐ litres
9. 3800 ml = ☐ litres
10. 1·4 litres = ☐ ml
11. 8·1 litres = ☐ ml
12. 0·3 litres = ☐ ml

Which metric unit would you use to measure the capacity of:

13. a hot water tank
14. a sachet of vinegar
15. a water pistol
16. a glass of orange
17. a swamp
18. a fire extinguisher?

C

Copy and complete.

1. 3530 ml = ☐ litres
2. 860 ml = ☐ litres
3. 2290 ml = ☐ litres
4. 5·01 litres = ☐ ml
5. 2·6 litres = ☐ ml
6. 7·12 litres = ☐ ml
7. 1580 ml = ☐ litres
8. 6940 ml = ☐ litres
9. 4310 ml = ☐ litres
10. 2·07 litres = ☐ ml
11. 5·63 litres = ☐ ml
12. 0·74 litres = ☐ ml

Choose the best estimate.

13. a squeezy lemon
 0·015 ℓ, 0·15 ℓ, 1·5 ℓ
14. a fish tank
 100 ml, 1000 ml, 10 000 ml
15. an ink bottle
 0·03 ℓ, 0·3 ℓ, 3 ℓl
16. a car's petrol tank
 40 ℓ, 400 ℓ, 4000 ℓ
17. a bottle of salad dressing
 2·5 ml, 25 ml, 250 ml
18. a bath
 10 ℓ, 100 ℓ, 1000 ℓ

I can draw and interpret bar line charts.

Examples

The number of elephants seen each day at a water hole in a Safari Park.

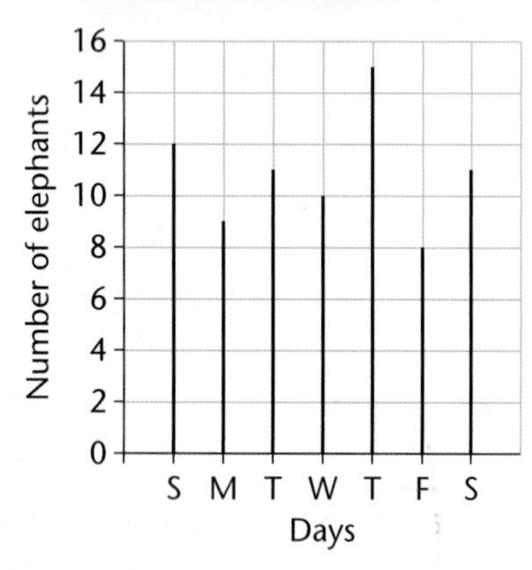

How many elephants were seen at the water hole on Monday?
What was the largest number of elephants seen on any one day?
What number of elephants was the mode?
(The mode is the most common value.)

This bar line chart shows the first 7 multiples of 5.

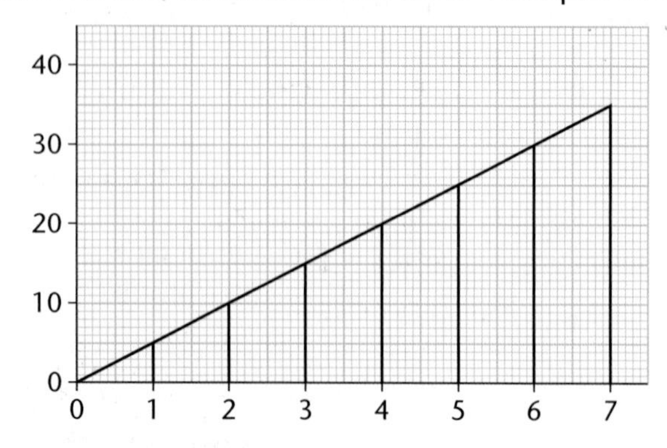

The tops of the bars have been joined to make a line graph showing the start of the 5 times table.

A

1 This bar line chart shows the destinations of holidays sold by a travel agent.

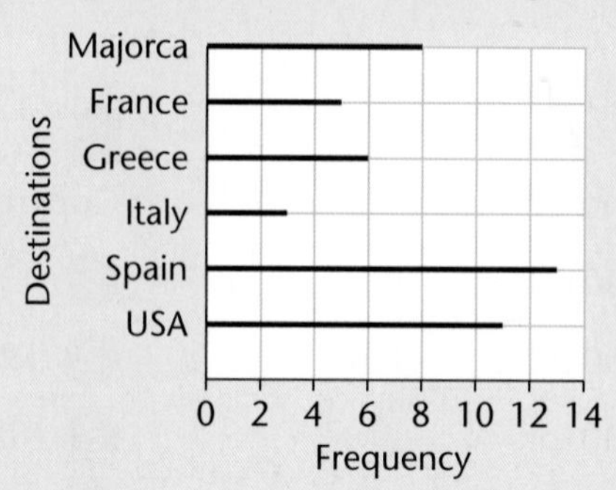

a) How many holidays were sold to the U.S.A.?

b) Which was the most popular destination?

c) Which was the least popular destination?

d) How many more holidays were sold to Majorca than to France?

e) How many holidays were sold altogether during the week?

2 Use graph paper.
Copy and complete this bar line chart showing all the multiples of 6 to $10 \times 6 = 60$.

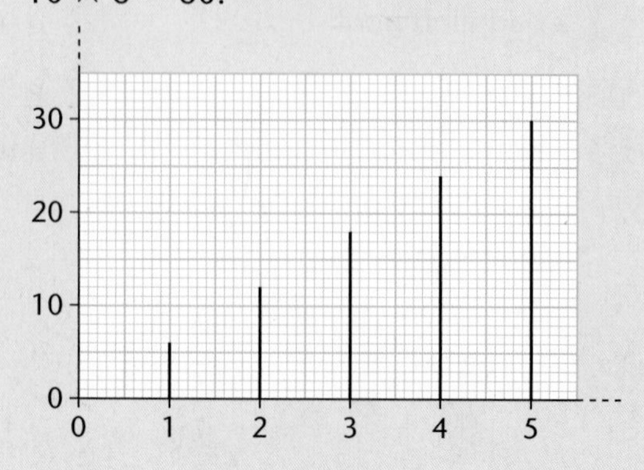

B

1 This bar line chart shows how many times each number was thrown when a dice was rolled repeatedly.

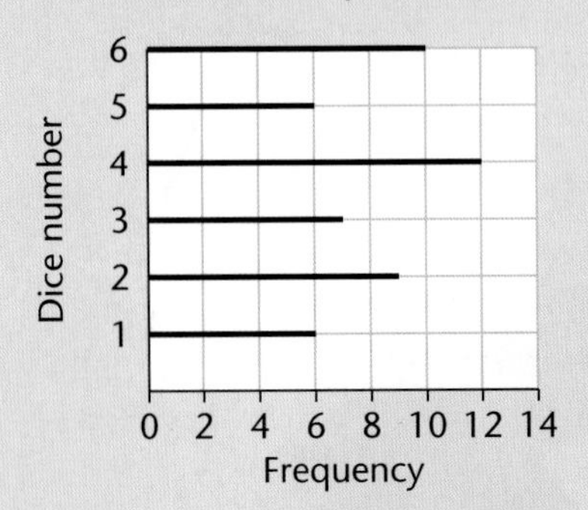

a) Which dice score was the mode?

b) How many times was 2 rolled?

c) How many more times was 6 rolled than 1?

d) How many times was a number less than 3 rolled?

e) How many times was an even number rolled?

f) How many times was the dice rolled altogether?

2 Use graph paper.
Copy and complete this line graph showing the 7 times table for all numbers to 12×7.

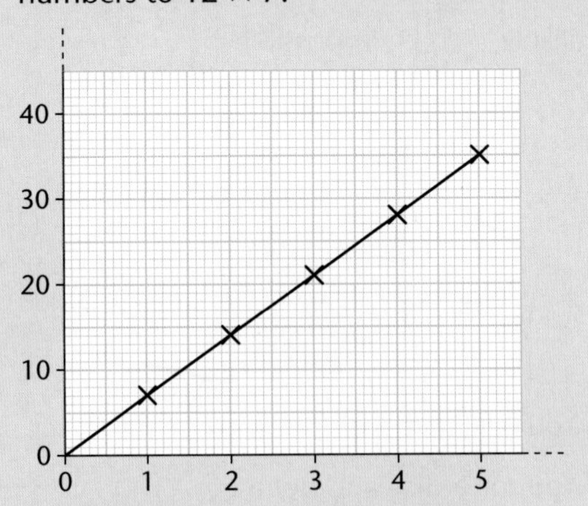

Use your graph to work out what is approximately:

a) $11{\cdot}4 \times 7$

b) $3{\cdot}7 \times 7$

c) $60 \div 7$

d) $40 \div 7$.

C

1 This line graph shows the outdoor temperature recorded hourly between 3 am and 3 pm on February 12th.

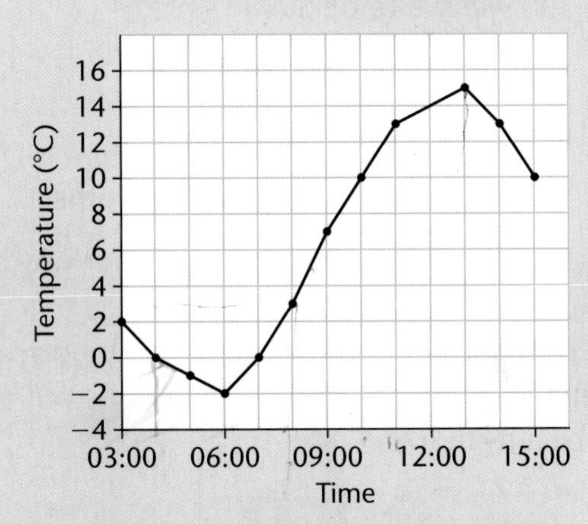

a) At what time was the temperature 5 °C?

b) What was the temperature at 11:00?

c) What was the highest temperature recorded?

d) What was the lowest temperature?

e) For how long was the temperature above 10 °C?

f) For how long was the temperature below 0 °C?

2 Roll two dice. Add the scores to give a total.
Repeat this 50 times keeping a tally of the total scores.
Draw a bar line chart to show the results.
What was the range of scores?
Which dice score was the mode?
Did this surprise you?

C2 PROBABILITY

I can use the language of probability and place events on a probability scale.

The probability of something happening is the likelihood or chance that it might happen.

Examples

What is the probability of these events?

1. The sun will rise tomorrow.
2. You will live to be 500.
3. You spin a coin and get a head.
4. It will rain tomorrow.
5. You will see a bus on your way home.
6. You will see an ambulance on your way home.

The probabilities of these events can be placed on a scale. You might choose to place them in these positions. Numbers 1 to 3 could not be put anywhere else but the last three statements depend upon the circumstances.

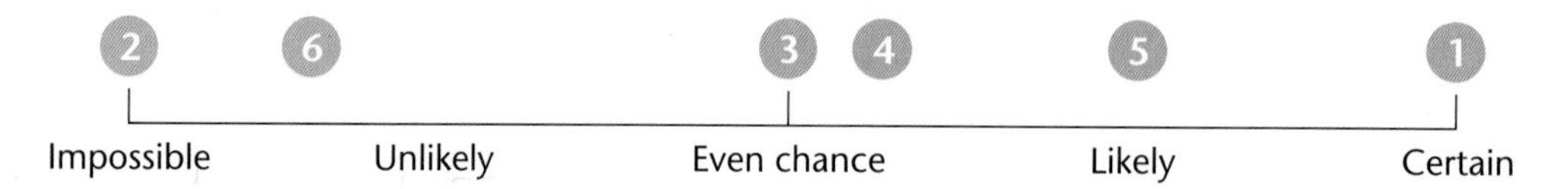

For each of these statements write one of these probabilities.

certain likely even chance unlikely impossible

1. You will get married next week.
2. You will watch television this evening.
3. The next match a football team play will be a home game.
4. Your teacher will win the Lottery and retire to the Bahamas.

5. You will have a birthday in the next year.
6. You roll a dice and get a 6.
7. The phone will ring this evening.
8. You will have a new pair of shoes in the next three months
9. You will learn to juggle in the next year.
10. It will snow next week.

B

Place the probability of these events on a scale like the one on the previous page.

1. You will get married when you grow up.
2. The Queen was born on a Thursday.
3. Someone in the family will receive a letter tomorrow.
4. You will pass your driving test next year.
5. You roll a dice and get an even number.
6. The next person to come into the classroom will be the Headteacher.
7. A baby will be born somewhere in the world today.
8. Everyone in the class will watch television next week.
9. Your television set will need to be repaired in the next five years.
10. A teacher at your school will have a Number 1 hit record.

1	2	3	4	5

11. The above cards are shuffled and then placed face down on a table. What is the probability of one card being turned over and it is:

a) 5
b) 6
c) odd
d) even
e) under 3
f) 3 or over 3?

12. One card is turned over.

2   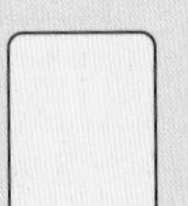 

What is the probability that the next card turned over will be:

a) odd
b) even
c) 2
d) 3
e) less than 3
f) greater than 3?

C

Work out these probabilities as a fraction and place each letter on the scale shown.

1. 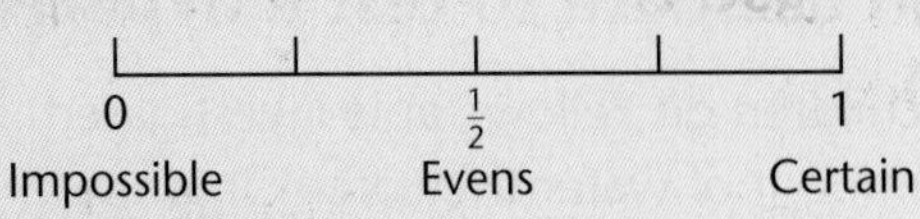

Spinning a coin and getting:

a) a head
b) a head or a tail
c) neither a head or a tail
d) a tail.

Spinning two coins and:

e) getting 2 heads
f) not getting 2 heads
g) getting one head and one tail
h) not getting one head and one tail.

2. 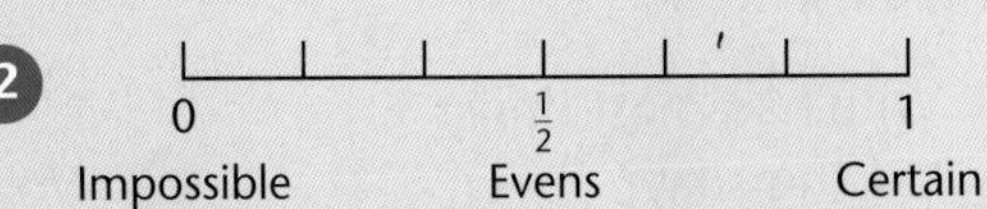

Rolling a 1 to 6 dice and getting:

a) an odd number
b) below 6
c) above 6
d) a 3
e) above 3
f) below 3

3. 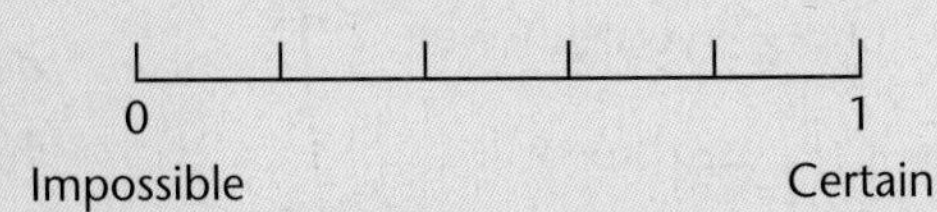

Using this spinner and getting:

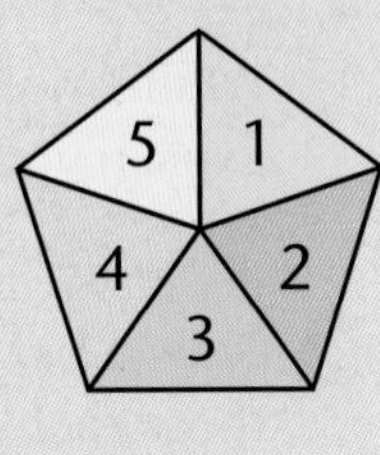

a) 1
b) below 1
c) above 1
d) an even number
e) an odd number
f) 6
g) below 6.

I can use data to test a hypothesis.

The children on Yellow Table investigated the amount of water they drank in one school day.
They worked out the amount of water in each child's average drink and then recorded the number of drinks they took each day for a week.
The table shows their results.

Name	Average drink	Number of drinks				
		M	Tu	W	Th	F
Adele	100 ml	4	8	7	5	6
Hugh	50 ml	12	15	9	8	11
Poppy	75 ml	4	6	8	5	7
Ryan	60 ml	5	7	9	6	8
Sanya	125 ml	2	3	5	4	6
Waqar	75 ml	9	10	7	11	8

A

Look at the table.

1. What is Poppy's average drink?
2. Who had most drinks on Thursday?
3. How much did Adele drink on Monday? Give your answer in millilitres.
4. Before the data was collected Hugh said
   I drink more than half a litre every day.
   Was he right?
   Explain your answer.
5. Ryan said
   I drink less than half a litre every day.
   Was he right?
   Explain your answer.
6. Draw a bar chart to show each child's average drink.

B

Look at the table.

1. On which day did:
   a) Poppy drink 375 ml
   b) Sanya drink 375 ml?
2. Which two children drank half a litre on Thursday?
3. On which day did the children have fewest drinks?
4. Who drank the most water on Wednesday?
5. Before the data was collected Sanya said
   We drink more on hotter days.
   Tuesday was the hottest day. Friday was the coldest. Does the data support her idea?
   Explain your answer.
6. Draw a bar line chart to show the total number of drinks for each child during the week.

C

Look at the table.

1. Which two children drank the same amount on Monday?
2. How much more did Sanya drink than Waqar on Wednesday?
3. In litres how much did:
   a) Adele drink in the week
   b) Hugh drink in the week?
4. Before the data was collected Adele said
   We all drink no less than 300 ml and no more than 800 ml every day.
   Explain why her theory is not supported by the data.
5. Who drank the most during the week?
6. Draw a bar line chart to show how much Waqar drank each day.

D2 ×/÷ DECIMALS BY 10, 100, 1000

I can multiply and divide whole numbers and decimals by 10, 100 and 1000.

		Examples
×10	digits move 1 place to the left	0·017 × 10 = 0·17
×100	digits move 2 places to the left	0·017 × 100 = 1·7
×1000	digits move 3 places to the left	0·017 × 1000 = 17
÷10	digits move 1 place to the right	36 ÷ 10 = 3·6
÷100	digits move 2 places to the right	36 ÷ 100 = 0·36
÷1000	digits move 3 places to the right	36 ÷ 1000 = 0·036

A

Work out

1. 40 × 10
2. 9100 ÷ 10
3. 28 × 100
4. 6500 ÷ 100
5. 9 × 1000
6. 70000 ÷ 1000
7. 511 × 10
8. 830 ÷ 10
9. 164 × 100
10. 20 000 ÷ 100
11. 34 × 1000
12. 21 000 ÷ 1000
13. 960 × 10
14. 4000 ÷ 10
15. 90 × 100
16. 19 300 ÷ 100
17. 20 × 1000
18. 50 000 ÷ 1000
19. 800 × 10
20. 1520 ÷ 10
21. 801 × 100
22. 60 000 ÷ 100
23. 68 × 1000
24. 47 000 ÷ 1000

B

×10	÷10	×100	÷100	×1000	÷1000
1. 3·2	7. 0·4	13. 5·2	19. 8	25. 0·3	31. 600
2. 0·006	8. 8	14. 0·97	20. 692	26. 2·08	32. 1978
3. 0·9	9. 1·07	15. 1·45	21. 30	27. 4·6	33. 250
4. 1·08	10. 405	16. 18·6	22. 480	28. 1·427	34. 16
5. 0·25	11. 36·9	17. 7·03	23. 106	29. 0·05	35. 40
6. 0·174	12. 22	18. 0·06	24. 75	30. 0·973	36. 121

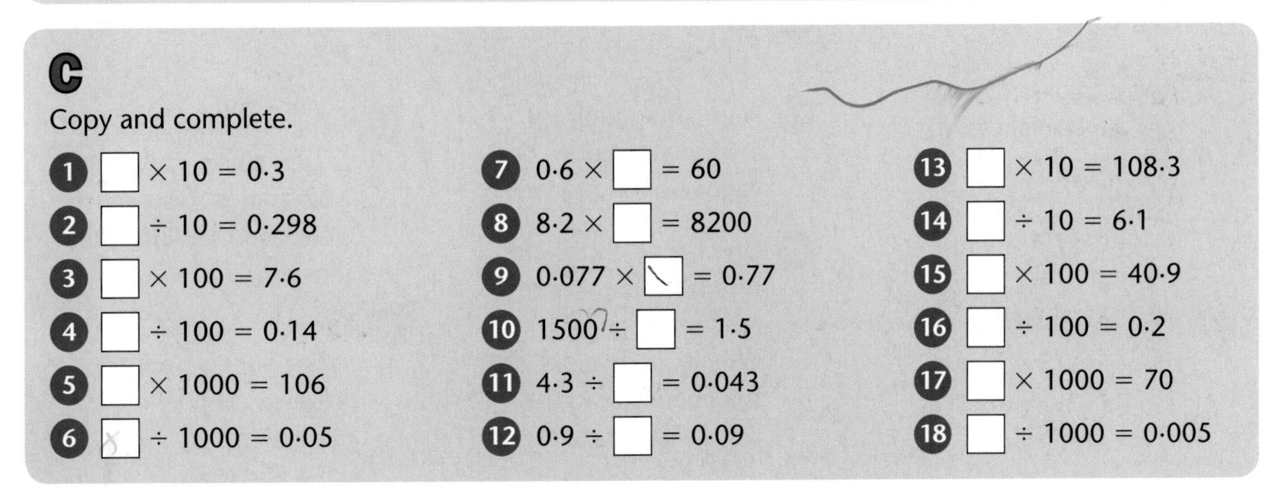

C

Copy and complete.

1. □ × 10 = 0·3
2. □ ÷ 10 = 0·298
3. □ × 100 = 7·6
4. □ ÷ 100 = 0·14
5. □ × 1000 = 106
6. □ ÷ 1000 = 0·05
7. 0·6 × □ = 60
8. 8·2 × □ = 8200
9. 0·077 × □ = 0·77
10. 1500 ÷ □ = 1·5
11. 4·3 ÷ □ = 0·043
12. 0·9 ÷ □ = 0·09
13. □ × 10 = 108·3
14. □ ÷ 10 = 6·1
15. □ × 100 = 40·9
16. □ ÷ 100 = 0·2
17. □ × 1000 = 70
18. □ ÷ 1000 = 0·005

D2 CONVERTING UNITS OF WEIGHT

I can convert grams to kilograms and vice versa.

Examples

1000 g = 1 kg	1000 g = 1 kg	4·3 kg = 4300 g
100 g = 0·1 kg	500 g = 0·5 kg	0·71 kg = 710 g
10 g = 0·01 kg	250 g = 0·25 kg	0·195 kg = 195 g
1 g = 0·001 kg	1750 g = 1·75 kg	2·013 kg = 2013 g

A

Copy and complete.

1. 2 kg = ☐ g
2. 5 kg = ☐ g
3. 1 kg = ☐ g
4. 9 kg = ☐ g
5. 7000 g = ☐ kg
6. 4000 g = ☐ kg
7. 3000 g = ☐ kg
8. 6000 g = ☐ kg
9. 2·5 kg = ☐ g
10. 1·25 kg = ☐ g
11. 0·5 kg = ☐ g
12. 4·25 kg = ☐ g
13. 3500 g = ☐ kg
14. 250 g = ☐ kg
15. 2750 g = ☐ kg
16. 1500 g = ☐ kg
17. A bag holds a 750 g box of cornflakes and half a kilogram of bananas. What is the weight of the shopping in kilograms?
18. A cake weighs one kilogram. One quarter is eaten. How much is left in grams?

B

Copy and complete.

1. 1·4 kg = ☐ g
2. 7·5 kg = ☐ g
3. 0·2 kg = ☐ g
4. 3·6 kg = ☐ g
5. 2800 g = ☐ kg
6. 1300 g = ☐ kg
7. 4500 g = ☐ kg
8. 900 g = ☐ kg
9. 5·7 kg = ☐ g
10. 2·3 kg = ☐ g
11. 1·4 kg = ☐ g
12. 0·1 kg = ☐ g
13. 3900 g = ☐ kg
14. 8800 g = ☐ kg
15. 600 g = ☐ kg
16. 4200 g = ☐ kg
17. Four cans weigh 1·6 kg. What does one can weigh in grams?
18. One bar of chocolate weighs 150 g. There are 24 bars in a box. What is the weight of the chocolate in the box in kilograms?

C

Copy and complete.

1. 2·37 kg = ☐ g
2. 4·63 kg = ☐ g
3. 1·28 kg = ☐ g
4. 6·05 kg = ☐ g
5. 3810 g = ☐ kg
6. 5140 g = ☐ kg
7. 520 g = ☐ kg
8. 9490 g = ☐ kg
9. 1·28 kg = ☐ g
10. 8·54 kg = ☐ g
11. 3·71 kg = ☐ g
12. 0·65 kg = ☐ g
13. 7090 g = ☐ kg
14. 4320 g = ☐ kg
15. 2960 g = ☐ kg
16. 5430 g = ☐ kg
17. A bag contains 1·2 kg of frozen chips. This makes 10 servings. How much does each serving weigh in grams?
18. One can weighs 225 g. What does a pack of 8 cans weigh in kilograms?

I can solve problems involving weight.

A

1. A tin of fruit weighs 200 g. What do 8 tins weigh in kilograms?
2. Four melons weigh 2 kg. What does one melon weigh?
3. Tom weighs 42·3 kg. Jerry weighs 1800 g less. What is their combined weight?
4. A sack of potatoes weighs 5 kg. Three quarters of the potatoes are eaten. What is the weight of the potatoes that are left?
5. A 200 g pack of ham contains 8 slices. How much does each slice weigh?
6. A cake is cut into 10 slices, each of which weighs 140 g. What is the weight of the cake in kilograms?

B

1. The 20 packets of biscuits in a box weigh 6 kg altogether. What is the weight of one packet in grams?
2. Each apple weighs 150 g. How much do 12 apples weigh in kilograms?
3. A pizza weighs 0·5 kg. One quarter is eaten. A further 175 g is eaten. How much is left?

4. A casserole is made with 800 g of meat and 1·2 kg of vegetables. What is the combined weight of the ingredients?
5. 10 packets of gravy powder weigh 3·5 kg. What does one packet weigh?
6. A box of lettuces weighs 2 kg. If the box weighs 100 g, how much do the lettuces weigh?

C

1. A loaf of bread weighs 0·8 kg. It is cut into 25 equal slices. How much does each slice weigh?
2. One parcel weighs 470 g. A second parcel weighs 200 g more. What is the combined weight of the parcels in kilograms?
3. A box containing 16 tins weighs 4 kg. How much does each tin weigh?
4. A recipe for 8 people requires using 1 kg of mince. How much mince would you use if you were cooking for 3 people?
5. A builder needs 2 kg of sand. He has 680 g left. How much more sand does he need?
6. A factory canteen serves 400 lunches. Each lunch requires 300 g of potatoes. What weight of potatoes is used?
7. A tray holding 24 eggs weighs 1·68 kg. Each egg weighs 65 g. What is the weight of the tray?

I can use a written method for addition of whole numbers and numbers with up to two decimal places.

Examples

```
  36 295        18·79     21·6 + 4·83      21·6      Line up the
+  6 487      +  3·45                    +  4·83     decimal points.
  42 782        22·24                      26·43
  1   11        11 1                        1
```

A

Copy and complete.

1. 3759 + 1246
2. 4818 + 2695
3. 7464 + 5928
4. 2374 + 682
5. 6533 + 1897
6. 47·3 + 30·9
7. 59·2 + 15·8
8. 86·4 + 27·3
9. 74·5 + 52·6
10. 48·7 + 43·9
11. Oliver weighs 35·6 kg. His father weighs 68·4 kg. What is their combined weight?
12. A bag of sand weighs 17·9 kg. A bag of cement weighs 32·8 kg more. How much does the cement weigh?
13. Belinda earns £2547 in January and £1987 in February. How much does she earn in the two months altogether?

B

Set out as in the examples.

1. 33 695 + 8276
2. 14 769 + 9523
3. 27 182 + 12 954
4. 16 437 + 13 895
5. 45 348 + 28 769
6. 26·38 + 97·52
7. 82·95 + 67·64
8. 30·81 + 75·46
9. 54·27 + 29·63
10. 93·56 + 48·79
11. Kate buys one present for £28·42 and another for £65·79. How much does she spend altogether?

12. A lorry weighs 12 134 kg. Its freight weighs 5984 kg. What is the combined weight?

C

Set out as in the examples.

1. 273·6 + 54·87
2. 78·18 + 4·967
3. 18·271 + 16·95
4. 602·4 + 9·858
5. 35·49 + 17·963
6. 12·065 + 7·835
7. 64·79 + 1·954
8. 884·3 + 57·96
9. 13·268 + 9·547
10. 486·7 + 17·943
11. One parcel weighs 538 g. A second parcel weighs 1·369 kg. What is their combined weight?
12. One year ago Niall weighed 25·35 kg. Since then his weight has increased by 3·785 kg. How much does he weigh now?
13. Joyce buys a chicken weighing 2·358 kg and 230 g of sausages. What is the combined weight of her meat?

I can use a written method for subtraction of whole numbers and numbers with up to two decimal places.

Do not write in this book

Examples

```
   2 14 6 12        4 14 6 13
 1 3  4 7  2        5  4 ·7 3
 −   1 7 6 9       −1  6 ·2 8
 -----------       ----------
  1 1 7 0 3         3  8 ·4 5
```

A

Work out

1. 592 − 125
2. 814 − 361
3. 650 − 284
4. 478 − 193
5. 726 − 407
6. 67·4 − 15·5
7. 51·6 − 27·2
8. 35·8 − 19·8
9. 89·2 − 43·6
10. 38·0 − 17·3
11. A large packet of cereal weighs 750 g. A smaller packet weighs 425 g. How much more does the larger packet weigh?
12. Asma weighs 32·4 kg. Her mother weighs 56·1 kg. How much less does Asma weigh?
13. Terry's father weighs 83·6 kg. Terry weighs 45·4 kg less. How much does Terry weigh?

B

Set out as in the examples.

1. 3619 − 1572
2. 5284 − 1346
3. 7051 − 5438
4. 14 369 − 7597
5. 11 472 − 2865
6. 24·09 − 13·85
7. 713·7 − 347·2
8. 95·81 − 29·65
9. 524·8 − 467·3
10. 73·95 − 39·86
11. Chelsea's new car weighs 2364 kg. This is 1187 kg more than her old car. What was the weight of her old car?

12. The apples in a barrel weigh 57·45 kg. Micky takes out 21·88 kg. What is the weight of the apples left in the barrel?

C

Set out as in the examples.

1. 2·349 − 0·867
2. 61·8 − 16·54
3. 9·572 − 7·836
4. 36·04 − 17·83
5. 5·29 − 2·455
6. 4·718 − 0·64
7. 75·29 − 66·83
8. 8·14 − 1·972
9. 3·87 − 2·9
10. 9·05 − 6·378
11. A round cheese weighs 2·58 kg. 325 g is cut off. How much is left?
12. The combined weight of the meat and vegetables in a casserole is 1·585 kg. 780 g of meat is used. What is the weight of the vegetables?
13. Eight unpeeled potatoes weigh 1·218 kg. After peeling they weigh 947 g. What is the weight of the removed skin?

I can use a written method to multiply HTU by U and U.t by U.

Examples

```
  264        264
×   8      ×   8
 1600       2112
  480        5 3
   32
 2112
 1 1
```

```
2·9 × 6
   29
×   6
  174
    5
```

2·9 × 6 = 17·4 (174 ÷ 10)

```
  12·9
×    6
  77·4
  1 5
```

A

Work out.

1. 34 × 5
2. 67 × 2
3. 72 × 6
4. 25 × 9
5. 59 × 3
6. 65 × 5
7. 89 × 2
8. 93 × 4
9. 48 × 6
10. 76 × 3
11. One bag of crisps weighs 28 g. What does a pack of six bags weigh?
12. Three children weigh 46 kg each. What is their combined weight?
13. One cake costs 45p. What do four cakes cost?

B

Work out.

1. 475 × 3
2. 296 × 6
3. 557 × 2
4. 364 × 7
5. 183 × 9
6. 592 × 8
7. 738 × 6
8. 356 × 4

Work out

9. 7·9 × 7
10. 6·5 × 5
11. 2·9 × 3
12. 7·8 × 4
13. 4·5 × 6
14. 5·6 × 9
15. 8·9 × 2
16. 3·7 × 8
17. 9·3 × 6
18. 6·8 × 7
19. A can of fish weighs 425 g. What is the weight of the eight cans in a box?
20. One bag of potatoes weighs 3·5 kg. How much do five bags weigh?

C

Work out.

1. 59·8 × 6
2. 47·2 × 9
3. 38·6 × 3
4. 47·3 × 8
5. 53·8 × 7
6. 25·6 × 9
7. 37·9 × 5
8. 48·7 × 7
9. 36·8 × 6
10. 29·4 × 8
11. One box weighs 46·7 kg. How much do four identical boxes weigh?

12. One car weighs 1597 kg. What is the weight of the seven cars on a transporter?

I can use a written method to divide HTU by U.

Examples

$131 \div 6$

$$\begin{array}{rl} 131 & \\ -\ 60 & (6 \times 10) \\ \hline 71 & \\ -\ 60 & (6 \times 10) \\ \hline 11 & \\ -\ 6 & (6 \times 1) \\ \hline 5 & \end{array}$$

Answer 21 r5

$431 \div 6$

$$\begin{array}{rl} 431 & \\ -420 & (6 \times 70) \\ \hline 11 & \\ -\ 6 & (6 \times 1) \\ \hline 5 & \end{array}$$

Answer 71 r5

$931 \div 6$

$$\begin{array}{rl} 931 & \\ -600 & (6 \times 100) \\ \hline 331 & \\ -300 & (6 \times 50) \\ \hline 31 & \\ -\ 30 & (6 \times 5) \\ \hline 1 & \end{array}$$

Answer 155 r1

A

Work out.

1. $36 \div 3$
2. $86 \div 8$
3. $34 \div 2$
4. $83 \div 5$
5. $77 \div 4$
6. $91 \div 7$
7. $138 \div 9$
8. $96 \div 8$
9. $57 \div 2$
10. $117 \div 5$
11. $105 \div 3$
12. $161 \div 6$
13. $94 \div 4$
14. $123 \div 8$
15. $112 \div 7$
16. $199 \div 9$
17. The five cereal bars in one pack weigh 120 g. What does one bar weigh?
18. Bella's father weighs four times as much as Bella. He weighs 68 kg. How much does Bella weigh?
19. There is 75 kg of potatoes in a sack. One third is eaten. How much has been eaten?

B

Work out.

1. $153 \div 6$
2. $324 \div 9$
3. $330 \div 8$
4. $202 \div 3$
5. $595 \div 7$
6. $355 \div 6$
7. $588 \div 8$
8. $339 \div 5$
9. $826 \div 7$
10. $465 \div 9$
11. $299 \div 2$
12. $768 \div 8$
13. $562 \div 4$
14. $872 \div 7$
15. $936 \div 6$
16. $660 \div 9$
17. Six slices of ham weigh 252 g. What does one slice weigh?
18. Nine televisions are loaded onto a van. They have a combined weight of 306 kg. What does each television weigh?
19. A pizza weighs 272 g. It is cut into eight slices. What does each slice weigh?

C

Work out.

1. $1382 \div 7$
2. $1198 \div 8$
3. $1185 \div 5$
4. $1568 \div 9$
5. $1011 \div 6$
6. $1168 \div 4$
7. $1262 \div 8$
8. $1185 \div 7$
9. $1219 \div 9$
10. $1056 \div 6$
11. $1351 \div 4$
12. $1020 \div 7$
13. $1343 \div 5$
14. $1384 \div 8$
15. $1078 \div 4$
16. $1681 \div 9$
17. There are four jars of peaches in a box. They weigh 1740 g altogether. What does one jar weigh?

18. A van carries 1164 kg of freight in six identical containers. How much does each container weigh?

I can read scales with some unnumbered divisions.

For each of the scales work out:

a) the measurement indicated by each of the arrows

b) the difference between the two arrows.

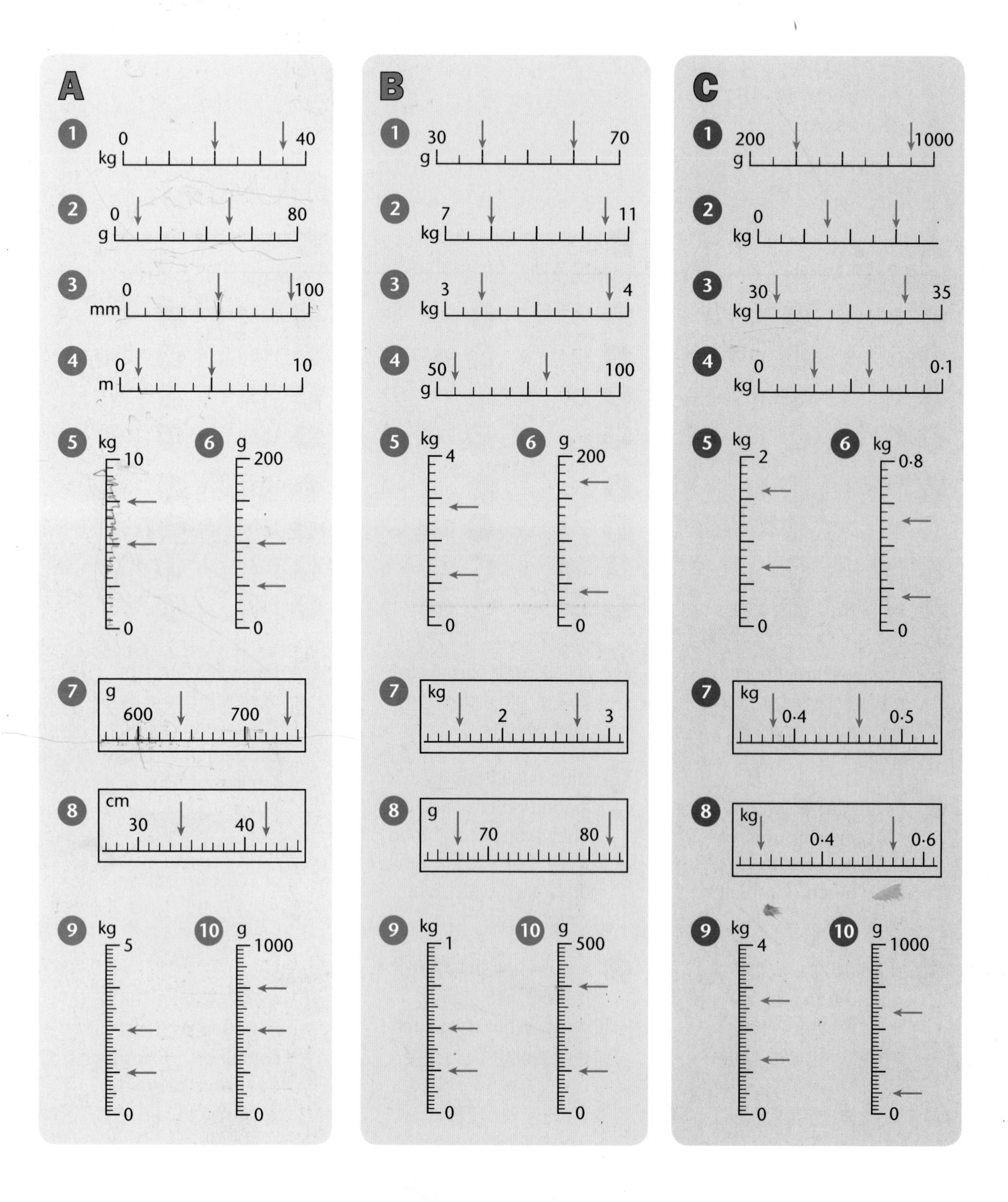

I can find the perimeter of regular and irregular polygons.

The perimeter of a shape is the distance around its edges.
It is a length and is measured in units of length such as metres or centimetres.

Examples

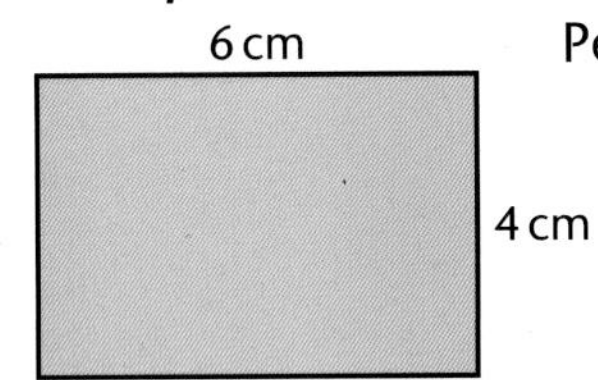

Perimeter $= 2 \times (6\,\text{cm} + 4\,\text{cm})$
$= 2 \times 10\,\text{cm}$
$= 20\,\text{cm}$

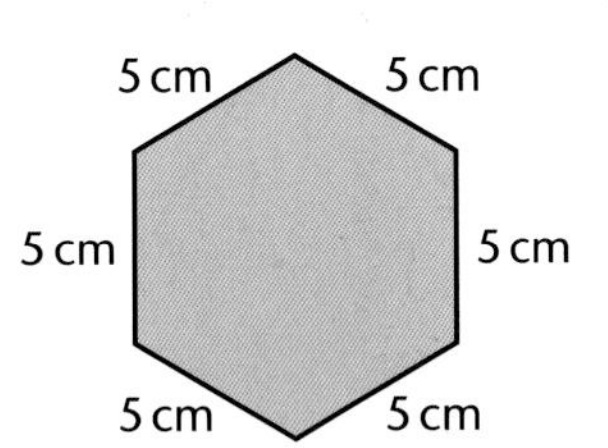

Perimeter $= 6 \times 5\,\text{cm}$
$= 30\,\text{cm}$

A

Measure each shape and work out the perimeter.

1. 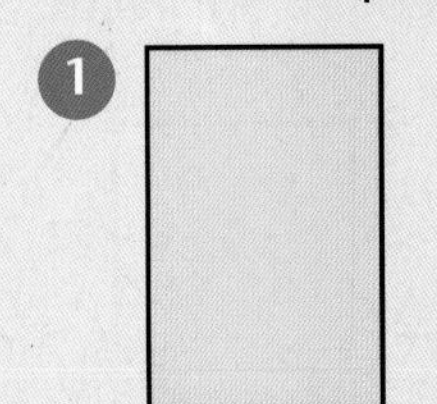
2. 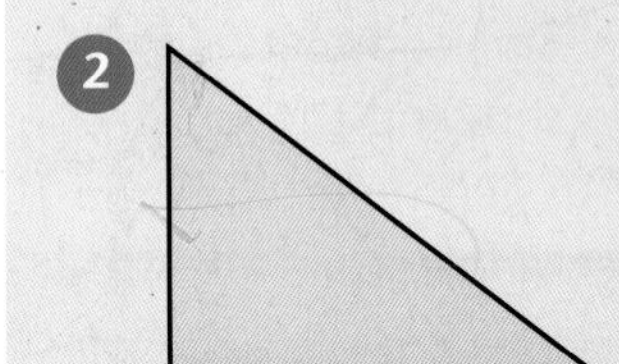
3. 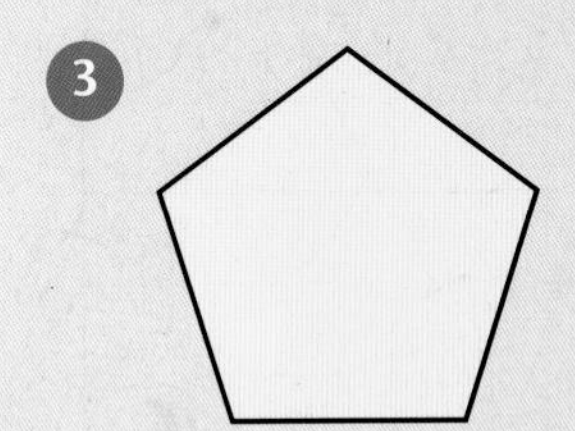

Work out the perimeter of each shape.

4. square
   sides 7 cm
5. rectangle
   sides 8 cm 4 cm
6. equilateral triangle
   sides 6 cm
7. regular pentagon
   sides 4 cm

B

Work out the perimeter of each shape.

1. rectangle
   sides 5 cm 12 cm
2. regular hexagon
   sides 7 cm
3. square
   sides 4·5 cm
4. regular octagon
   sides 8 cm
5. Copy and complete this table showing the measurements of rectangles.

Length	Width	Perim.
5 cm	4 cm	
7 cm	3 cm	
	5 cm	26 cm
	4 cm	28 cm
8 cm		22 cm
9 cm		32 cm

6. Work out the perimeter. All lengths are in cm.

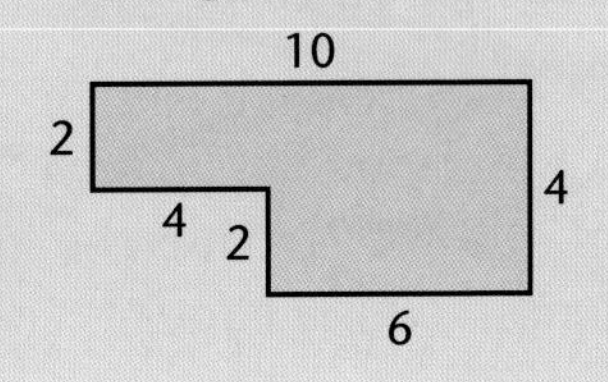

C

Work out the perimeter of each shape. All lengths are in cm.

1. 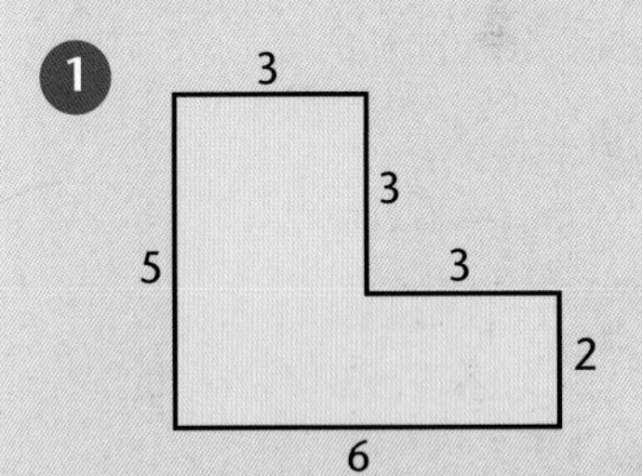

2. 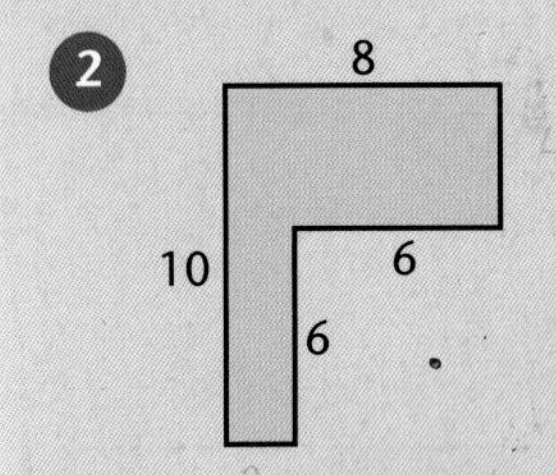

3. 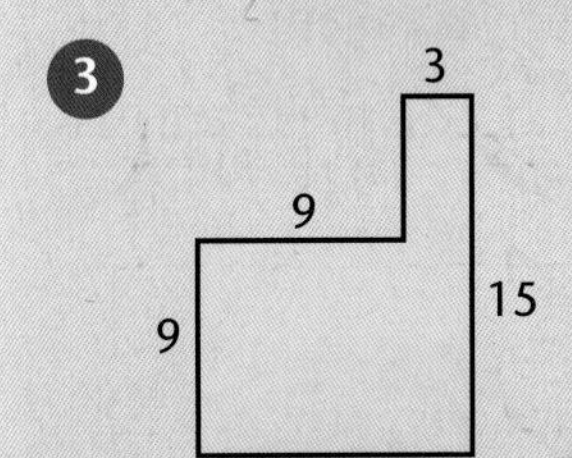

4. Copy and complete the table.

Length	Width	Perim.
12 cm		46 cm
4 cm	3·5 cm	
	2·5 cm	17 cm
7·5 cm		26 cm

I can find the area of a square or a rectangle.

The area of a shape is the amount of surface it covers.
It is measured in squares, usually square metres (m^2) or square centimetres (cm^2).

Example

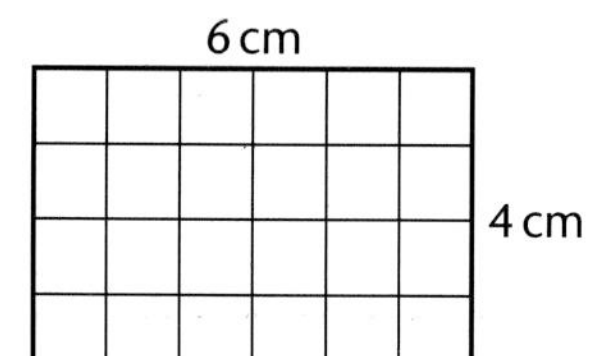

Area = length × width
$= (6 \times 4)\,cm^2$
$= 24\,cm^2$

A

Use 1 cm squared paper. Draw these shapes and work out each area by counting squares.

1. square sides 6 cm
2. rectangle sides 5 cm 7 cm
3. square sides 4 cm
4. rectangle sides 4 cm 9 cm

Use 1 cm squared paper.

5. Draw a square with an area of $25\,cm^2$. Work out the perimeter.
6. Draw a rectangle with a length of 8 cm and a perimeter of 22 cm. Work out the area.
7. Draw two different rectangles with an area of $8\,cm^2$. Work out the perimeters.

B

1. Copy and complete this table showing the measurements of rectangles.

Length	Width	Area
7 cm	3 cm	
8 cm	5 cm	
12 cm		$48\,cm^2$
9 cm		$54\,cm^2$
	4 cm	$32\,cm^2$
	5 cm	$65\,cm^2$

2. Use squared paper. Draw three different rectangles each with an area of $30\,cm^2$. Work out the perimeters.
3. Use squared paper. Draw three different rectangles each with a perimeter of 30 cm. Work out the areas.
4. A square playground has a perimeter of 200 metres. What is its area?
5. A square tile has an area of $400\,cm^2$. What is the length of one edge?

C

1. Work out the area of each shape. All lengths are in cm.

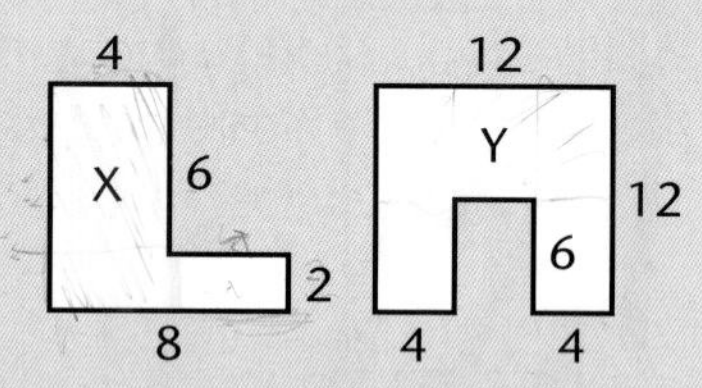

2. Copy and complete the table showing the length, width, perimeter and area of rectangles.

L cm	W cm	P cm	A cm^2
7	5		
12			96
	6	30	
		28	48

3. How many square centimetres are there in a square metre?
4. How many square metres are there in a square kilometre?
5. A carpet costs £20 per square metre. A room is 7 metres long and 4 metres wide. How much would it cost to carpet the room?

I can say whether an angle is acute, obtuse or a right angle, order a set of angles and measure them to within 5°.

Angles measure the amount something turns or rotates. Angles are measured in degrees (°).

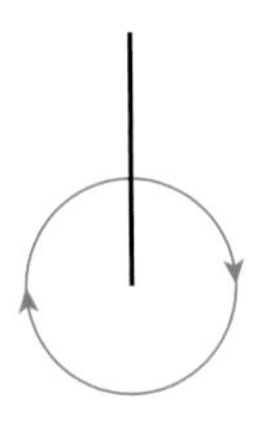

A whole turn
360°

A right angle
90°

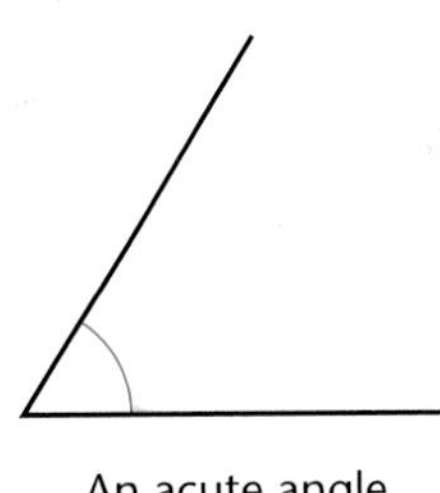

An acute angle
Less than 90°

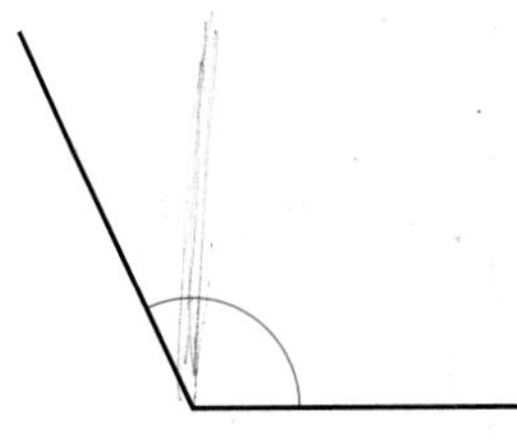

An obtuse angle
Greater than 90° and less than 180°

USING A PROTRACTOR

A protractor is used to measure or draw angles accurately. Most protractors have two scales, a clockwise outer scale and an anti-clockwise inner scale.
It is important to use the correct scale.

Examples

Outer Scale

$A\hat{O}B = 50°$

$A\hat{O}C = 140°$

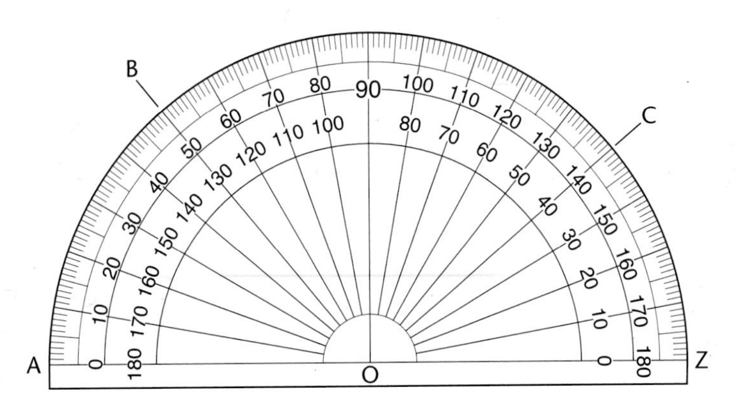

Inner Scale

$Z\hat{O}C = 40°$

$Z\hat{O}B = 130°$

COMMON MISTAKES

1. Using the wrong scale.
   Before measuring, decide if the angle is greater than or less than 90°.

2. Reading the scale in the wrong direction.
   The angle in the example is 125° but could be read wrongly as 135°.
   Make sure you look at the numbers on both sides of the line.

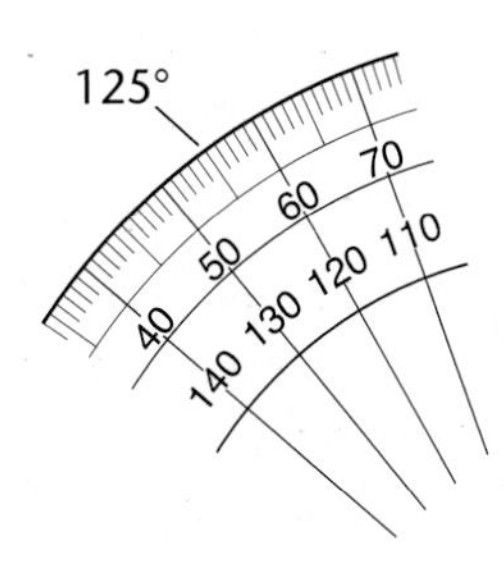

Decide which is the correct angle from the two answers.

1

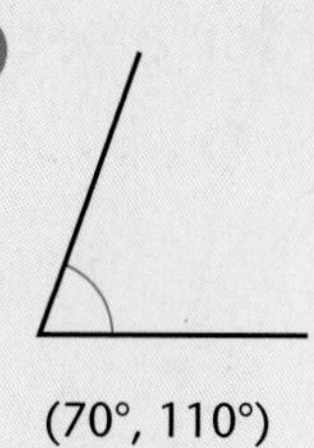

(70°, 110°)

3

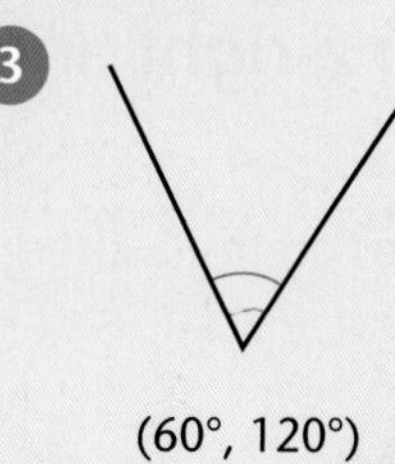

(60°, 120°)

5

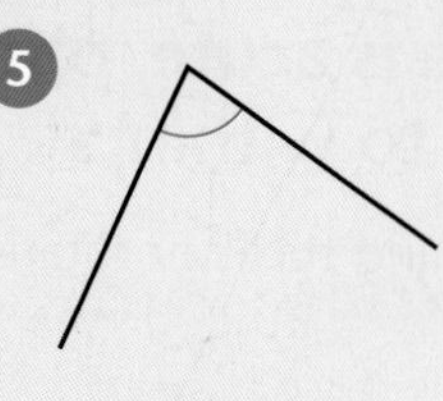

(80°, 100°)

7

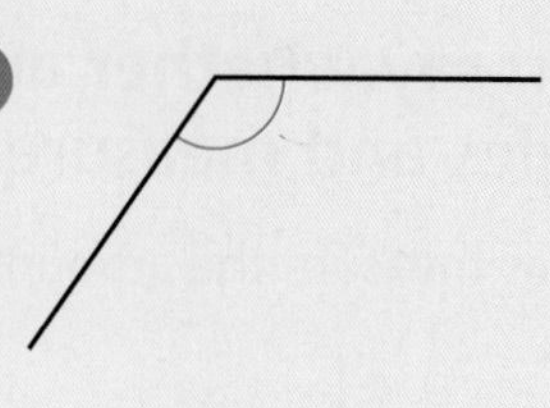

(55°, 125°)

2

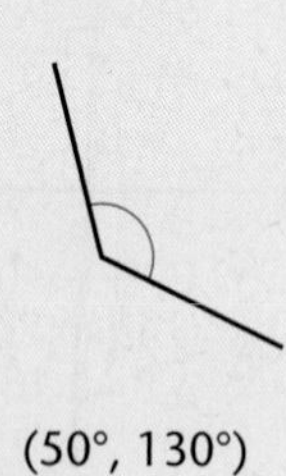

(50°, 130°)

4

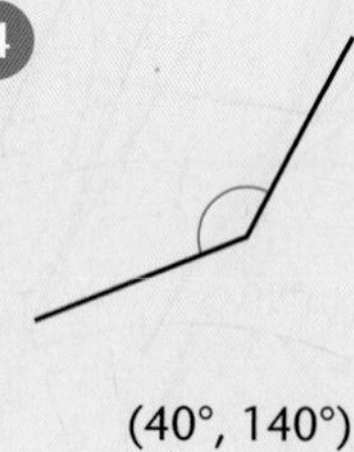

(40°, 140°)

6

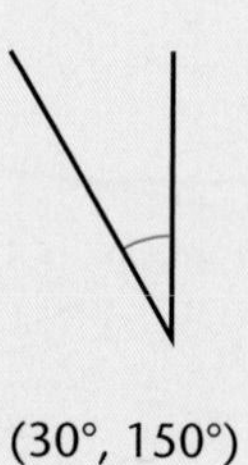

(30°, 150°)

8

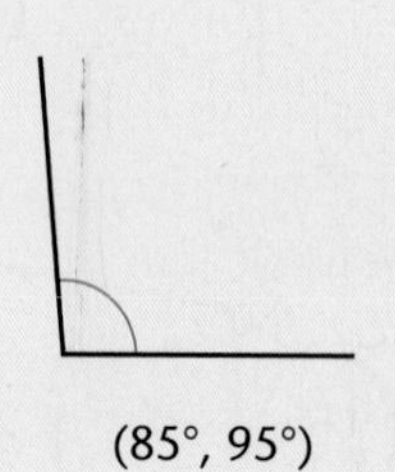

(85°, 95°)

Give the measurement of each angle.

9 $A\hat{O}E$

10 $A\hat{O}C$

11 $A\hat{O}I$

12 $A\hat{O}M$

13 $A\hat{O}B$

14 $A\hat{O}H$

15 $A\hat{O}D$

16 $A\hat{O}J$

17 $Z\hat{O}L$

18 $Z\hat{O}I$

19 $Z\hat{O}F$

20 $Z\hat{O}C$

21 $Z\hat{O}K$

22 $Z\hat{O}B$

23 $Z\hat{O}M$

24 $Z\hat{O}G$

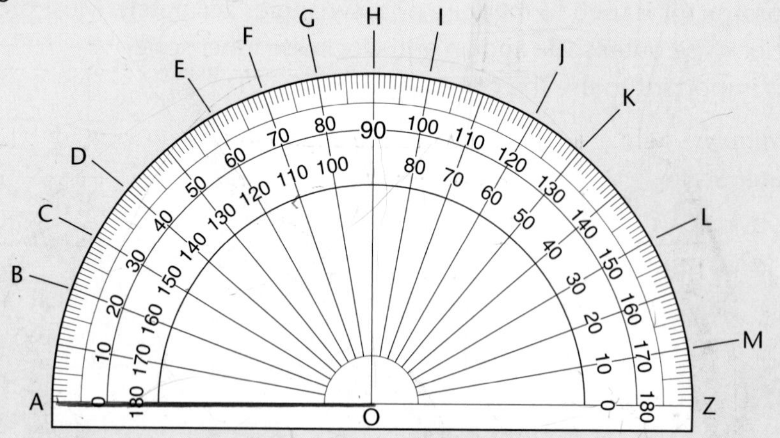

25 For each triangle write the angles in order of size, smallest first.

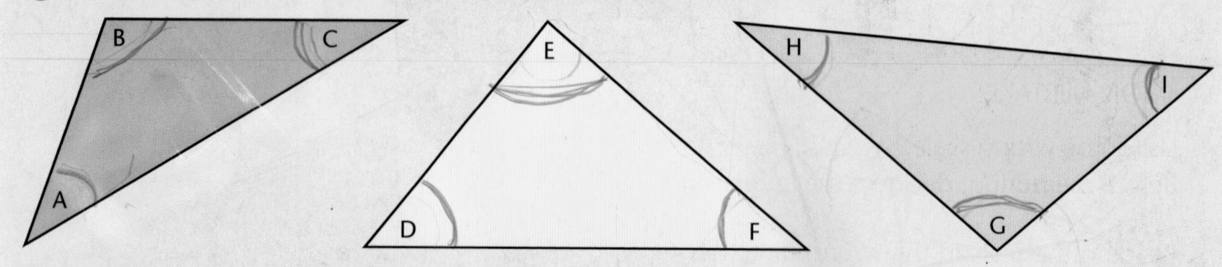

26 For each of the angles in the above triangles:

a) say whether the angle is acute, obtuse or a right angle

b) estimate the size of the angle to the nearest 10°

c) measure the angle to the nearest 10°.

B

Say whether the following angles are acute or obtuse. Do not measure the angles.

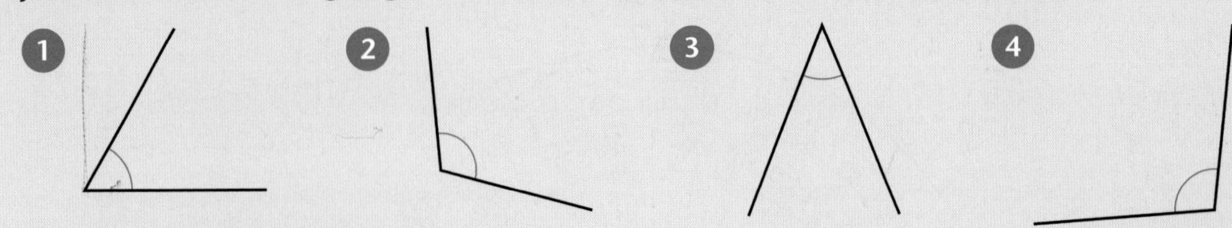

Give the measurement of each angle to the nearest 5°.

5 AÔD
6 AÔJ
7 AÔG
8 AÔM
9 AÔB
10 AÔH
11 AÔE
12 AÔC
13 ZÔL
14 ZÔI
15 ZÔF
16 ZÔC
17 ZÔK
18 ZÔB
19 ZÔM
20 ZÔE

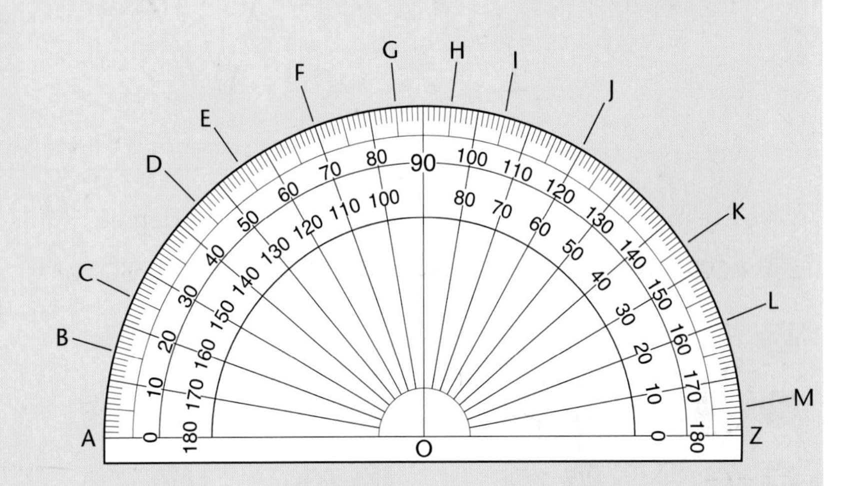

21 For each quadrilateral write the angles in order of size, smallest first.

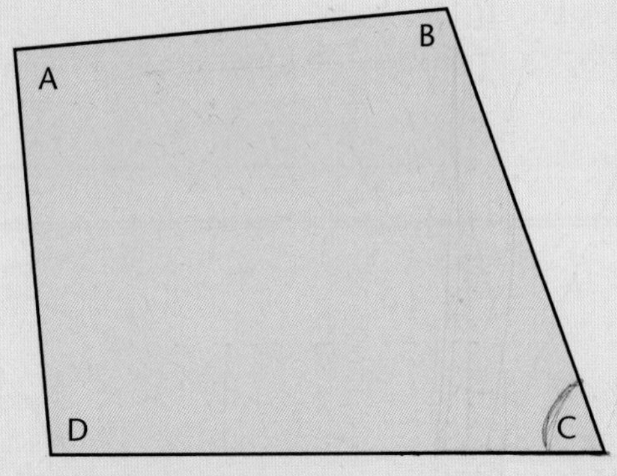

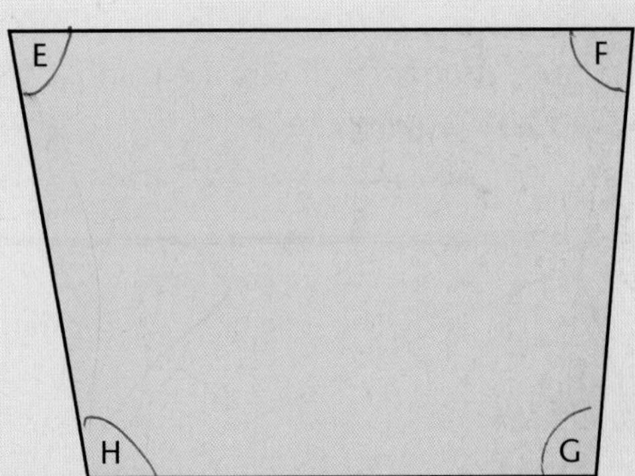

22 For each of the angles in the above quadrilaterals:

a) say whether the angle is acute, obtuse or a right angle
b) estimate the size of the angle to the nearest 5°
c) measure the angle to the nearest 5°.

23

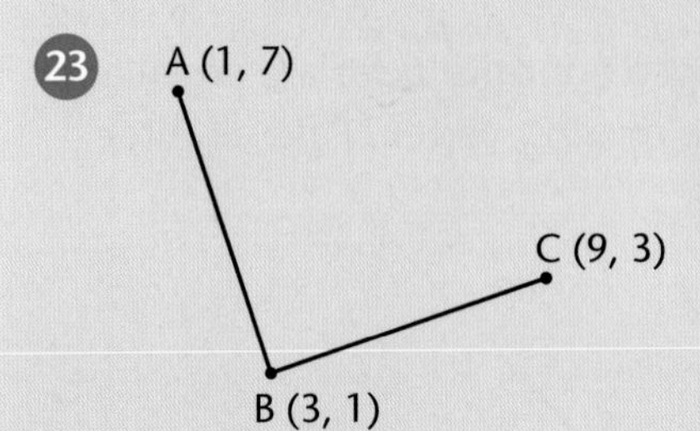

A, B and C are three vertices of a square.

a) Use squared paper. Plot the points on a grid.
b) Find the missing vertex and complete the square.
c) Use a protractor to check that the angles are 90°.

24 (0, 2), (1, 6) and (9, 4) are three vertices of a rectangle. Plot the co-ordinates on a grid and find the missing vertex. Complete the rectangle and check that the angles are 90°.

C

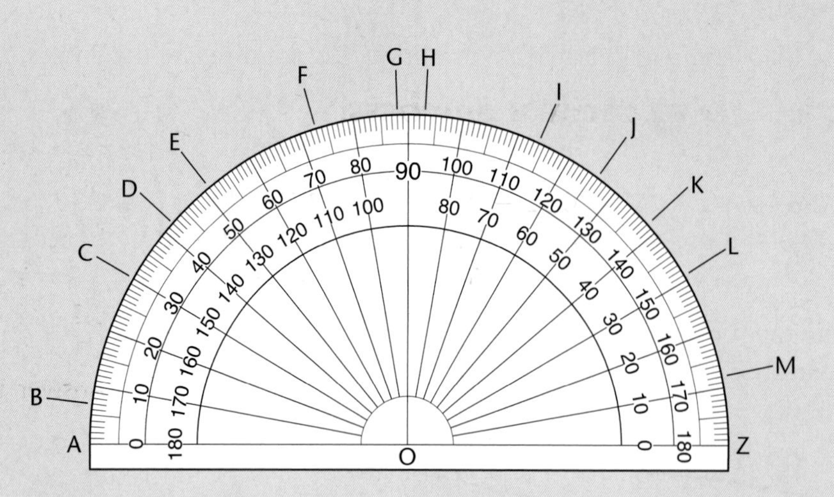

Give the measurement of each angle to the nearest degree.

1 AÔE
2 ZÔL
3 AÔC
4 ZÔI
5 AÔI
6 ZÔF
7 AÔM
8 ZÔD
9 AÔH
10 ZÔJ
11 AÔB
12 ZÔG
13 ZÔM
14 AÔJ
15 ZÔE
16 AÔF
17 ZÔH
18 AÔK
19 ZÔC
20 AÔG
21 ZÔK
22 AÔL
23 ZÔB
24 AÔD

25 Estimate the size of these angles and then measure them to the nearest degree. Use a 360° protractor. If you are using a 180° protractor, measure the inner angle and calculate the required angle.

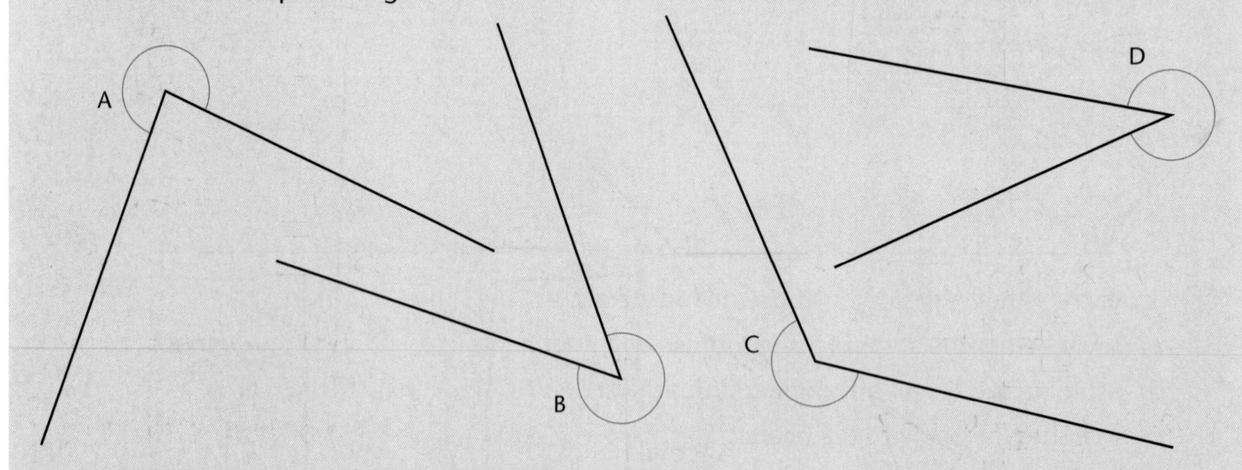

26 (4, 5), (9, 5) and (5, 1) are three vertices of a quadrilateral whose opposite sides are equal and parallel. There are three possibilities for the co-ordinates of the missing vertex. Find all three, and draw the three quadrilaterals on a grid.

27 Measure the angles of each quadrilateral. What do you notice?

27 a) Draw five different triangles.
b) Measure the angles.
c) Work out the sum of the angles for each triangle. What do you notice?

E2 DOUBLING AND HALVING DECIMALS

I can double and halve decimal numbers.

Examples

$3{\cdot}8 \times 2$	$0{\cdot}67 \times 2$	$0{\cdot}92 \div 2$	$3{\cdot}7 \div 2$	Find the number halfway between 1·5 and 1·8.
$(3 + 0{\cdot}8) \times 2$	$(0{\cdot}6 + 0{\cdot}07) \times 2$	$(0{\cdot}9 + 0{\cdot}02) \div 2$	$(3 + 0{\cdot}7) \div 2$	$1{\cdot}8 - 1{\cdot}5 = 0{\cdot}3$
$6 + 1{\cdot}6$	$1{\cdot}2 + 0{\cdot}14$	$0{\cdot}45 + 0{\cdot}01$	$1{\cdot}5 + 0{\cdot}35$	$0{\cdot}3 \div 2 = 0{\cdot}15$
$7{\cdot}6$	$1{\cdot}34$	$0{\cdot}46$	$1{\cdot}85$	$1{\cdot}5 + 0{\cdot}15 = 1{\cdot}65$
				Answer 1·65

A

Double these numbers.

1. 0·7
2. 0·9
3. 0·5
4. 0·8

Halve these numbers.

5. 3
6. 5
7. 1
8. 7

Copy and complete.

9. $1{\cdot}3 \times 2 = (1 + 0{\cdot}3) \times 2$
   $= \square + 0{\cdot}6$
   $= \square$
10. $4{\cdot}6 \times 2 = (4 + 0{\cdot}6) \times 2$
   $= 8 + \square$
   $= \square$
11. $2{\cdot}9 \times 2 = (2 + 0{\cdot}9) \times 2$
   $= \square + \square$
   $= \square$
12. $2{\cdot}4 \div 2 = (2 + 0{\cdot}4) \div 2$
   $= \square + 0{\cdot}2$
   $= \square$
13. $6{\cdot}8 \div 2 = (6 + 0{\cdot}8) \div 2$
   $= 3 + \square$
   $= \square$
14. $1{\cdot}6 \div 2 = (1 + 0{\cdot}6) \div 2$
   $= \square + \square$
   $= \square$

B

Double

1. 0·47
2. 3·6
3. 0·09
4. 5·5
5. 0·83
6. 2·7
7. 0·38
8. 1·9
9. 0·75
10. 8·8
11. 0·26
12. 4·5

Halve

13. 6·4
14. 0·28
15. 0·3
16. 5·0
17. 0·56
18. 7·8
19. 0·92
20. 3·4
21. 0·72
22. 1·4
23. 0·38
24. 9·6

Find the number halfway between:

25. 5·8 and 6·4
26. 0·7 and 0·8
27. 2·5 and 3
28. 2·2 and 1·9
29. 3 and 5·5
30. 4·8 and 4·1
31. 0·45 and 0·15
32. 1·04 and 1·1

C

Copy and complete

1. $\square \times 2 = 1{\cdot}98$
2. $\square \times 2 = 3{\cdot}5$
3. $\square \times 2 = 5{\cdot}24$
4. $\square \times 2 = 0{\cdot}19$
5. $\square \times 2 = 0{\cdot}176$
6. $\square \times 2 = 1{\cdot}32$
7. $\square \div 2 = 0{\cdot}073$
8. $\square \div 2 = 2{\cdot}45$
9. $\square \div 2 = 2{\cdot}86$
10. $\square \div 2 = 0{\cdot}67$
11. $\square \div 2 = 1{\cdot}55$
12. $\square \div 2 = 3{\cdot}65$

Find the number halfway between:

13. 0·38 and 0·39
14. 0·82 and 0·828
15. 1·013 and 1·005
16. 2·02 and 1·99
17. 0·27 and 0·45
18. 3·15 and 3·1
19. 0·85 and 0·76
20. 2·23 and 2·3

E2 IMPROPER FRACTIONS

I can change an improper fraction to a mixed number and vice versa.

Examples

Change $\frac{17}{5}$ to a mixed number.

$\frac{17}{5} = 17 \div 5$

$= 3$ remainder 2

$= 3\frac{2}{5}$

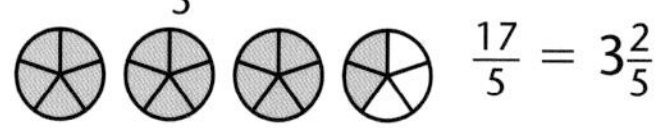

$\frac{17}{5} = 3\frac{2}{5}$

Change $5\frac{3}{4}$ to an improper fraction.

$5\frac{3}{4} = (5 \times 4)$ quarters plus 3 quarters

$=$ 20 quarters plus 3 quarters

$=$ 23 quarters

$= \frac{23}{4}$

$5\frac{3}{4} = \frac{23}{4}$

A

Write the next five pairs of numbers in each number line.

1. $0 \quad \frac{1}{4} \quad \frac{2}{4} \quad \frac{3}{4} \quad \frac{4}{4} \quad \frac{5}{4}$
   $0 \quad \frac{1}{4} \quad \frac{2}{4} \quad \frac{3}{4} \quad 1 \quad 1\frac{1}{4}$
2. $0 \quad \frac{1}{3} \quad \frac{2}{3} \quad \frac{3}{3} \quad \frac{4}{3} \quad \frac{5}{3}$
   $0 \quad \frac{1}{3} \quad \frac{2}{3} \quad 1 \quad 1\frac{1}{3} \quad 1\frac{2}{3}$
3. $0 \quad \frac{1}{5} \quad \frac{2}{5} \quad \frac{3}{5} \quad \frac{4}{5} \quad \frac{5}{5} \quad \frac{6}{5}$
   $0 \quad \frac{1}{5} \quad \frac{2}{5} \quad \frac{3}{5} \quad \frac{4}{5} \quad 1 \quad 1\frac{1}{5}$
4. $0 \quad \frac{1}{6} \quad \frac{2}{6} \quad \frac{3}{6} \quad \frac{4}{6} \quad \frac{5}{6} \quad \frac{6}{6}$
   $0 \quad \frac{1}{6} \quad \frac{2}{6} \quad \frac{3}{6} \quad \frac{4}{6} \quad \frac{5}{6} \quad 1$

Use your number lines to write these improper fractions as mixed numbers.

5. $\frac{4}{3}$
6. $\frac{6}{5}$
7. $\frac{10}{4}$
8. $\frac{7}{6}$
9. $\frac{9}{5}$
10. $\frac{7}{3}$
11. $\frac{9}{6}$
12. $\frac{7}{4}$

Use your number lines to write these mixed numbers as improper fractions.

13. $1\frac{2}{6}$
14. $2\frac{1}{4}$
15. $1\frac{2}{3}$
16. $2\frac{1}{5}$
17. $1\frac{3}{4}$
18. $1\frac{4}{6}$
19. $1\frac{3}{5}$
20. $2\frac{2}{3}$

B

Copy and complete.

1. $\frac{5}{3} = 1\square$
2. $\frac{7}{4} = \square\frac{3}{4}$
3. $3\frac{1}{2} = \square$
4. $4\frac{3}{5} = \square$

Change to mixed numbers.

5. $\frac{13}{2}$
6. $\frac{19}{6}$
7. $\frac{22}{5}$
8. $\frac{21}{8}$
9. $\frac{25}{4}$
10. $\frac{23}{7}$
11. $\frac{10}{3}$
12. $\frac{17}{10}$

Change to improper fractions

13. $3\frac{4}{5}$
14. $2\frac{5}{9}$
15. $1\frac{3}{7}$
16. $4\frac{1}{4}$
17. $6\frac{2}{3}$
18. $5\frac{3}{10}$
19. $1\frac{7}{8}$
20. $2\frac{2}{6}$

Write as both mixed numbers and improper fractions.

21.
22.
23.
24.
25.

C

Change to mixed numbers.

1. $\frac{25}{4}$
2. $\frac{17}{3}$
3. $\frac{29}{6}$
4. $\frac{37}{7}$
5. $\frac{44}{5}$
6. $\frac{50}{8}$
7. $\frac{57}{9}$
8. $\frac{123}{10}$
9. $\frac{65}{12}$
10. $\frac{116}{50}$
11. $\frac{712}{100}$
12. $\frac{92}{25}$
13. $\frac{50}{11}$
14. $\frac{79}{20}$
15. $\frac{94}{15}$
16. $\frac{50}{16}$

Change to improper fractions

17. $5\frac{1}{5}$
18. $5\frac{1}{3}$
19. $6\frac{3}{4}$
20. $9\frac{3}{6}$
21. $2\frac{6}{7}$
22. $7\frac{1}{8}$
23. $12\frac{9}{10}$
24. $3\frac{11}{12}$
25. $4\frac{7}{9}$
26. $7\frac{8}{100}$
27. $2\frac{11}{16}$
28. $9\frac{27}{50}$
29. $3\frac{9}{30}$
30. $2\frac{5}{14}$
31. $4\frac{4}{19}$
32. $6\frac{6}{11}$

I can write a fraction as a decimal and use a calculator to change a fraction to a decimal.

Examples

Write fractions with a denominator of 10, 100 or 1000 in the right column.

	U · t h th
$\frac{7}{10}$	0 · 7
$\frac{12}{100}$	0 · 1 2
$\frac{428}{1000}$	0 · 4 2 8

Find an equivalent fraction with a denominator of 10, 100 or 1000.

$\frac{2}{5} = \frac{4}{10} = 0{\cdot}4$

$\frac{3}{4} = \frac{75}{100} = 0{\cdot}75$

$\frac{1}{8} = \frac{125}{1000} = 0{\cdot}125$

Use a calculator to divide the numerator by the denominator.

$\frac{1}{3} = 1 \div 3 = 0{\cdot}333...$

$\frac{2}{9} = 2 \div 9 = 0{\cdot}222...$

$\frac{5}{7} = 5 \div 7 = 0{\cdot}714...$

A

Write as decimals.

1. $\frac{43}{100}$
2. $\frac{7}{10}$
3. $\frac{35}{100}$
4. $\frac{2}{10}$
5. $\frac{5}{10}$
6. $\frac{6}{100}$
7. $\frac{9}{10}$
8. $\frac{81}{100}$

Write as fractions.

9. 0·3
10. 0·51
11. 0·29
12. 0·6
13. 0·8
14. 0·06
15. 0·4
16. 0·73

Draw a number line 10 cm long. Above the line mark it from 0 to 1 in steps of 0·1. Below the line mark it from 0 to 1 in steps of $\frac{1}{5}$.

0 0·1 0·2 0·3 ...

0 $\frac{1}{5}$

Use your number line to copy and complete.

17. 0·4 = □ fifths
18. 0·8 = □ fifths
19. □ = 1 fifth
20. □ = 3 fifths

B

1. Copy and continue the number line from 0 to 1.

0 0·1 0·2 0·3 ...

0 $\frac{1}{20}$ $\frac{2}{20}$ $\frac{3}{20}$ $\frac{4}{20}$ $\frac{5}{20}$ $\frac{6}{20}$ $\frac{7}{20}$

Use your number line to copy and complete.

2. $0{\cdot}5 = \frac{\square}{20} = \frac{\square}{2}$
3. $0{\cdot}9 = \frac{\square}{20} = \frac{\square}{10}$
4. $\square = \frac{14}{20} = \frac{\square}{10}$
5. $\square = \frac{8}{20} = \frac{\square}{10} = \frac{\square}{5}$

Write as fractions.

6. 0·68
7. 0·17
8. 0·25
9. 0·3
10. 0·75
11. 0·59
12. 0·01
13. 0·1

Write as decimals. Use a calculator to check or work out.

14. $\frac{1}{2}$
15. $\frac{3}{4}$
16. $\frac{3}{5}$
17. $\frac{3}{8}$
18. $\frac{1}{4}$
19. $\frac{4}{5}$
20. $\frac{7}{8}$
21. $\frac{19}{20}$

C

Give the answer as a decimal.

1. $0{\cdot}5 + \frac{4}{10}$
2. $\frac{31}{100} - 0{\cdot}28$
3. $0{\cdot}8 - \frac{1}{2}$
4. $\frac{3}{4} - 0{\cdot}12$
5. $0{\cdot}2 + \frac{1}{2}$
6. $\frac{1}{4} + 0{\cdot}53$

Write in ascending order.

7. $\frac{3}{4}$ 0·43 0·344
8. 0·91 $\frac{19}{100}$ $\frac{9}{10}$
9. $\frac{3}{5}$ 0·5 $\frac{27}{100}$
10. $\frac{81}{100}$ 0·188 0·8
11. $\frac{2}{7}$ 0·2 $\frac{27}{100}$
12. 0·56 $\frac{5}{6}$ 0·556

Use a calculator to write as a decimal, rounding to the nearest hundredth.

13. $\frac{1}{3}$
14. $\frac{1}{6}$
15. $\frac{1}{12}$
16. $\frac{3}{7}$
17. $\frac{6}{11}$
18. $\frac{5}{9}$

I can solve problems involving finding fractions of amounts.

Examples

Find $\frac{1}{5}$ of 90p

$\frac{1}{5}$ of 90p = 90p ÷ 5
= 18p

Find $\frac{3}{5}$ of 90p

$\frac{3}{5}$ of 90p = (90p ÷ 5) × 3
= 18p × 3
= 54p

A

Find $\frac{1}{10}$ of:

1. 70
2. 100
3. 40 m
4. £1·00

Find $\frac{1}{5}$ of:

5. 15
6. 50
7. 30p
8. 45 cm

Find $\frac{1}{3}$ of:

9. 15
10. 27
11. £30
12. 24p

Find $\frac{1}{4}$ of:

13. 16
14. 28
15. 40 m
16. 20 cm

17. There are 80 drawing pins in a packet. One tenth are yellow. How many yellow pins are there?

18. Phil has £40. He spends one fifth of his money. How much does he have left?
19. There are 21 sweets in a packet. One third are eaten. How many are left?

B

Find

1. $\frac{2}{3}$ of 18
2. $\frac{4}{5}$ of 35
3. $\frac{9}{10}$ of 60
4. $\frac{6}{7}$ of 28
5. $\frac{3}{4}$ of 32 cm
6. $\frac{7}{9}$ of £36
7. $\frac{5}{6}$ of 18 kg
8. $\frac{3}{8}$ of 24p

9. There are 20 cards in a packet. Two fifths have been used. How many cards have been used?
10. A bottle holds 2 litres of milk. Three tenths is drunk. How much milk is left?
11. A pizza weighs 360 g. One half is eaten. A further one sixth is eaten. How much is left?
12. Five eighths of the 40 children in Drama Club are girls. How many boys are there?

C

Find

1. $\frac{7}{10}$ of 500 g
2. $\frac{5}{9}$ of 72
3. $\frac{12}{100}$ of 2 m
4. $\frac{3}{7}$ of 42
5. $\frac{4}{5}$ of 60
6. $\frac{69}{1000}$ of 1 kg
7. $\frac{7}{8}$ of 400 ml
8. $\frac{4}{15}$ of 90

9. Gemma has to drive 385 miles. She completes five sevenths of her journey before stopping. How much further does she have to go?
10. A jar contains 450 g of jam. Two ninths is used. How much is left?
11. A saucepan holds 1·5 litres of water. Nine hundredths evaporates. How much water is left?
12. A bag holds 4 kg of flour. Three fifths is used. How much is left?

E2 PERCENTAGES OF AMOUNTS

I can find 10% of an amount and use it to find 5%, 20%, 30%, etc.

Examples

10% of 40	30% of 40	5% of 40	3% of 400
$\frac{1}{10}$ of 40	(10% of 40) × 3	(10% of 40) ÷ 2	(1% of 400) × 3
40 ÷ 4	4 × 3	4 ÷ 2	($\frac{1}{100}$ of 400) × 3
4	12	2	4 × 3
			12

A

Find 10% of:

1. 40
2. 70
3. 20
4. 90
5. 130
6. 400
7. 250
8. 1000.

Find 10% of:

9. 20p
10. 80p
11. £3·00
12. £2·40
13. £1·00
14. £5·90
15. £22·00
16. £60.

Find 10% of:

17. 50 cm
18. 90 cm
19. 100 g
20. 600 g
21. 1 m
22. 2 m
23. 1 kg
24. 5 kg.

25. A shirt costs £14·00. In a sale there is 10% off. What is the new price?
26. Reece has 70 out of 100 in a test. Isla's score is 10% better. How many marks did Isla get?

B

For each of the following amounts find:

a) 10% **b)** 5% **c)** 20%.

1. £5·00
2. 700 ml
3. 2 kg
4. 25 m

Find

5. 30% of £6·00
6. 60% of £1·50
7. 40% of 75 cm
8. 90% of 3 m
9. 5% of 800 g
10. 5% of 4 kg
11. 5% of 1 litre
12. 5% of 420 ml
13. The price of a car is £4000. It is reduced by 20%. What is the new price?
14. A factory employs 350 people. Seventy percent are women. How many men work at the factory?
14. A school has 200 pupils. 5% are absent. How many children are at school?

C

Find

1. 1% of £360
2. 6% of £25
3. 15% of 4 m
4. 25% of 50 cm
5. 99% of 600 g
6. 20% of 1·5 kg
7. 15% of 200 ml
8. 95% of 10 litres

Copy and complete.

9. 10% of ☐ = 4
10. 20% of ☐ = 28
11. 25% of ☐ = 20
12. 40% of ☐ = 8
13. 1% of ☐ = 0·5
14. 5% of ☐ = 10
15. 75% of ☐ = 60
16. 2% of ☐ = 4
17. Ed leaves £2000 in a savings account which earns 5% interest each year. How much is in the account after:
    a) 1 year
    b) 2 years?

I write fractions and decimals as percentages.

Per cent means out of 100.
Percentages are fractions with a denominator of 100.
The symbol for per cent is %.

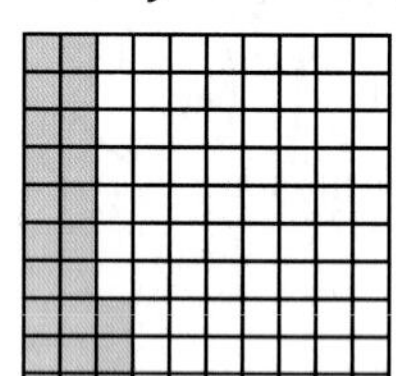

$\frac{23}{100} = 23\%$

To express fractions as percentages, change them to equivalent fractions with denominators of 100.

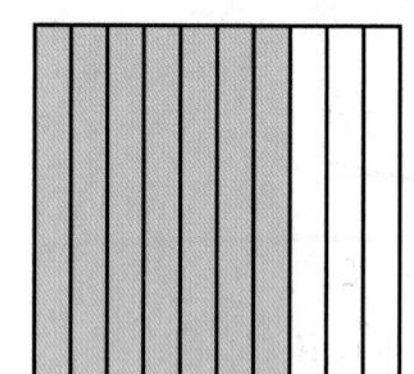

$\frac{7}{10} = \frac{70}{100} = 70\%$

$\frac{1}{2} = \frac{50}{100} = 50\%$

To express decimals as percentages, multiply by 100.

$0{\cdot}2 = (0{\cdot}2 \times 100)\%$
$= 20\%$

$0{\cdot}53 = (0{\cdot}53 \times 100)\%$
$= 53\%$

It is useful to know that:

$\frac{1}{100} = 0{\cdot}01 = 1\%$, $\frac{2}{100} = 0{\cdot}02 = 2\%$, etc.

$\frac{1}{10} = 0{\cdot}1 = 10\%$, $\frac{2}{10} = 0{\cdot}2 = 20\%$, etc.

$\frac{1}{4} = 25\%$, $\frac{1}{2} = 50\%$, $\frac{3}{4} = 75\%$

A

Use 10 × 10 grids of small squares. Shade in:

1. 27 squares
2. 80 squares
3. 9 squares
4. 50 squares.

Express each shaded area as:

a) a fraction
b) a decimal
c) a percentage.

5. Copy and complete the table.

Fraction	Decimal	Percentage
$\frac{1}{2}$		
$\frac{1}{10}$		
1		
$\frac{1}{4}$		
$\frac{3}{4}$		
$\frac{1}{100}$		
	0·3	
	0·62	

Copy the sentences changing each fraction to a percentage.

6. *One tenth* of the cars were blue.
7. Ellie has read *three quarters* of her book.
8. *One half* of the class saw the programme.
9. One pence is *one hundredth* of one pound.
10. Bruce lost *one quarter* of his golf balls.

B

Express each shaded area as:

a) a fraction

b) a decimal

c) a percentage.

1 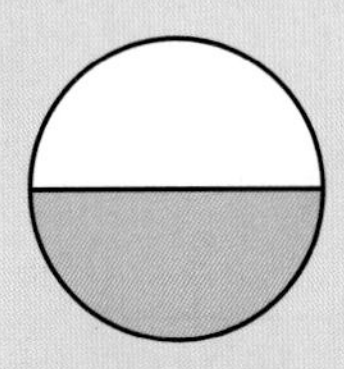

2 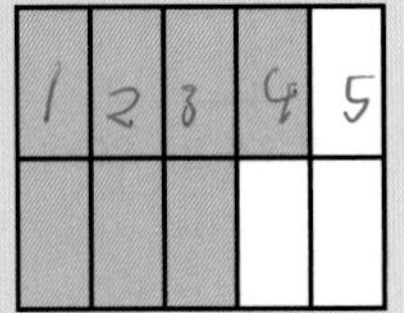

3 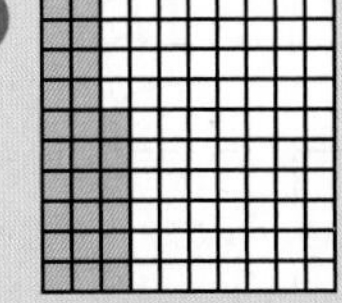

4 

5 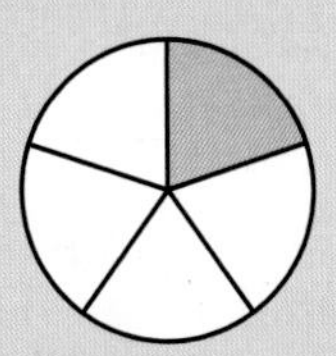

6 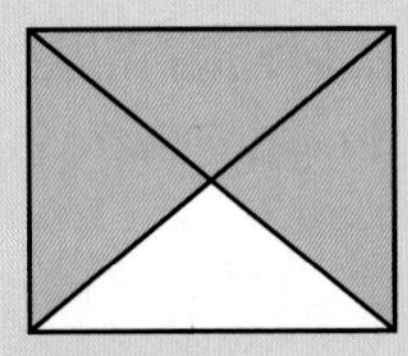

7 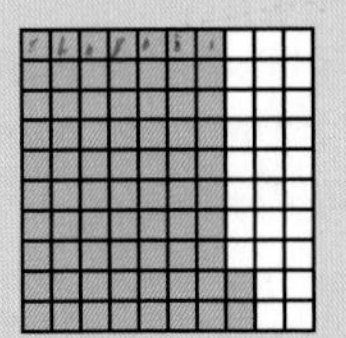

8 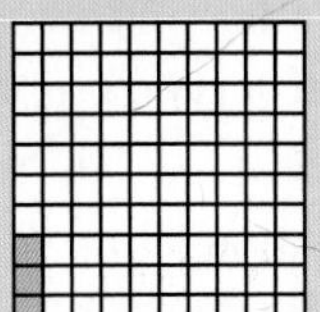

9 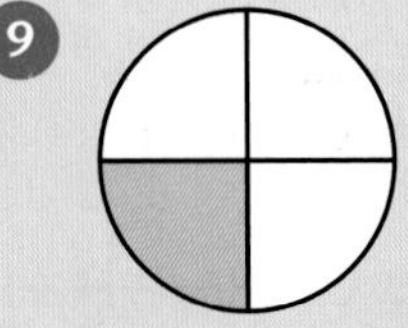

10 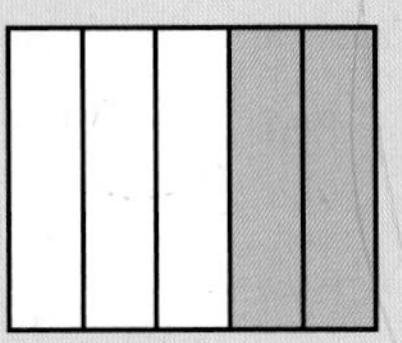

11 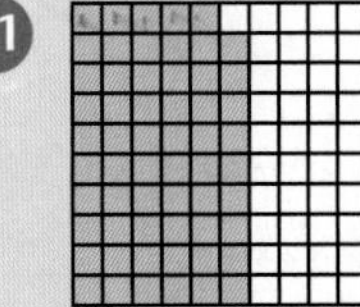

12 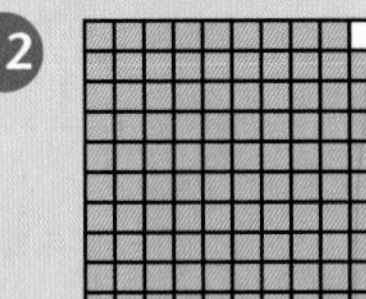

13 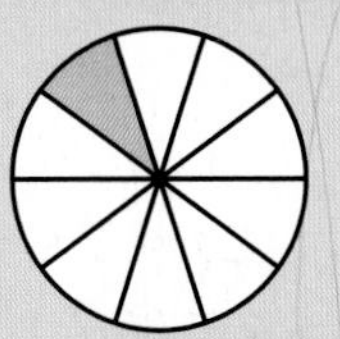

14 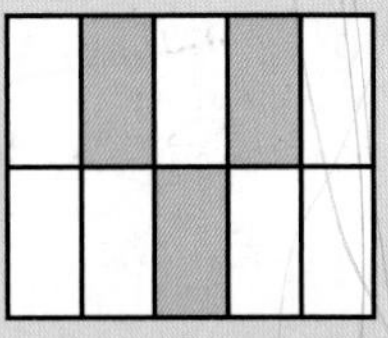

15 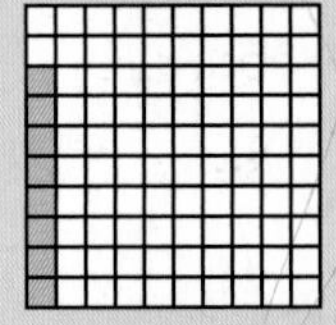

16 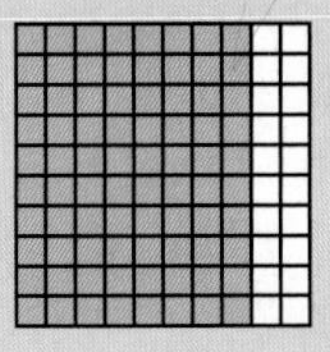

C

Write each fraction as

a) a decimal

b) a percentage.

1. $\frac{1}{10}$
2. $\frac{3}{10}$
3. $\frac{1}{100}$
4. $\frac{69}{100}$
5. $\frac{7}{100}$
6. $\frac{1}{5}$
7. $\frac{2}{5}$
8. $\frac{1}{4}$
9. $\frac{4}{50}$

Write each percentage as:

a) a fraction in its simplest form

b) a decimal.

10. 50%
11. 91%
12. 8%
13. 90%
14. 80%
15. 95%
16. 75%
17. 39%
18. 16%

19. 83% of the passengers on a coach are children. What percentage are adults?

20. 65% of the footballers in the Premiership are foreign. What percentage are English?

21. Copy the table but give each of the marks achieved as a percentage of the total marks for that test.

Subject	Total	Ali	Dan	Mia	Fay
English	100	61	39	58	47
Maths	200	140	168	70	94
Science	50	23	36	39	42
R.E.	20	12	11	15	14
History	25	20	19	16	13

22. One quarter of the customers in a shop buy one item. 18% buy two items. What percentage buy more than two items?

23. Three fifths of a bag of flour is used. A further 15% is used. What percentage is left?

I can solve a problem involving scaling up a number.

Scaling a number makes it bigger by a given factor. Scaling by a factor of 3 makes a number three times bigger.

Example

A necklace is made using this pattern of beads. There are 16 yellow beads. How many red beads are there?

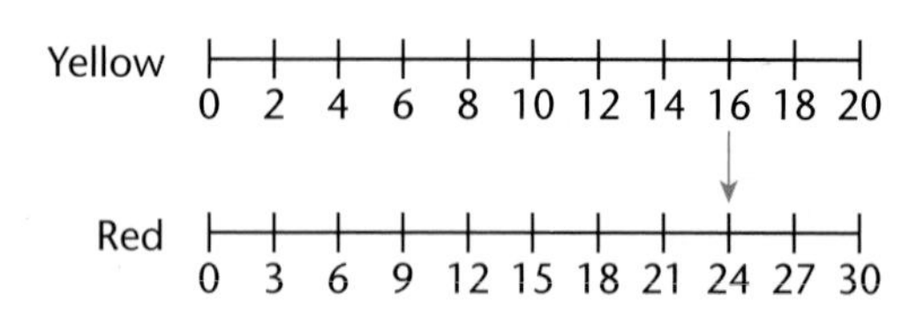

Answer *There are 24 red beads.*

A

1. A necklace is made using this pattern of beads. Copy and complete the pair of number lines.

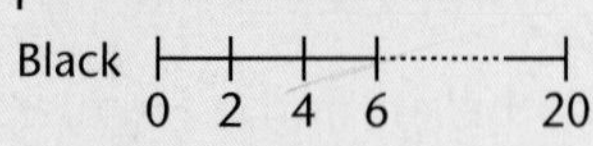

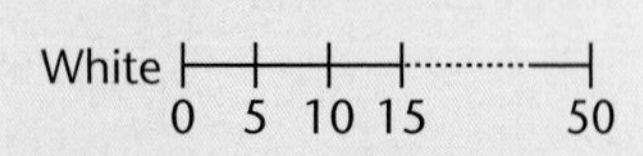

Use your number lines.

2. Find how many white beads there are if there are:
   a) 14 black beads
   b) 10 black beads
   c) 70 beads altogether?
3. How many black beads are there for every:
   a) 15 white beads
   b) 40 white beads?
4. How many white beads are there in every:
   a) 7 beads
   b) 14 beads
   c) 42 beads?

B

1. Peggy has 4 stickers for every 3 that Gary has. Peggy has 24 stickers. How many does Gary have?
2. There are 2 green apples for every 5 red apples. How many green apples are there if there are 21 apples altogether?
3. A football team scored 5 goals for every 4 they let in. They scored 40 goals. How many did they let in?
4. A market stall sold 3 white towels for every 2 blue towels. They sold 10 blue towels. How many white towels were sold?
5. In a box of chocolates there are 4 soft centres for every 3 hard centres. Sixteen chocolates have soft centres. How many have hard centres?

C

1. There are 35 people on a bus. Two in every seven go upstairs. How many people are downstairs?
2. Four in every nine shirts sold are white. 36 white shirts are sold. How many shirts are sold altogether?
3. In 5M two in every five children have fair hair. Twelve children have fair hair. How many children are there in the class?
4. Five books in every eight are fiction. There are 200 books altogether. How many of these are non-fiction?
5. Two children in every three at a swimming club are girls. There are 30 girls. How many boys are there?

I can arrange a set of decimals in order.

Examples

Arrange 5·3, 0·35, 8 and 5·8 in order.

Write in column.	Put in zeros.	Arrange in order.
5·3	5·30	0·35
0·35	0·35	5·3
8	8·00	5·8
5·8	5·80	8

What number is halfway between 1·3 and 1·9?

1·9 − 1·3 = 0·6
0·6 ÷ 2 = 0·3
1·3 + 0·3 = 1·6
Answer 1·6

A

Write the larger of these pairs of numbers.

1. 1·7 7·0
2. 35 5·3
3. 4·0 2·4
4. 21 2·1
5. 1·0 1·1
6. 2·5 25
7. 7·0 3·7
8. 0·3 3·0
9. 8·0 6·8
10. 5·4 4·5
11. Copy the number line.
    Put each number from the box on the line.

    1·0 0·3 1·2 0·5 1·8 1·5

    0 ——— 2

B

Arrange these decimals in order.
Write the smallest first:

1. 5·62, 6·52, 5·26, 6·5, 6·25
2. 3·18, 1·8, 3·81, 3·8, 1·38
3. 6·76, 6·6, 6·06, 6·7, 6·07
4. 21·8, 2·8, 2·18, 2·08, 28

What number lies halfway between:

5. 9 and 10
6. 3 and 6
7. 2 and 2·5
8. 3·1 and 3·2
9. 1·4 and 1·8
10. 1·55 and 1·75
11. 6·7 and 7·1
12. 7·1 and 5·4?
13. Copy the line and locate the numbers.

    2·95 3·06 3·0 2·91 2·98 3·04

    2·9 ——— 3·1

C

Arrange these decimals in order.
Write the smallest first.

1. 4·2, 4·25, 0·45, 4·5, 4·52
2. 6·1, 6·71, 0·67, 6·7, 6·17
3. 3·39, 0·93, 3·09, 3·3, 0·39
4. 8·4, 8·22, 8·24, 8·44, 8·42

What number lies halfway between:

5. 2·15 and 2·45
6. 0·67 and 0·68
7. 4·355 and 4·359
8. 1·266 and 1·272
9. 0·8 and 0·85
10. 4 and 4·75
11. 0·97 and 1·0
12. 7·55 and 7·6?
13. Draw a number line from 2·9 to 3·0 with 20 divisions. Put these numbers on your line.

    2·95 2·99 2·91 2·975 2·925 2·94

A3 ROUNDING DECIMALS

I can round decimals to the nearest whole number.

To round a decimal fraction to the nearest whole number look at the tenths column.
If the number in that column is less than 5, round down.
If the number in that column is greater than 5, round up.

Examples

3·5 rounds to 4
£2·70 rounds to £3
5·49 rounds to 5
£6·28 rounds to £6
3·62 m rounds to 4 m
5·379 km rounds to 5 km

A

Choose one of the numbers in the brackets.

1. 1·9 rounds to (1, 2).
2. 8·1 rounds to (8, 9).
3. 15·2 rounds to (15, 16).
4. 9·8 rounds to (9, 10).
5. 7·1 rounds to (7, 8).
6. 14·2 rounds to (14, 15).
7. 3·9 rounds to (3, 4).
8. 17·7 rounds to (17, 18).
9. 14·3 rounds to (14, 15).
10. 18·5 rounds to (18, 19).

Copy and complete.

11. £12·30 rounds to ☐.
12. £5·80 rounds to ☐.
13. £6·10 rounds to ☐.
14. £3·90 rounds to ☐.
15. £7·20 rounds to ☐.
16. £8·60 rounds to ☐.
17. £4·50 rounds to ☐.
18. £3·40 rounds to ☐.
19. £5·30 rounds to ☐.
20. £9·80 rounds to ☐.

B

Round to the nearest pound.

1. £8·63
2. £27·27
3. £3·91
4. £6·36
5. £12·80
6. £7·52
7. £4·49
8. £9·78
9. £15·15
10. £6·61

Round to the nearest whole number.

11. 4·8
12. 6·2
13. 3·5
14. 11·7
15. 8·4
16. 13·3
17. 0·52
18. 5·46
19. 27·91
20. 12·5

Round to the nearest metre.

21. 5·6 m
22. 3·9 m
23. 9·7 m
24. 6·3 m
25. 2·8 m
26. 1·49 m
27. 7·5 m
28. 11·9 m
29. 8·26 m
30. 4·81 m

Round to the nearest kilogram.

31. 4·3 kg
32. 3·6 kg
33. 12·2 kg
34. 8·7 kg
35. 5·4 kg
36. 3·5 kg
37. 16·38 kg
38. 7·61 kg
39. 11·91 kg
40. 9·19 kg

C

Round to the nearest 10p.

1. £1·27
2. £5·83
3. £9·61
4. £31·39
5. £7·45
6. £4·52
7. £0·06
8. £2·74
9. £8·17
10. £6·95

Round to the nearest tenth.

11. 2·55
12. 3·26
13. 14·14
14. 0·72
15. 5·63
16. 8·47
17. 29·91
18. 1·35
19. 52·09
20. 6·82

Round to the nearest 10 cm.

21. 4·19 m
22. 1·62 m
23. 7·48 m
24. 2·81 m
25. 0·53 m
26. 3·37 m
27. 5·94 m
28. 12·05 m
29. 0·29 m
30. 8·76 m

Round to the nearest 100 ml.

31. 6·46 litres
32. 9·09 litres
33. 18·932 litres
34. 35·184 litres
35. 20·250 litres

A3 COUNTING IN DECIMAL STEPS

I can count in decimal steps and find the missing numbers in a sequence involving decimals.

Examples

Count on four steps of 0·6

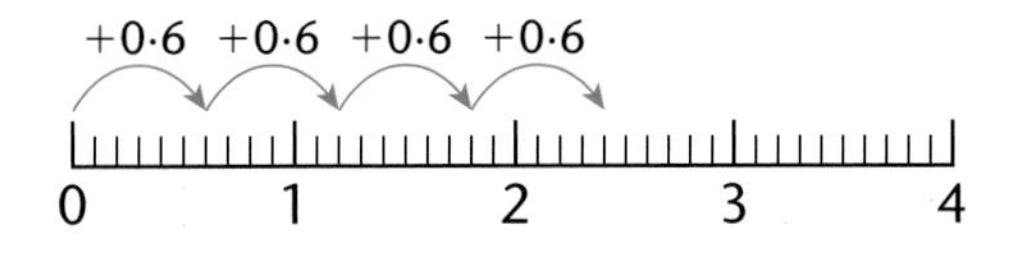

0·6 × 4 = 2·4

Count back in steps of 0·05 from 0·3

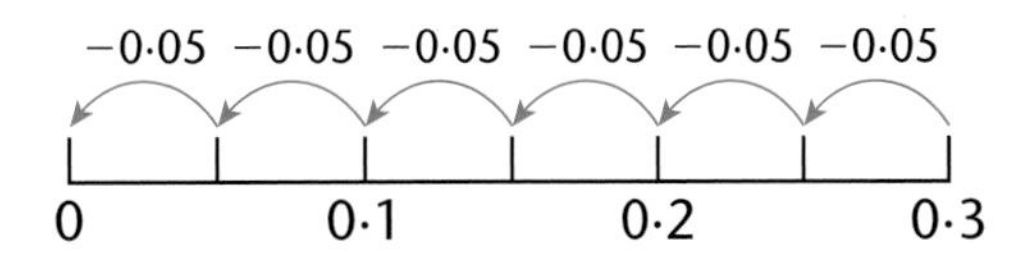

0·3 ÷ 0·05 = 6

A

Write out each sequence.

Start at 0 each time.

1. Count on 4 steps of 0·5
2. Count on 6 steps of 0·2
3. Count on 7 steps of 0·3
4. Count on 4 steps of 0·9
5. Count on 5 steps of 0·6

Write out each sequence.

6. Count back in steps of 0·8 from 3·2
7. Count back in steps of 0·4 from 2·4
8. Count back in steps of 0·7 from 3·5
9. Count back in steps of 0·5 from 3·5
10. Count back in steps of 0·2 from 1·8
11. Count back in steps of 0·3 from 1·8

B

Complete each sequence.

1. 3·6 4·2 □ □ □ 6·6
2. 8·1 7·2 □ □ 4·5 □
3. 0·02 0·04 □ □ □ □
4. 0·15 □ 0·09 □ □ □
5. □ 0·1 □ 0·2 □ 0·3

Work out

6. 0·6 × 2
7. 0·5 × 9
8. 0·8 × 6
9. 0·9 × 3
10. 0·7 × 8

Work out

11. 5·6 ÷ 0·7
12. 3·6 ÷ 0·4
13. 2·5 ÷ 0·5
14. 0·14 ÷ 0·02
15. 0·54 ÷ 0·09

C

Complete each sequence.

1. □ 2·0 □ 3·5 □ 5·0
2. 0·3 □ 0·6 □ 0·9 □
3. 1·91 1·93 1·95 □ □ □
4. 0·05 □ 0·1 □ 0·15 □
5. □ 1·1 □ 2·4 □ 3·7

Copy and complete

6. 0·07 × □ = 0·21
7. 0·05 × □ = 0·2
8. 0·09 × □ = 0·54
9. 0·008 × □ = 0·072
10. 0·007 × □ = 0·042

Copy and complete

11. 0·72 ÷ □ = 0·09
12. 0·49 ÷ □ = 0·07
13. 0·4 ÷ □ = 0·05
14. 0·03 ÷ □ = 0·005
15. 0·027 ÷ □ = 0·009

I can use a calculator to solve one- and two-step problems involving decimals.

Remember to match the units of measurement.

Example What is the cost of two towels at £3·69 each and a rubber duck costing 92p?

[C] [3] [·] [6] [9] [×] [2] [+] [0] [·] [9] [2] [=] → 8·3

The total cost is £8·30.

1. Zoe saves £2·40 each week. How much has she saved after 14 weeks?
2. A plank is 2·6 m long. Lengths of 75 cm and 65 cm are cut off. How long is the plank now?
3. A bath is filled with 32·5 litres of hot water and 23·8 litres of cold water. How much water is in the bath?
4. There are 150 tea bags in a packet. They weigh 480 g altogether. How much does each bag weigh?
5. Chas buys two games for £2·35 each. How much change does he have from £10?
6. How many 75p pens can you buy for £20?

1. A school buys a set of books for £178·20. Each book costs £4·95. How many books does the school buy?
2. At the Equator the temperature is 34·6 °C. At the North Pole it is 86·7 °C colder. What is the temperature at the North Pole?
3. Chickens cost £2·80 for one kilogram. Estelle buys a chicken weighing 1·6 kg. How much change will she receive from £10?
4. Eight lengths of 2·15 metres are cut from a 40 metre rope. How much rope is left?
5. A shower uses 9 litres of water every minute. How much water is used in 25 seconds.

C

1. A burger bar sells 276 burgers. The takings for the burgers is £372·60. How much does each burger cost?
2. Tickets for a charity concert cost £4·50. 629 people attend the concert. How much money is raised by the sale of tickets?
3. A lake is 127·4 metres deep. The surface of the lake is 73 metres above sea level. How many metres below sea level is the bottom of the lake?
4. The 250 pins in a packet weigh 20 g altogether. What is the weight of 6 pins?
5. Twenty-eight 150 ml glasses and a jug holding 1·385 litres are filled from a 6 litre pack of orange juice. How much juice is left?
6. Every day the four members of the Tunkel family eat a 35 g portion of breakfast cereal each. How many days will a 1 kilogram box last?

I can multiply a two-digit number by a two-digit number.

Examples

68 × 27

Estimate first

68 × 27 rounds to 70 × 30

70 × 30 = 2100

68 × 27 is less than 2100

×	20	7	
60	1200	420	1620
8	160	56	216
			1836

```
   68
 × 27
 1200   60 × 20
  420   60 × 7
  160    8 × 20
   56    8 × 7
 1836
 1
```

```
   68
 × 27
 1360   68 × 20
  476   68 × 7
 1836
  1
```

A

Copy and complete.

1.

×	10	5	
20			
4			

24 × 15 = ☐

2.

×	20	3	
30			
6			

36 × 23 = ☐

3.

×	10	6	
40			
7			

47 × 16 = ☐

4.

×	20	4	
20			
9			

29 × 24 = ☐

Work out

5. 25 × 18
6. 34 × 27
7. 52 × 19
8. 38 × 22

B

Copy and complete.

1.
```
   28
 × 17
        20 × 10
         8 × 10
        20 × 7
         8 × 7
```

2.
```
   32
 × 29
        30 × 20
         2 × 20
        30 × 9
         2 × 9
```

3.
```
   46
 × 34
        40 × 30
         6 × 30
        40 × 4
         6 × 4
```

Work out

4. 35 × 16
5. 29 × 23
6. 47 × 26
7. 38 × 35

C

Copy and complete.

1. 38 × 19
2. 53 × 28
3. 85 × 13
4. 48 × 45
5. 67 × 36
6. 72 × 54
7. 43 × 39
8. 58 × 52
9. 93 × 24
10. 65 × 41
11. 56 × 37
12. 74 × 63

Work out

13. 215 × 14
14. 146 × 27
15. 271 × 35
16. 483 × 16
17. 149 × 55
18. 527 × 29
19. 368 × 18
20. 492 × 36

I can multiply three-digit numbers and decimals by a one-digit number.

Examples

```
  368                   368        6·8               1·68
×   7                 ×   7      ×   7             ×    7
 2100  300 × 7         2576      42·0    6 × 7      7·00      1 × 7
  420   60 × 7           45       5·6  0·8 × 7      4·20    0·6 × 7
   56    8 × 7                   47·6               0·56   0·08 × 7
 2576                                              11·76
```

A

Copy and complete.

1.
```
   278
 ×   5
         200 × 5
          70 × 5
           8 × 5
```

2.
```
   352
 ×   9
         300 × 9
          50 × 9
           2 × 9
```

3.
```
   3·5
 ×   7
           3 × 7
         0·5 × 7
```

4.
```
   6·9
 ×   3
           6 × 3
         0·9 × 3
```

Work out

5. 148 × 2
6. 234 × 6
7. 5·7 × 4
8. 2·6 × 9

B

Copy and complete.

1. 249 × 2
2. 373 × 4
3. 185 × 7
4. 356 × 3
5. 2·8 × 3
6. 9·5 × 9
7. 6·7 × 2
8. 5·9 × 6

Work out

9. 238 × 9
10. 469 × 5
11. 193 × 8
12. 275 × 6
13. 4·8 × 5
14. 7·6 × 8
15. 8·9 × 4
16. 7·2 × 7
17. A bucket holds 8·7 litres of water. How much water would 6 buckets hold?
18. A baby weighs 6·4 kilograms. His mother is nine times heavier. How much does his mother weigh?

C

Work out

1. 1354 × 8
2. 2769 × 9
3. 3918 × 7
4. 4267 × 4
5. 23·7 × 9
6. 75·9 × 4
7. 14·6 × 8
8. 38·2 × 6
9. 1·59 × 3
10. 2·73 × 7
11. 6·48 × 5
12. 3·92 × 8
13. A roll of wallpaper is 3·16 metres in length. How long are 8 rolls altogether?
14. One gallon is 4·55 litres. How much is three gallons in litres?
15. A cross-country circuit is 1·78 km long. An athlete runs the circuit five times. How far does he run altogether?

I can divide a three-digit number by a one-digit number.

Examples

Estimate
$6 \times 30 = 180$
$6 \times 40 = 240$
$180 < 231 < 240$
$30 < \text{Answer} < 40$

$$
\begin{array}{rl}
 & 231 \\
- & \underline{\ 60} \quad (6 \times 10) \\
 & 171 \\
- & \underline{\ 60} \quad (6 \times 10) \\
 & 111 \\
- & \underline{\ 60} \quad (6 \times 10) \\
 & 51 \\
- & \underline{\ 48} \quad (6 \times 8) \\
 & 3
\end{array}
$$

Answer 38 r3

For a more efficient method of chunking start by subtracting this figure.
↓
$180 < 231 \div 6 < 240$

$$
\begin{array}{rl}
 & 231 \\
- & \underline{180} \quad (6 \times 30) \\
 & 51 \\
- & \underline{\ 48} \quad (6 \times 8) \\
 & 3
\end{array}
$$

Answer 38 r3

A

Work out

1. $36 \div 2$
2. $85 \div 5$
3. $74 \div 6$
4. $140 \div 8$
5. $93 \div 4$
6. $100 \div 7$
7. $53 \div 3$
8. $61 \div 4$
9. $120 \div 9$
10. $114 \div 6$
11. $98 \div 8$
12. $75 \div 4$
13. $69 \div 5$
14. $121 \div 7$
15. $160 \div 9$
16. $49 \div 3$
17. In one week a vet treated 112 animals. One quarter were dogs. How many were not dogs?

18. Five friends share a prize of £130. How much should they each receive?

B

Work out

1. $86 \div 4$
2. $93 \div 6$
3. $159 \div 7$
4. $173 \div 8$
5. $129 \div 9$
6. $114 \div 4$
7. $167 \div 6$
8. $205 \div 7$
9. $301 \div 8$
10. $294 \div 9$
11. $173 \div 4$
12. $211 \div 6$
13. $293 \div 7$
14. $254 \div 8$
15. $350 \div 9$
16. $267 \div 4$
17. Chairs are stacked in groups of 6. How many stacks are needed to store 138 chairs?
18. There are eight screws in each packet. How many packets can be filled with 208 screws?
19. One ninth of the 162 children in a school can speak a language other than English. How many children only speak English?

C

Work out

1. $314 \div 5$
2. $360 \div 8$
3. $441 \div 6$
4. $513 \div 9$
5. $385 \div 4$
6. $453 \div 7$
7. $731 \div 9$
8. $624 \div 8$
9. $220 \div 18$
10. $299 \div 13$
11. $180 \div 12$
12. $360 \div 15$
13. $250 \div 22$
14. $650 \div 25$
15. $400 \div 32$
16. $800 \div 34$
17. The 14 sweets in a packet weigh 322 g. What is the weight of each sweet?
18. One in every fifteen raffle tickets wins a prize. 435 tickets are sold. How many prizes are needed?
19. How many 25 ml doses of medicine are there in a 600 ml bottle?
20. How many days is 600 hours?

A3 NUMBER PROBLEMS

I can solve number problems and puzzles.

A

Place a decimal in each box to make the calculation correct.

1. 0·☐ + 0·☐ = 1
2. 4·☐ + ☐·2 = 10
3. I think of a number. I multiply by 3. I add 65. The answer is 107. What is my number?
4. I think of a number. I subtract 156. I divide by 4. The answer is 36. What is my number?
5. The perimeter of a square is 68 cm. How long is each side?
6. The perimeter of an equilateral triangle is 45 cm. How long is each side?

Copy and complete.

7. 5☐ + ☐7 = 85
8. ☐3 − 2☐ = 18
9. ☐7 × 2 = 13☐
10. ☐6 × 4 = 34☐

B

Copy and complete.

1. ☐ + 0·4 + ☐ = 1
2. ☐ + ☐ + 0·18 = 1
3. 10 = 8·☐ + ☐·63
4. 10 = ☐·51 + 3·☐
5. I think of a number. I multiply by 6. I subtract 138. The answer is 84. What is my number?
6. I think of a number. I divide it by 4. I multiply by 9. The answer is 423. What is my number?
7. The perimeter of a regular pentagon is 215 cm. How long is each side?
8. Find two consecutive numbers with a product of:
   a) 702 **b)** 210.
9. Find two numbers between 10 and 20 with a product of:
   a) 224 **b)** 247.
10. Find two numbers between 20 and 30 with a product of:
    a) 700 **b)** 462.

C

Copy and complete.

1. ☐ + 3·67 + ☐ = 10·5
2. 5·1 − ☐ − ☐ = 3·62
3. 2 4 5 8

   Use the above digits once only. Place one digit in each box so that the answer is a whole number.

   ☐·☐☐ × ☐
4. The perimeter of a regular octagon is 368 cm. How long is each side?

Copy and complete.

5. ☐ + 0·16 − 0·7 = 4·4
6. ☐ × 6 − 3·7 = 1·7
7. ☐ ÷ 13 ÷ 10 = 0·2
8. ☐ × 3 − 2·1 = 3·6
9. ☐ × 9 − 856 = 278
10. ☐ − 29·6 ÷ 7 = 4·5
11. ☐ ÷ 8 − 5·24 = 16·46
12. ☐ + 1·76 × 15 = 300
13. Find two consecutive numbers with a product of 2352.
14. Find two numbers between 30 and 40 with a product of 1254.

I can continue sequences involving diagrams and numbers.

Pattern 1

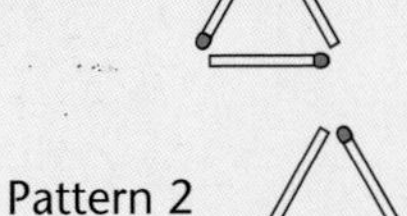

Pattern 2

Pattern 3

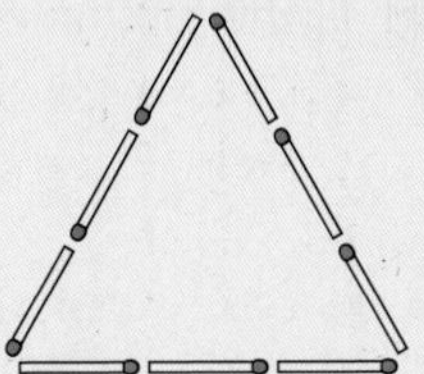

1. Draw the next two diagrams in the above pattern.
2. Copy and complete the table.

Pattern	Matches
1	3
2	
3	
4	
5	

3. Copy and complete this sentence.
   The rule for the number of matches is ________ times the number of patterns.
4. How many matches would there be in:
   a) the 6th pattern
   b) the 10th pattern
   c) the 20th pattern
   d) the 100th pattern?

Pattern 1

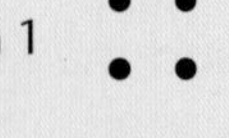

Pattern 2

Pattern 3

1. Use squared paper. Draw the next two diagrams in the above pattern.
2. Copy and complete the table.

Pattern	Dots
1	4
2	
3	
4	
5	

3. Copy and complete.
   The rule for the number of dots is ________ times the number of the pattern plus ________.
4. How many dots would there be in:
   a) the 9th pattern
   b) the 14th pattern
   c) the 36th pattern?
5. Which pattern has
   a) 16 dots
   b) 24 dots
   c) 40 dots?

C

Pattern 1

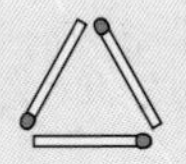

Pattern 2

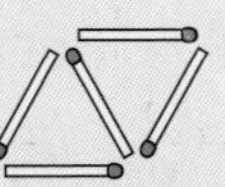

Pattern 3

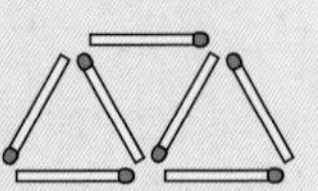

1. How many matches would there be in:
   a) the 7th pattern
   b) the 16th pattern
   c) the 39th pattern?
2. Which pattern has:
   a) 27 matches
   b) 53 matches
   c) 215 matches?

Pattern 1

Pattern 2

Pattern 3

3. How many dots would there be in:
   a) the 8th pattern
   b) the 24th pattern
   c) the 100th pattern?
4. Which pattern has:
   a) 21 dots
   b) 65 dots
   c) 129 dots?
5. Write a rule for each of the above patterns.

I can find all the factors of a two-digit number.

Factors are numbers that divide exactly into another number. It is often useful to think of factors as pairs of numbers whose product is the target number.

Examples

Find the factors of 12.
1×12 2×6 3×4
The factors of 12 are 1, 2, 3, 4, 6, 12

Find the factors of 9.
1×9 3×3
The factors of 9 are 1, 3, 9

A

Copy and complete the second factor in each pair.

1. 24 → 8 and □
2. 15 → 3 and □
3. 42 → 6 and □
4. 18 → 9 and □
5. 28 → 7 and □
6. 40 → 5 and □
7. 54 → 9 and □
8. 72 → 8 and □

Find all the factors of the following numbers. The number of factors is shown in brackets.

9. 10 (4)
10. 14 (4)
11. 20 (6)
12. 24 (8)
13. 27 (4)
14. 16 (5)
15. 30 (8)
16. 42 (8)

36 40 24 45

Which of the above numbers have a factor of:

17. 2
18. 3
19. 4
20. 5?

B

Find all the factors of the following numbers.

1. 36
2. 44
3. 51
4. 65
5. 99
6. 75
7. 48
8. 90

9. Nick says

   Every whole number has an even number of factors.

   Laila disagrees.
   a) Who is right?
   b) Explain why?

10. Sharon notices that the number of chocolates in a full box is a multiple of 9. She eats one. The number of chocolates is now a multiple of 7. How many chocolates are there in the full box?

11. Find five numbers that have a factor of 2 and a factor of 3. What do you notice?

12. Investigate numbers which have a factor of 3 and a factor of 4.

C

Find all the factors of:

1. 49
2. 60
3. 57
4. 68
5. 92
6. 72
7. 98
8. 100.

9. Yunis is under 40. Both his age and his mother's age are multiples of 6. Next year both ages will be multiples of 5. How old are Yunis and his mother?

10. Milly's great grandmother's age is a multiple of 9. Next year it will be a multiple of 7. How old is she?

Find the highest factor shared by:

11. 24 and 60
12. 38 and 57
13. 32 and 48
14. 30 and 75.

Make a statement about numbers that have a factor of both:

15. 3 and 5
16. 4 and 5.

I can recognise multiples of 2, 5, 10 or 100.

Multiples are the numbers in a multiplication table.
Whole numbers are multiples of:

2 if the number is even
5 if the last digit is 0 or 5
10 if the last digit is 0
100 if the last two digits are 00.

A

Write down the first six multiples of:

1. 3
2. 8
3. 11
4. 7
5. 4
6. 9

Which number should not be in the box?

7. Multiples of 2: 34 25 78 90
8. Multiples of 5: 95 30 54 70
9. Multiples of 10: 780 110 205
10. Multiples of 100: 300 60 1000

Write Yes or No

11. Is 36 a multiple of 2?
12. Is 52 a multiple of 5?
13. Is 70 a multiple of 10?
14. Is 210 a multiple of 100?
15. Is 45 a multiple of 5?
16. Is 87 a multiple of 2?
17. Is 400 a multiple of 100?
18. Is 804 a multiple of 10?

B

Write True or False.

1. 390 is a multiple of 10.
2. 185 is a multiple of 5.
3. 245 is a multiple of 2.
4. 1300 is a multiple of 100.
5. 3210 is a multiple of 5.
6. 209 is a multiple of 10.
7. 194 is a multiple of 2.
8. 640 is a multiple of 100.
9. 750 is a multiple of 10.
10. 1501 is a multiple of 5.
11. 430 is a multiple of 2.
12. 3000 is a multiple of 100.

Dani says

Any number that ends in the digits 52 is divisible by 4.

13. Divide 152, 252 and 352 by 4. Is Dani's statement true for these numbers?
14. Use a calculator. Test Dani's statement using 3-digit and 5-digit numbers.

C

A number is a multiple of 4 if its last two digits are divisible by 4.

1. Test the above statement for five 3-digit numbers.
2. Use a calculator and test the statement for five 4-digit numbers.
3. Can you explain why this statement is true?

A number is a multiple of 3 if the sum of its digits is divisible by 3.

4. Test this statement for:
   a) five 2-digit numbers
   b) five 3-digit numbers
   c) five 4-digit numbers.

Use these cards.

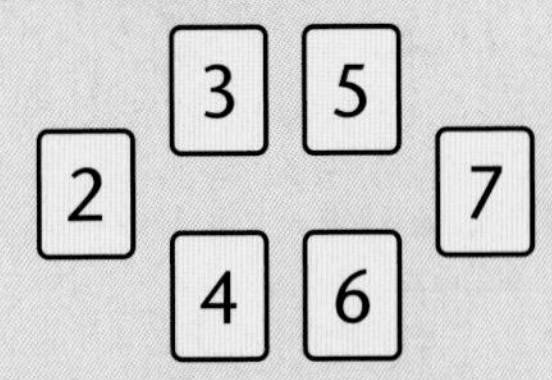

Make as many 3-digit numbers as you can that are:

5. multiples of 3
6. multiples of 4.

I can use my calculation skills and understanding of place value to solve number problems.

A

Copy and complete.

1. $1 \cdot 7 + \square = 4 \cdot 4$
2. $\square \times 5 = 3 \cdot 5$

Find the number that lies halfway between:

3. 5·4 and 8
4. 2·7 and 4·5.

Find all the possible ways to complete these calculations by placing one digit in each box.

5. $\square \times \square = 24$
6. $\square \cdot 3 + \square \cdot 7 = 4$

7. I think of a number.
   I add 17.
   I double it.
   The answer is 46.
   What is my number?

Use a calculator.
Copy and complete.

8. $7 \cdot 6 + \square = 14 \cdot 5$
9. $\square + 5 \cdot 9 = 21 \cdot 3$
10. $22 \cdot 4 - \square = 8 \cdot 7$
11. $\square - 9 \cdot 4 = 13 \cdot 2$

12. Find two consecutive numbers with a product of:
    a) 380 **b)** 182.

B

Copy and complete.

1. $6 \cdot 1 - \square = 5 \cdot 25$
2. $\square \div 7 = 2 \cdot 4$

Find the number that lies halfway between:

3. 3·9 and 6·2
4. 5·41 and 4·73.

Find all the possible ways to complete these calculations by placing one digit in each box.

5. $0 \cdot \square \times \square = 2$
6. $60 \div 1\square = \square$

7. I think of a number.
   I multiply by 3.
   I take 0·77.
   The answer is 6·73.
   What is my number?

Use a calculator.
Copy and complete.

8. $\square 3 \times 2\square = 1118$
9. $1890 \div \square 5 = 5\square$
10. $(\square \times 3) + 0 \cdot 6 = 9 \cdot 3$
11. $(\square \div 8) - 25 = 37$

12. Find two consecutive numbers with a product of:
    a) 5852 **b)** 2970.

C

Copy and complete.

1. $3 \cdot 792 + \square = 5 \cdot 1$
2. $\square \times 4 = 9 \cdot 4$

Find the number that lies halfway between:

3. 1·4 and 2·56
4. 2·67 and 3.

Find all the possible ways to complete these calculations by placing one digit in each box.

5. $100 \div \square\square = \square \cdot \square$
6. $\square \cdot \square \times \square = 3$

7. I think of a number.
   I halve it.
   I add 3·59.
   The answer is 5·74.
   What is my number?

Use a calculator.
Copy and complete.

8. $\square + (3 \cdot 56 \div 4) = 1 \cdot 71$
9. $(\square \div 9) \times 4 \cdot 8 = 30 \cdot 24$
10. $\square\square \times 3\square = 3393$
11. $2812 \div 7\square = \square\square$

12. Find a pair of two-digit numbers with a product of:
    a) 221 **b)** 437.

I can solve word problems.

Example

Mr. and Mrs. Flynn's plane tickets to Venice cost £239 each. They spent a further £647 while they were there. How much did their holiday cost?

£239 × 2 = £478
£478 + £647 = £1025
The holiday cost £1025 altogether.

A

1. There are four children in each tent. How many tents are needed for 72 children?
2. Kenny buys three pencils and a ruler for 75p. Pencils cost 15p. How much is the ruler?
3. All of Mrs. Carter's seven children had four children themselves. All of her grandchildren had three children each. How many great grandchildren does Mrs. Carter have?
4. There are 42 cars in a car park. In the next hour 29 enter and 53 leave. How many cars are there now in the car park?
5. Komal has read one fifth of her book. She has just read page 24. How many pages does the book have?

B

1. How many minutes are there in a day?
2. There are 116 passengers on a train. At the next station 48 people get off and 57 get on. How many passengers are there now?
3. Sharon has 200 chocolate buttons. On Monday she eats one fifth of the sweets. On Tuesday she eats one half of the rest. How many chocolate buttons are left?
4. Louis flew 2564 miles and then travelled 287 miles by train. How long was his journey?
5. Jodie buys eight ice creams at 79p each. She pays with a £10 note. How much change will she receive?
6. Five biscuits weigh 225 g. What does one weigh?

C

1. There are 24 Jaffa cakes in each box. How many boxes are needed for 1200 cakes?
2. There are 342 passengers on a flight leaving London.
   At New York 153 people get off the plane and 79 new passengers get on. How many people are on the plane when it flies on to Los Angeles?
3. There are 4 wards on every floor of a hospital. Each ward has 20 beds. How many floors are there if the hospital has 560 beds altogether?
4. In London a car costs £9249. This is £1768 more than the price of the same car in Holland. What does the car cost in Holland?
5. Beef costs £6·40 for one kilogram. What would 350 g cost?
6. There are 16 pencils in each packet and 48 packets in each box.
   A school buys two boxes. How many pencils has it bought?

I can measure the angles of 2-D shapes and use this to investigate their properties.

A

1. Use triangular paper. Draw three different equilateral triangles. Measure the angles of each triangle. What do you find?
2. What is each angle of a square?
3. Use a ruler and a protractor only. Draw:
   - **a)** an equilateral triangle with sides of 5 cm
   - **b)** a square with sides of 3·5 cm.
4. Use a small rectangle of card.
   - **a)** Join the mid points of the longer sides.
   - **b)** Draw a diagonal in one half.
   - **c)** Cut the card into three shapes along the lines.

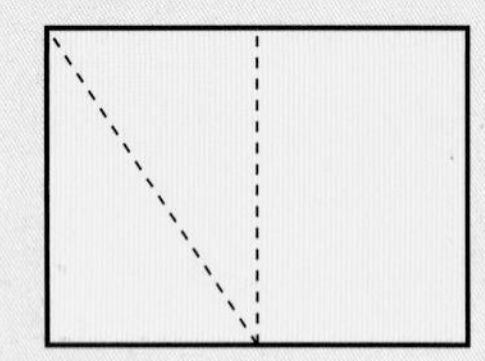

5. Make different shapes using your three pieces. Draw round and label each shape.

B

1. Use triangular paper. Draw three different regular hexagons. Measure the angles of each shape. What do you find?
2. Draw round a regular pentagon. Measure each of the angles. What do you find?
3. Use a protractor and a ruler only. Draw:
   - **a)** a regular hexagon with sides of 3 cm
   - **b)** a regular pentagon with sides of 2·5 cm.
4. Use squared paper. Draw different parallelograms. (Opposite sides equal and parallel.)

   Measure the angles of each shape. What do you find?

Use triangular paper.

5. Make different shapes using four equilateral triangles side to side. Label each shape.
6. Make different shapes using six equilateral triangles side to side. Label each shape and draw any lines of symmetry.

C

1. Copy and complete this table showing the sum of the angles of regular polygons.

Sides	Angle	Sum of Angles
3		
4	90°	360°
5		
6		
7	128·6°	900°

2. Can you see a pattern in your table? Use the pattern to write the next three rows.
3. Use a ruler and a protractor only. Draw:
   - **a)** a regular octagon with sides of 2 cm
   - **b)** a regular nonagon (9 sides) with sides of 2·5 cm
   - **c)** a regular decagon (10 sides) with sides of 2·2 cm
   - **d)** a parallelogram with sides of 3 cm and 5 cm and a 60° angle.
4. A trapezium has one pair of parallel sides. Investigate the angles of a symmetrical trapezium.

B3 NETS

I can draw accurate nets for 3-D shapes.

1. Copy this net onto squared paper. Cut it out. Cut off one square and fold to make a net for an open cube.

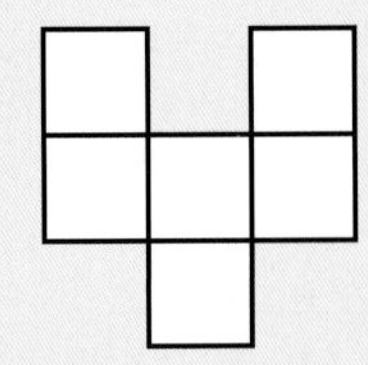

2. Copy this net and cut it out. Cut off one square and fold to make a net for a closed cube.

3. Copy this net onto squared paper. Cut it out and make the cuboid.

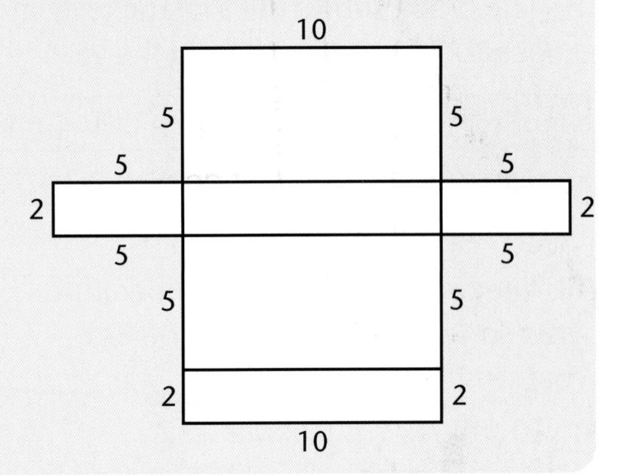

B

1. Make nets for these cuboids.

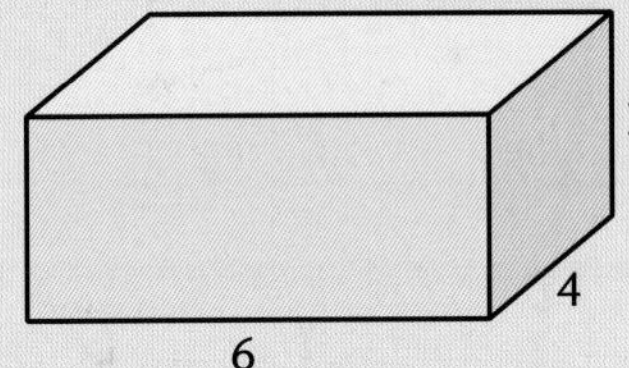

2. Use triangular paper. Make this net for a tetrahedron. Find different nets that make a tetrahedron.

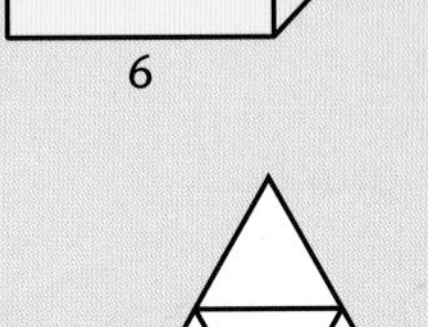

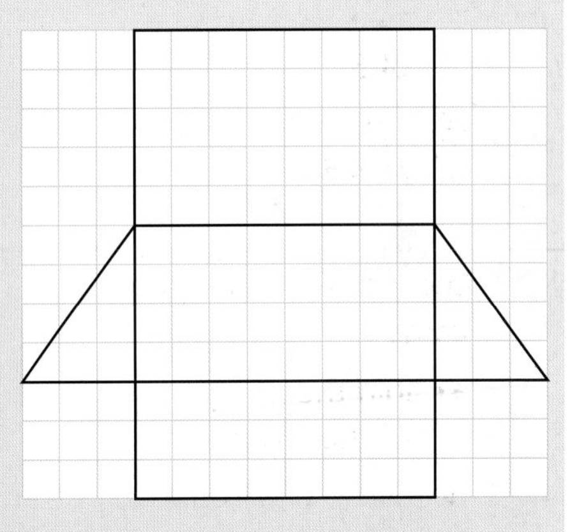

3. Copy the above net onto squared paper. Cut it out and make the triangular prism.

1. Copy this net onto squared paper. Cut it out and make the pyramid.

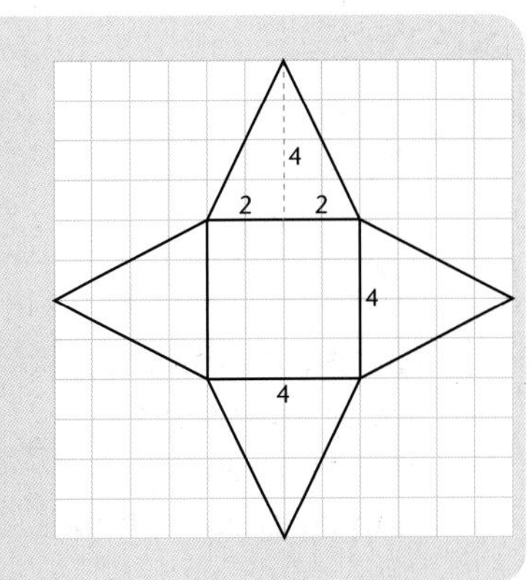

2. Make a net for a square based pyramid with a base area of 25 cm^2 and a height of 5 cm.
3. Make a net for a hexagonal based prism with a length of 6 cm and edges of 2 cm.

I can draw and interpret line graphs.

Line graphs are graphs in which a set of data is plotted and the points are joined up with a line.
Line graphs often show a trend.

Examples

This line graph shows the average daily maximum temperature in London during the year.

Month	J	F	M	A	M	J	J	A	S	O	N	D
Temperature (°C)	4	5	7	9	12	16	18	17	15	11	8	5

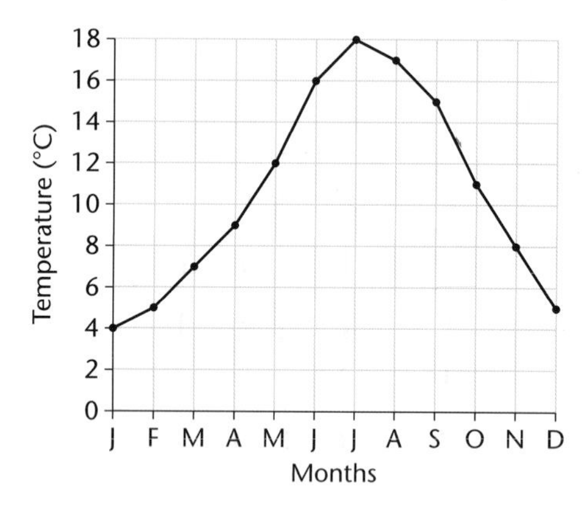

This line graphs shows the temperature between 6 am and 6 pm on June 8th.
What was the temperature at:

a) 10 am Answer *12°C*

b) 11 am? Answer *15°C*

At what time was the temperature 10 °C?
Answer *9 am*

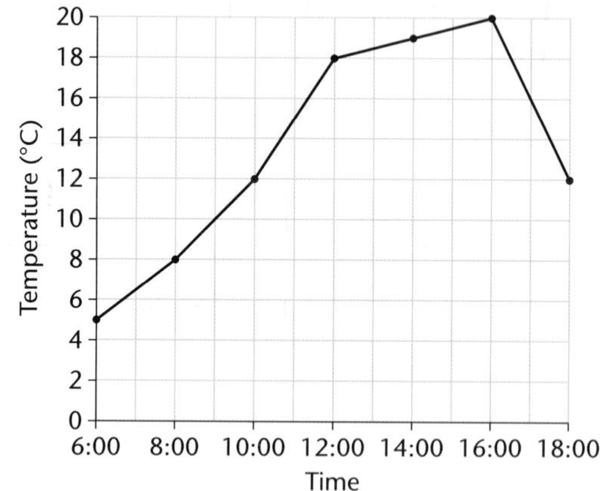

Match each of these statements to one of the graphs.

1. The pulse rate rises steadily.
2. The pulse rate begins to rise and then falls quickly.
3. The pulse rate rises more and more quickly.
4. The pulse rate stays the same and then falls quickly.
5. The pulse rate falls faster and faster.
6. The pulse rate rises, stays the same and then rises quickly.
7. The table shows the results of Sara's weekly tables test. Use the data to draw a line graph. Label the axes.

Week	1	2	3	4	5	6	7	8
Mark	3	5	5	6	7	8	8	9

A

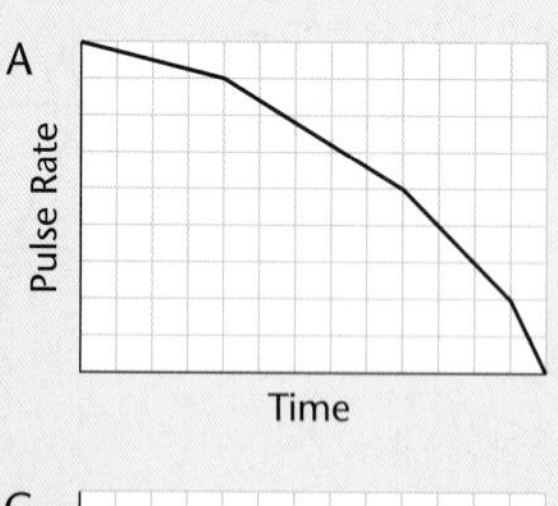

B

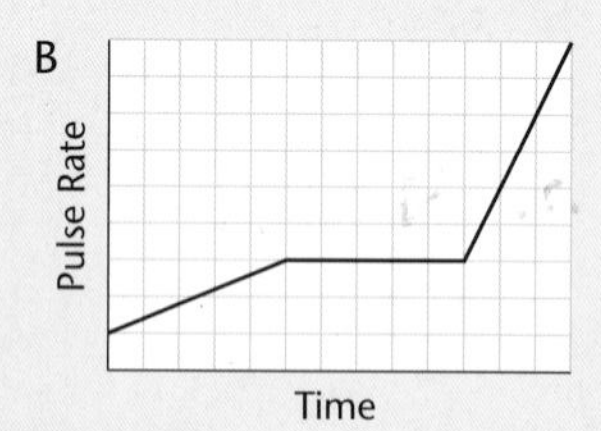

C

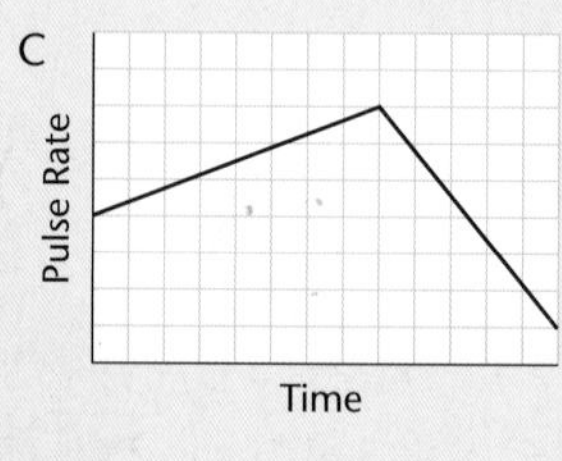

D

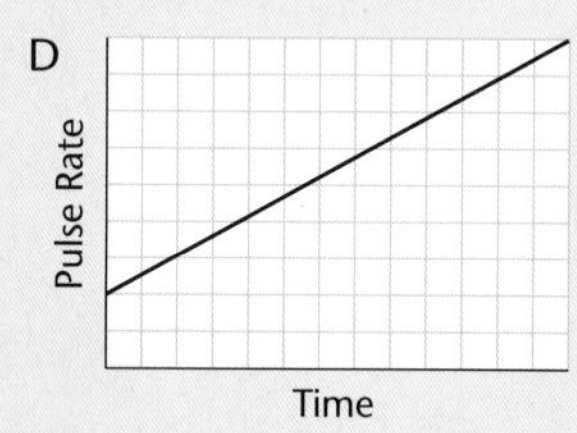

E

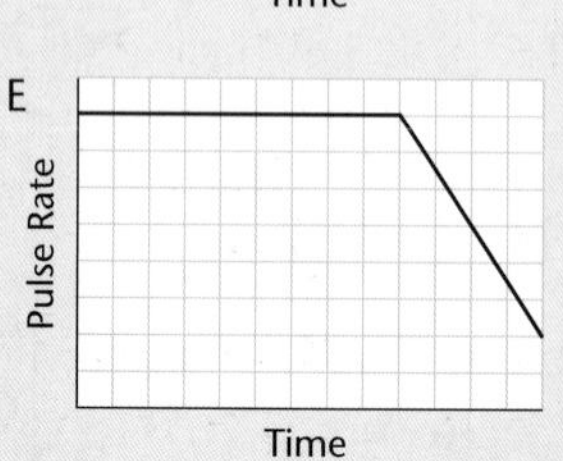

F

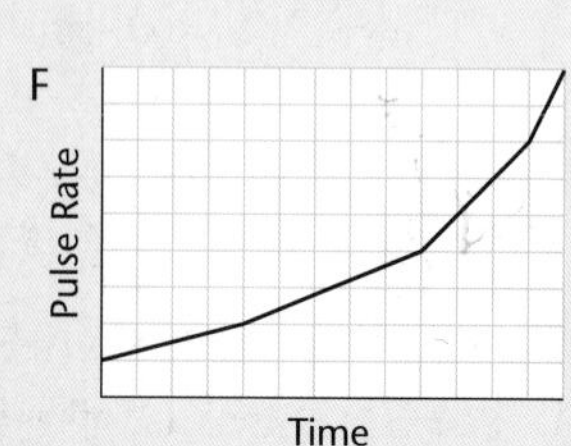

B

This line graph shows Natasha's heart rate during a 50 minute PE lesson.

1. What was Natasha's pulse at:
   a) 11:15 **b)** 11:20?
2. When did Natasha's pulse:
   a) rise to 120 beats per minute
   b) fall to 130 beats per minute?
3. When did her pulse start to fall?
4. What was Natasha's highest pulse rate during the lesson?
5. What is her resting pulse rate?
6. Use the table below to draw a line graph showing the temperature in a room in a school over 24 hours in January. Remember to label the axes.

Time	0400	0600	0800	1000	1200	1400	1600	1800	2000	2200	0000	0200	0400
Temperature in room (°C)	3	2	14	18	19	19	17	14	8	5	5	4	3

7. When did the temperature increase most rapidly? Why do you think this happened?

C

1. This line graph shows the average maximum daily temperature in Sweden.
   a) What was the temperature in June?
   b) In which month was the temperature 7 °C?
   c) In which two months was the temperature 3 °C?
   d) Which two months saw the largest fall in temperature?
   e) What was the range of temperature over the year?
   f) For how many months was the temperature below 3 °C?

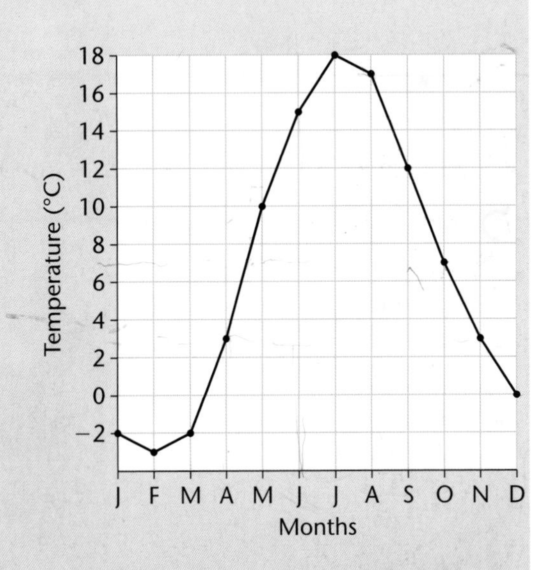

2. Use the table to draw a line graph to show the improvement in an athlete's time for running 400 m. You will need to use graph paper.

Week	1	2	3	4	5	6	7	8	9	10	11	12
400 m time (seconds)	58·6	58·2	57·3	56·9	56·1	55·5	54·6	54·9	53·5	53·1	52·9	52·8

   a) In which week did she make the greatest improvement in time?
   b) In which week do you think she had a slight cold?

C3 METRIC UNITS OF LENGTH

I can choose and use metric units to measure length.

Examples

10 mm = 1 cm	100 cm = 1 m	1000 m = 1 km
5 mm = 0·5 cm	20 cm = 0·2 m	700 m = 0·7 km
68 mm = 6·8 cm	240 cm = 2·4 m	1300 m = 1·3 km
168 mm = 16·8 cm	379 cm = 3·79 m	4520 m = 4·52 km

A

Copy and complete.

1. 50 mm = ☐ cm
2. 20 mm = ☐ cm
3. 3 cm = ☐ mm
4. 6 cm = ☐ mm
5. 800 cm = ☐ m
6. 100 cm = ☐ m
7. 9 m = ☐ cm
8. 4 m = ☐ cm
9. 2000 m = ☐ km
10. 7000 m = ☐ km
11. 6 km = ☐ m
12. 3 km = ☐ m

Suggest a suitable metric unit to measure these lengths.

13. a lollipop stick
14. a ladybird
15. the Channel tunnel
16. a pea
17. a straw
18. the height of a skyscraper

B

Copy and complete.

1. 21 mm = ☐ cm
2. 72 mm = ☐ cm
3. 1·8 cm = ☐ mm
4. 0·6 cm = ☐ mm
5. 510 cm = ☐ m
6. 870 cm = ☐ m
7. 3·1 m = ☐ cm
8. 9·3 m = ☐ cm
9. 6500 m = ☐ km
10. 2900 m = ☐ km
11. 4·4 km = ☐ m
12. 0·2 km = ☐ m

Suggest a suitable metric unit to measure these lengths.

13. a plane journey
14. the length of the River Nile
15. a school corridor
16. an ear stud
17. a fork
18. a staple

C

Copy and complete.

1. 434 cm = ☐ m
2. 799 cm = ☐ m
3. 21 cm = ☐ m
4. 2·52 m = ☐ cm
5. 1·07 m = ☐ cm
6. 5·83 m = ☐ cm
7. 450 m = ☐ km
8. 3180 m = ☐ km
9. 4620 m = ☐ km
10. 1·24 km = ☐ m
11. 0·06 km = ☐ m
12. 1·73 km = ☐ m

Choose the best estimate.

13. a pen
    140 mm, 140 cm, 140 m
14. a marathon
    420 m, 4200 m, 42 000 m
15. a computer screen's width
    0·3 m, 0·03 m, 0·003 m
16. an oval running track
    4 km, 0·4 km, 0·04 km
17. the diameter of a CD
    12 mm, 1·2 cm, 0·12m

I can present data and use it to investigate a problem.

The children on Orange Table investigated whether the distance they could throw a rounders ball would improve with practice.

They measured the longest throw of each child for five days.

The table shows the results.

Name	Distance Thrown (m)				
	M	Tu	W	Th	F
Amit	12	16	16	19	21
Carol	10	12	14	14	16
Jake	24	24	28	29	30
Naomi	16	18	21	20	24
Stu	20	25	27	28	31
Zena	25	28	30	31	35

A

1. How far did:
   a) Carol throw on Tuesday?
   b) Stu throw on Thursday?
2. On which day did:
   a) Amit throw 19 m
   b) Naomi throw 16 m?
3. What was the difference between Zena's throws on Monday and Tuesday?
4. What was the difference between Stu's throws on Thursday and Friday?
5. On which day did Jake:
   a) make his longest throw
   b) make his greatest improvement?
6. On which day did:
   a) Carol not improve
   b) Naomi not improve?
7. Draw a bar chart labelled in 2s to show Amit's throws on each day.

B

1. Who improved most between:
   a) Monday and Tuesday
   b) Tuesday and Wednesday
   c) Wednesday and Thursday
   d) Thursday and Friday?
2. How much further did Jake throw than Naomi:
   a) on Monday
   b) on Wednesday
   c) on Friday?
3. Look only at the distances thrown on Monday and Friday.
   a) Who made the greatest improvement in distance thrown in the 5 days?
   b) Who made the least improvement in distance?
4. Work out the improvement made by each child in the 5 days and present the data in a bar line chart.

C

Naomi's improvement in distance (DI) was 8 m. We can also work out her improvement as a percentage (PI) of her first throw (FT) by using this formula:

$PI = (DI \div FT) \times 100$

$PI = (8 \div 16) \times 100$

$= 0{\cdot}5 \times 100$

$= 50$

Naomi improved by 50% on her first throw.

1. Use a calculator. Work out the percentage improvement for each child using the above formula.
2. Draw a bar line chart to show the percentage improvement made by each child.
3. Which chart is better at showing how much each child has improved? Give a reason for your answer.

I can predict how likely an event is to happen.

The probability of an event can be placed on a probability scale.

Impossible — Unlikely — Even chance — Likely — Certain

For each of these statements write one of the above five probabilities.

1. Your TV needs to be repaired in the next 5 years.
2. Your teacher becomes a pop star.
3. You spin a coin and get a head.
4. It will snow next year at the South Pole.
5. You will roll a dice and get a 6.
6. You will have two children.
7. Your holiday next year will be on Mars.
8. Tomorrow the Headteacher will come to school on an elephant.

1. Make this spinner.

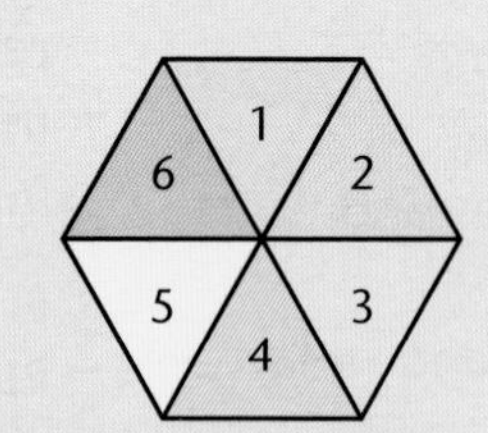

2. Copy and complete this table for 60 spins.

Spinner Number	Expected Frequency	Actual Frequency
1	10	
2	10	
3	10	
4	10	
5	10	
6	10	

3. Which number is the mode?
4. Draw a bar line chart to show the frequency of each spinner number in 60 spins.
5. Make this spinner. Complete a table like that in Question 2 for 30 spins.

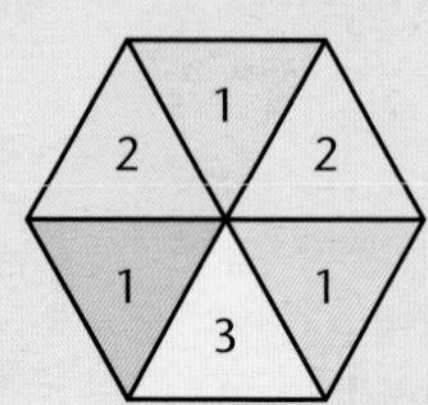

C

Work out the probability of each spinner landing on orange as a fraction.

1. 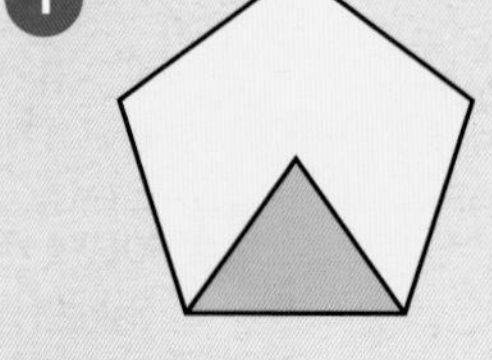
2. 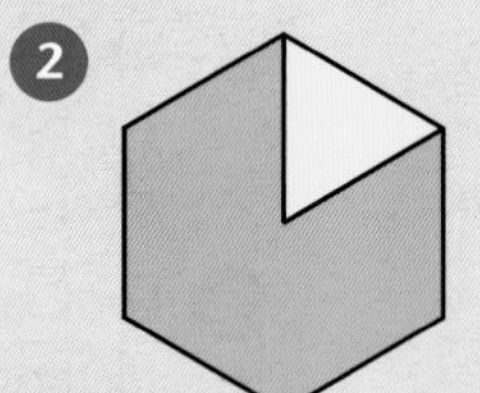
3. 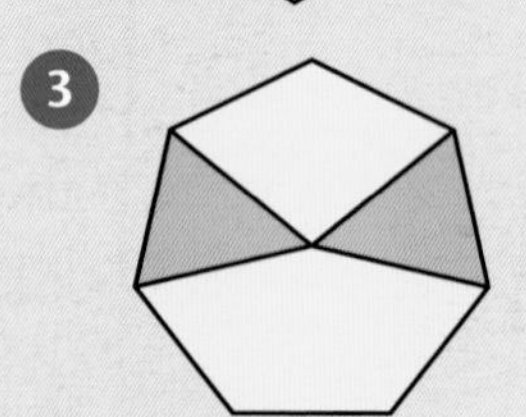
4. 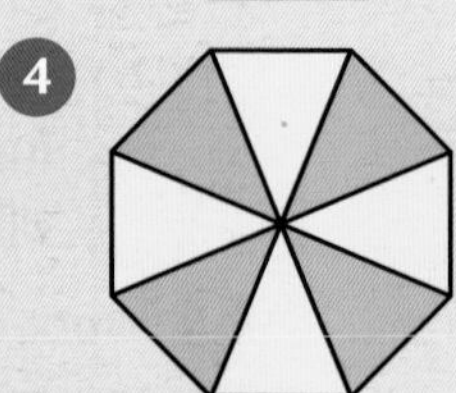
5. 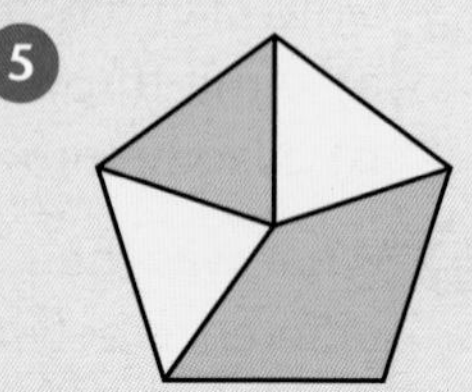
6. 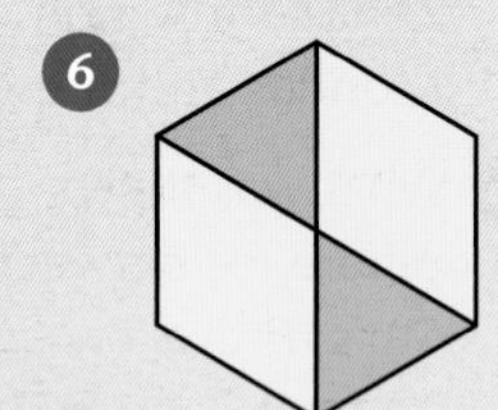
7. 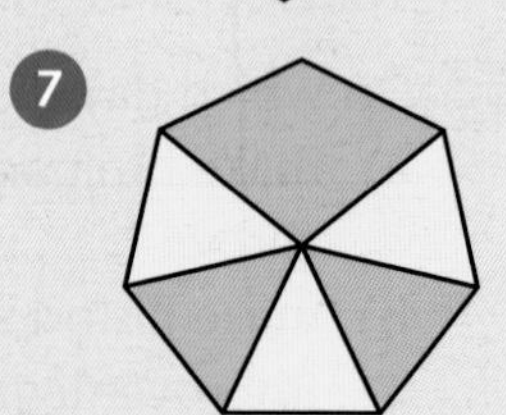
8. 
9. Place the numbers 1 to 8 on a probability scale to show the likelihood of each spinner landing on orange.

I can read scales with some unnumbered divisions.

For each of the scales work out:

a) the measurement indicated by each of the arrows.

b) the difference between the two arrows.

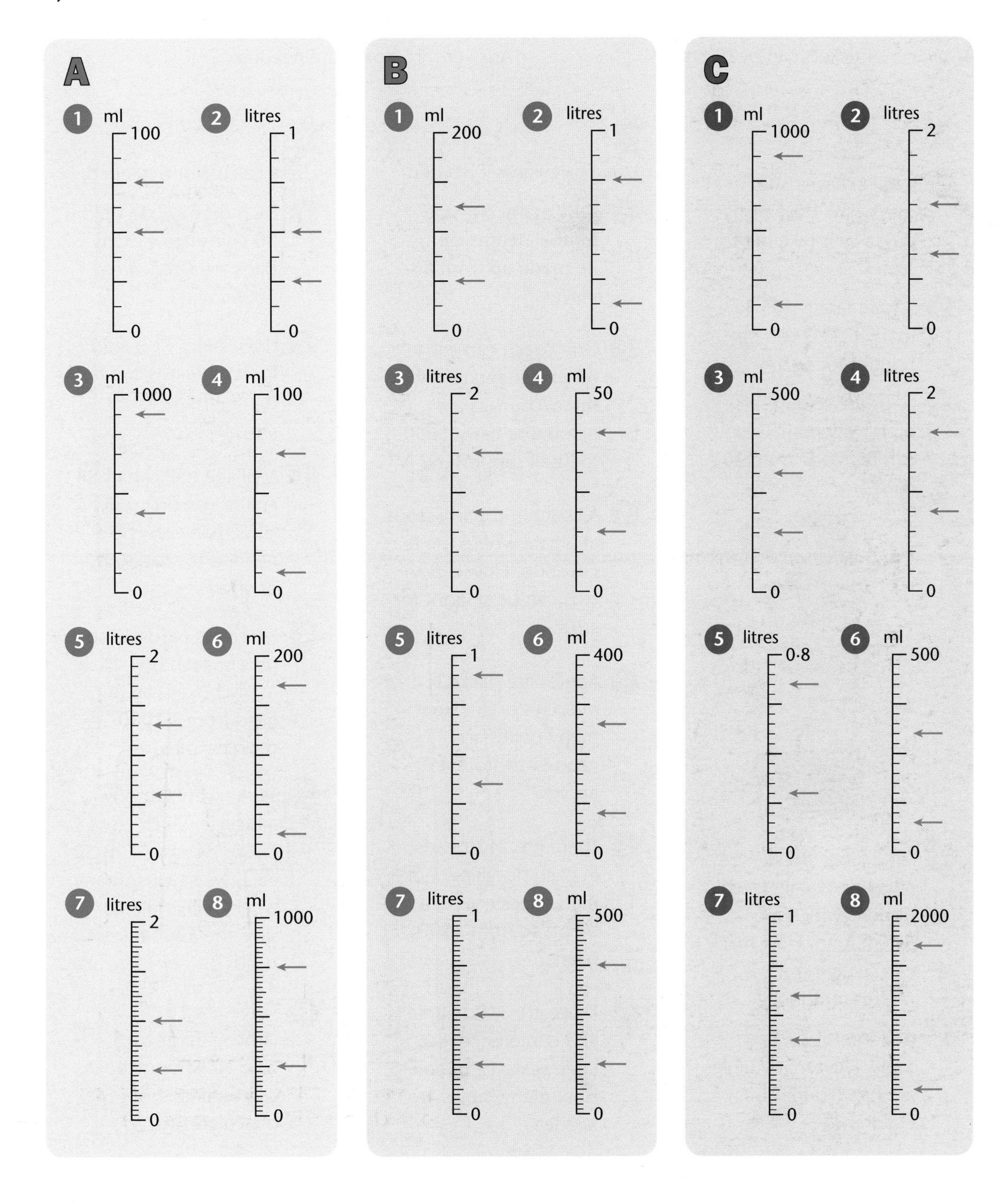

D3 ROUNDING REMAINDERS UP OR DOWN

I can decide whether to round up or down after division.

Examples

How many £6 tickets can I buy with £87?

87 ÷ 6 = 14 remainder 3

Answer 14 tickets can be bought.

An egg box holds 6 eggs.
How many boxes do I need to hold 87 eggs?

87 ÷ 6 = 14 remainder 3

Answer 15 boxes are needed.

A

1. Jennifer saves 30p every day. How many days will it take her to save £2?
2. A train fare is £5. How many tickets can be bought for £78?
3. Cups are sold in sets of 4. How many sets can be made from 30 cups?

4. For a fancy dress costume Natalie needs ribbons which are 80 cm long. How many can she cut from 5 metres of ribbon?
5. Children sit six to a table. How many tables are needed for 100 children?

B

Use a calculator if needed.

1. How many 6-a-side football teams can be made up from 83 players?
2. One coach can carry 65 passengers. How many coaches are needed to carry 1600 football supporters?
3. A coach trip party stops at a cafe where the teas cost 60p. How many teas can be bought for £20?
4. Apples are packed in boxes of 20. How many boxes are needed to store 450 apples?
5. There are 218 pearls in each necklace. How many necklaces can be made from 3500 pearls?
6. There are 340 people at a conference. Each table seats 12 people. How many tables are needed?

C

Use a calculator if needed.

1. Each money bag holds 30 coins. How many bags are needed for 1000 coins?
2. How many 11-a-side football teams can be made up from 140 players?
3. A village hall can fit 24 chairs into one row. How many rows are needed to seat 300 people?
4. There are 60 drawing pins in each box. How many boxes can be filled from 10 000 drawing pins?
5. Safraz wants to buy a bicycle which costs £200. He saves £13·50 each week. How many weeks will it take to save the £200 he needs?
6. There are 16 chocolates in each box. How many boxes can be filled from 500 chocolates?

I can solve problems involving capacity.

A

1. A bottle of lemonade holds one litre. One quarter of it is drunk. How much lemonade is left in the bottle?
2. An ink cartridge holds 15 ml. It can be filled twenty times from an ink bottle. How much ink is in the bottle?
3. Five children share a 2 litre bottle of cola. How much cola does each child have?
4. There is 200 ml of water in a bowl. One and a half litres is added. How much water is in the bowl now?
5. A shower uses 50 ml of water every second. How much water does it use in one minute?
6. Hannah pours 0·2 litres of water into her steam iron. When she has finished ironing there is 40 ml of water left. How much water has turned to steam?
7. One cup holds 150 ml. How many litres will fill 20 cups?

B

1. One quarter of a 2 litre tub of ice cream is used on Tuesday. 350 ml is used on Wednesday. How much ice cream is left?
2. A water pistol holds 120 ml of water. It is filled up 15 times. How much water is squirted from the pistol in litres?
3. Goldy's bowl holds 1600 ml of water. His tank holds 8 times more. What is the capacity of Goldy's tank in litres?

4. A motor mower has 800 ml of petrol left. 2·7 litres is added. How much petrol is there now in the mower?
5. Nathan uses 40 ml of washing up liquid every day. How long will his one litre bottle last?
6. A cafe makes 20 litres of tea in an urn. How many 250 ml cups can be filled?

C

1. 1·2 litres of water and 400 ml of orange are used to make orange squash. It is poured into eight glasses. How much does each glass hold?
2. Twenty-four 150 ml glasses are filled from four one litre bottles of wine. How much wine is left?
3. A sprinkler uses 60 ml of water every second. How many litres does it use in one minute?
4. A puddle contains 12·4 litres of water. 700 ml evaporates. How much water is left?
5. A bottle of handwash contains 300 ml. How many bottles can be filled from 12 litres?
6. A dripping tap loses 35 ml of water every minute. How many litres does it lose in 10 hours?
7. A chemist makes a medicine by mixing 0·8 litres of one liquid with 675 ml of another liquid. How much medicine is made?

I can find information in a timetable.

Waterloo (London)	07:10	08:35	11:35	13:50
Woking	07:35	–	12:00	14:15
Basingstoke	07:55	09:21	12:21	–
Andover	08:16	–	12:42	–
Salisbury	08:36	09:54	13:17	15:08
Yeovil	09:24	10:42	14:07	15:48
Honiton	10:01	–	14:53	16:34
Exeter	10:27	11:42	15:18	16:59

Examples

How long does it take the 12:42 from Andover to reach Salisbury?

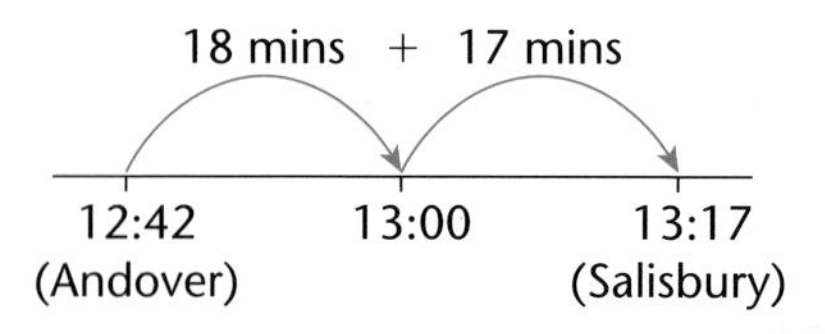

Answer *35 minutes*

A

1. How long does it take the 07:10 from Waterloo to travel to:
   a) Woking
   b) Basingstoke
   c) Andover?
2. At how many stations does the 11:35 from Waterloo stop?
3. At what time does the 08:35 from Waterloo reach Salisbury?
4. If you had to be in Exeter by 15:30 which train would you catch from Waterloo?
5. You arrive at Waterloo at 08:20. How long do you have to wait for the next train to Exeter?
6. The 11:35 from Waterloo runs 10 minutes late. At what time will it reach Andover?

B

1. How long does it take the 11:35 from Waterloo to travel to:
   a) Salisbury
   b) Yeovil
   c) Exeter?
2. At how many stations does the 08:16 from Andover stop before it reaches Honiton?
3. At what time does the 12:21 from Basingstoke reach Yeovil?
4. If you had to be in Exeter by 12:00 which train would you catch from Basingstoke?
5. You arrive at Waterloo at 11:08. How long do you have to wait for the next train to Exeter?
6. The 08:35 from Waterloo runs 19 minutes late. At what time will it reach Exeter?

C

1. How long does it take the 07:55 from Basingstoke to travel to:
   a) Salisbury
   b) Yeovil
   c) Exeter?
2. At how many stations does the 09:21 from Basingstoke stop before it reaches Exeter?
3. At what time does the 14:15 from Woking reach Honiton?
4. If you had to be in Honiton by 16:00 which train would you catch from Salisbury?
5. You arrive at Waterloo at 10:42. How long do you have to wait for the next train to Exeter?
6. The 11:35 from Waterloo runs 38 minutes late. At what time will it reach Honiton?

I can work out angles on a straight line.

Examples

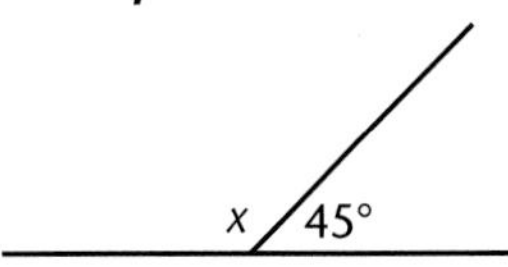

$x° + 45° = 180°$
$x° = 135°$

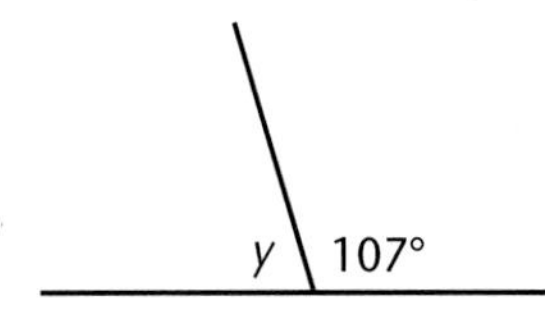

$y° + 107° = 180°$
$y° = 73°$

A

Calculate the missing angles.

1. 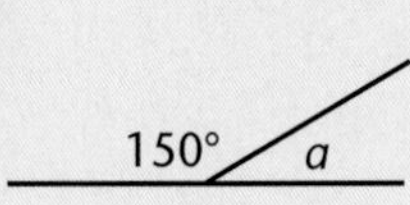

2. 

3. 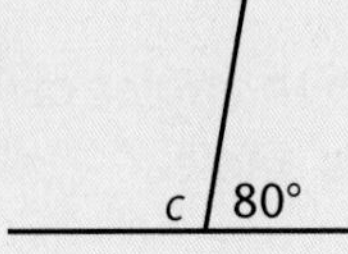

4. 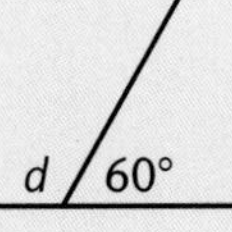

5. 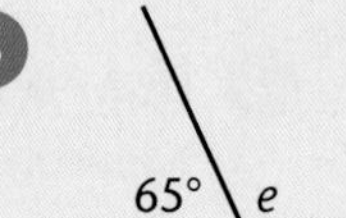

6. 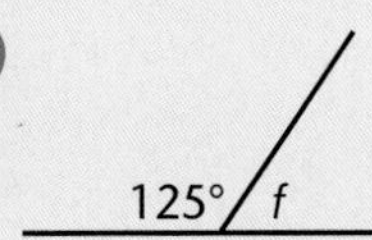

7. 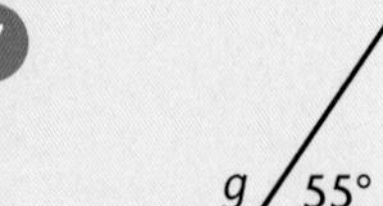

8. 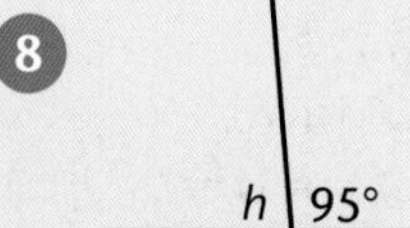

B

Calculate the missing angles.

1. 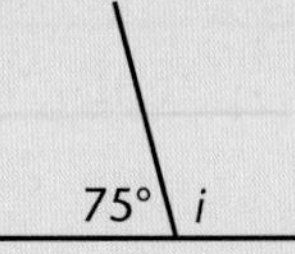

2. 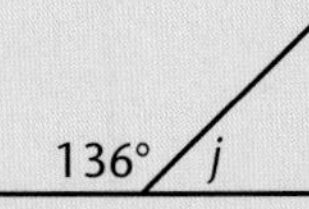

3. 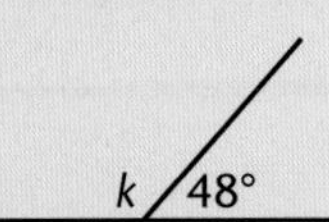

4. 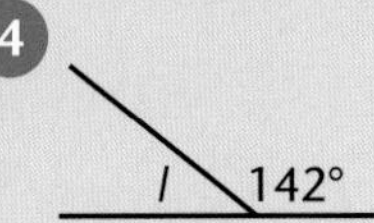

5. 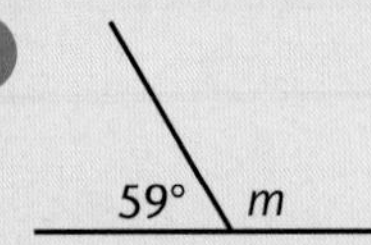

6. 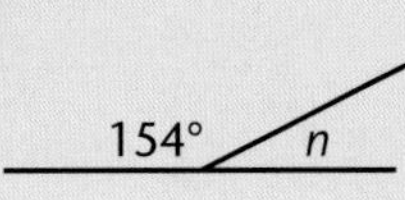

7. 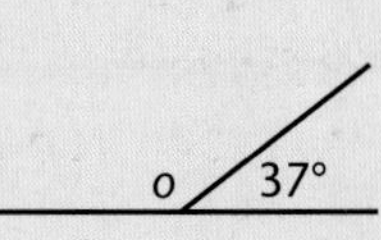

8. 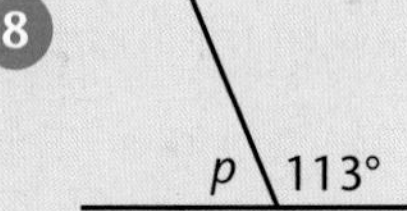

C

Calculate the missing angles.

1. 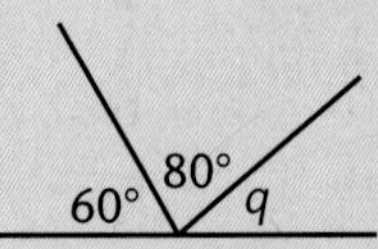

2. 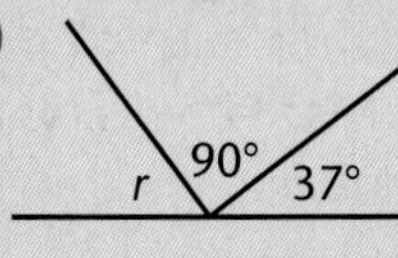

3. 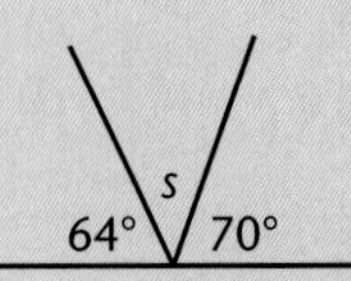

4. 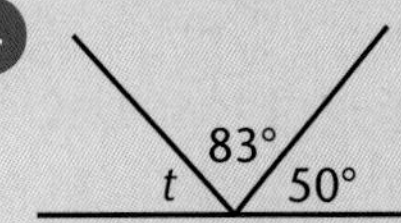

5. 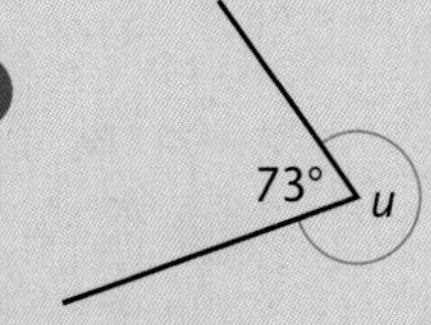

6. 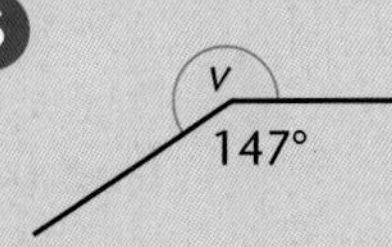

7. 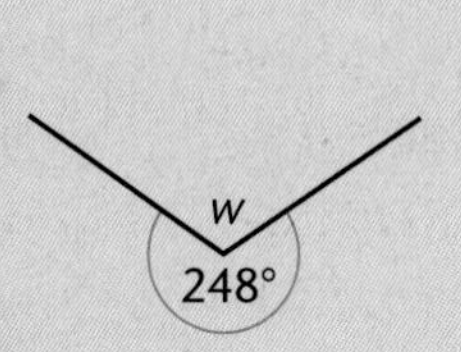

8. 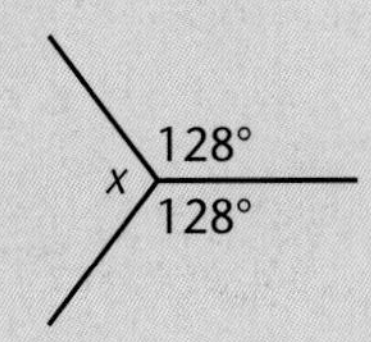

D3 MEASURING ANGLES

I can draw and measure angles using a protractor.

A

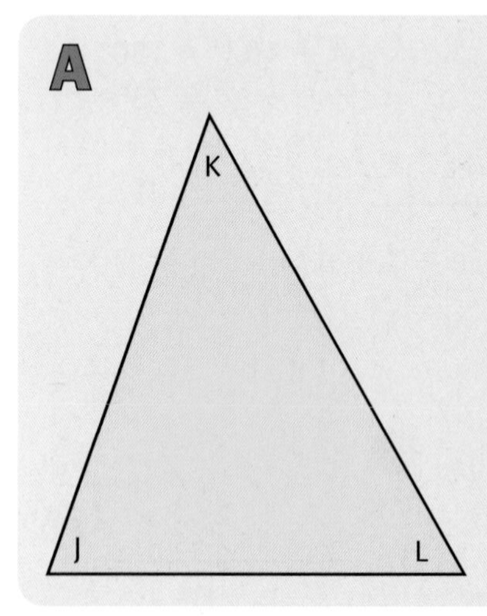

1. Estimate the size of each angle in the triangle to the nearest 10°.
2. Measure the angles.
3. Use a protractor to draw the following angles.
   a) 30° **c)** 10° **e)** 60°
   b) 100° **d)** 150° **f)** 160°
4. Draw a triangle with angles of 110° and 30°.
   Measure the third angle.

B

1. Estimate the size of each angle in the quadrilateral to the nearest 5°.
2. Measure the angles.
3. Use a protractor to draw the following angles.
   Write acute or obtuse by each angle.
   a) 45° **c)** 25° **e)** 75°
   b) 145° **d)** 125° **f)** 155°
4. Draw a quadrilateral with angles of 65°, 115° and 55°.
   Measure the fourth angle.

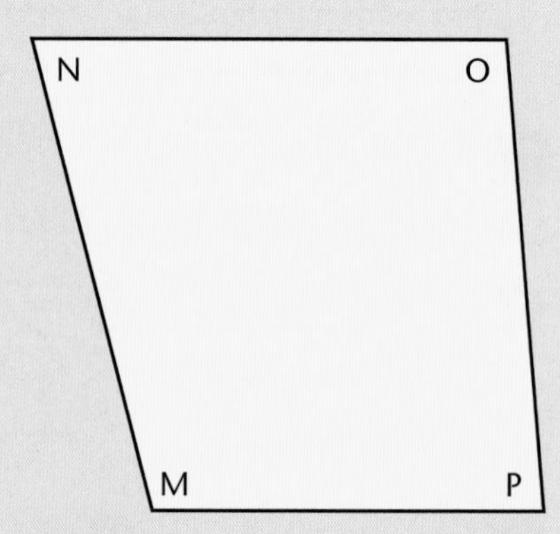

C

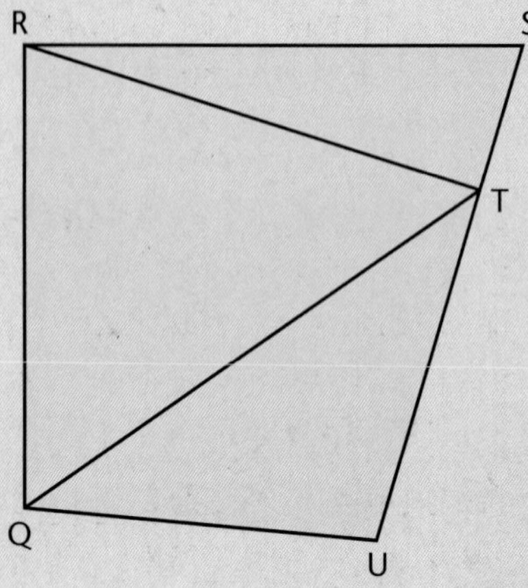

1. Estimate and then measure to the nearest degree the angles of:
   a) triangle SRT **c)** triangle QTU
   b) triangle QTR **d)** quadrilateral RSUQ.
2. Draw the following angles.
   a) 53° **c)** 108° **e)** 79°
   b) 131° **d)** 167° **f)** 124°
3. Draw three different triangles.
   Find the sum of the angles of each shape.
   What do you notice?

I can solve problems involving area and perimeter.

To understand the difference between area and perimeter think of a field. The perimeter is the length of the fence. The area is the field itself.

Example

Perimeter = (6 + 4 + 6 + 4) cm
= 20 cm

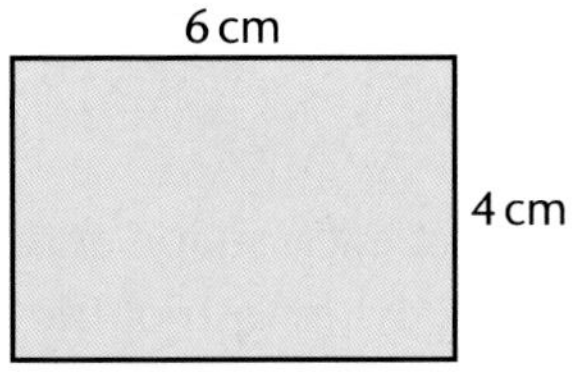

Area = length × width
= (6 × 4) cm^2
= 24 cm^2

A

For each of these shapes work out:

a) the perimeter

b) the area.

1. square
sides 2 cm
2. rectangle
sides 5 cm 4 cm
3. square
sides 6 cm
4. rectangle
sides 8 cm 2 cm

Use 1 cm squared paper.

5. Find as many rectangles as you can with an area of 12 cm^2. Work out the perimeters.
6. Find as many rectangles as you can with a perimeter of 14 cm. Work out the areas.
7. Draw a square with a perimeter of 12 cm. Work out the area?

B

1. Copy and complete the table showing the length, width, perimeter and area of rectangles.

L cm	W cm	P cm	A cm^2
7	2		
10			30
	6		48
	3	24	
15		38	
		18	18

2. Find as many rectangles as you can with an area of 36 cm^2. Work out the perimeters.
3. Find as many rectangles as you can with a perimeter of 22 cm. Work out the areas.

These rectangles are drawn on a 1 cm grid. Find:

a) the missing co-ordinates
b) the perimeter
c) the area.

4. (2, 2) (2, 6) (4, 2) (☐, ☐)
5. (4, 4) (9, 4) (9, 1) (☐, ☐)

C

1. For each shape work out:
a) the perimeter
b) the area.
All lengths are in cm.

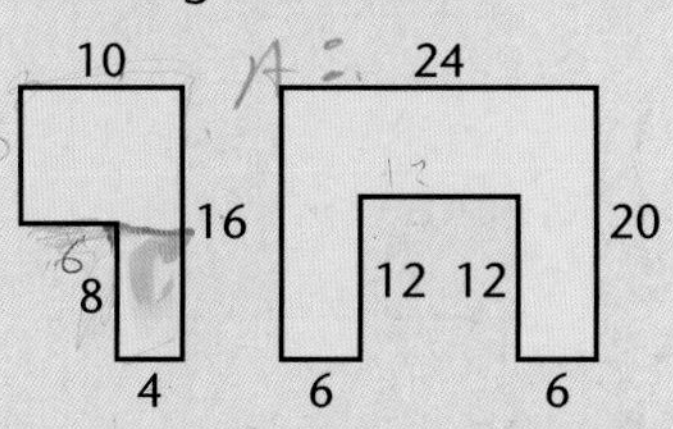

2. Use 1 cm^2 paper. Make different L shapes with an area of 24 cm^2. Work out the perimeters.
3. A square picture frame has an outer perimeter of 76 cm. The frame is 2 cm wide.
a) Find the inner perimeter of the frame.
b) Find the area of the picture.

These rectangles are drawn on a 1 cm grid. Find:

a) the missing co-ordinates
b) the perimeter
c) the area.

4. (4, 3) (1, 6) (3, 8) (☐, ☐)
5. (7, 2) (6, 5) (0, 3) (☐, ☐)

I can construct shapes that have parallel or perpendicular sides.

Use a set square and a ruler to construct each shape.
All lengths shown are in centimetres.
All angles are right angles except where shown with an arc as in this example.

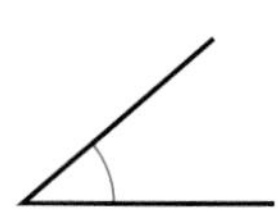

Construct each shape and check that the opposite sides are equal.

1
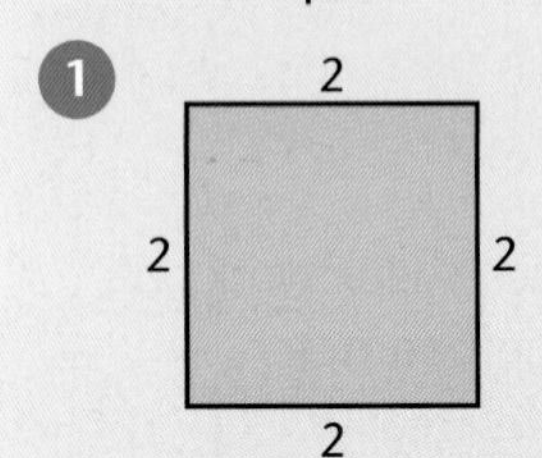

2
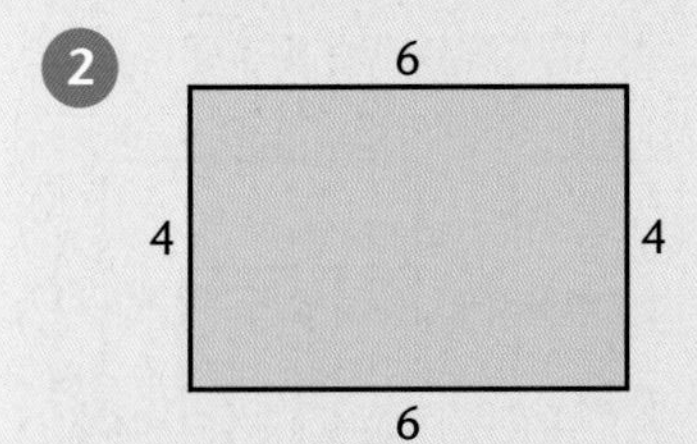

3
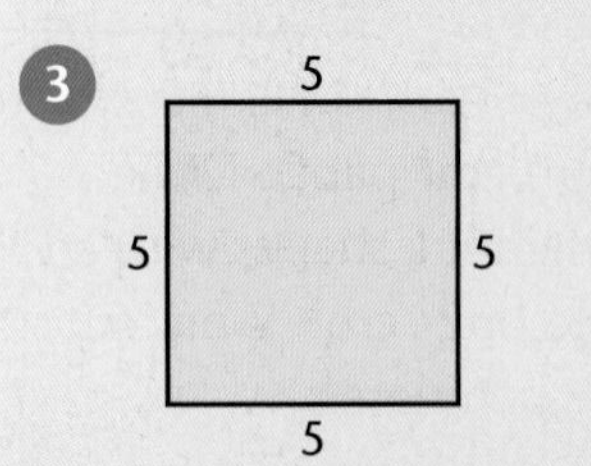

4
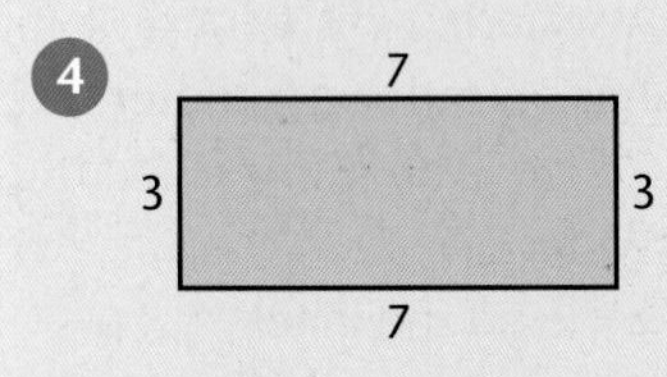

5 Construct a square with a perimeter of 64 cm.

6 Construct a rectangle with a perimeter of 14 cm and a longest side of 5 cm.

7 Construct a rectangle with a perimeter of 24 cm and a shortest side of 4 cm.

B

Construct each shape and measure the length of the diagonal to the nearest mm.

1
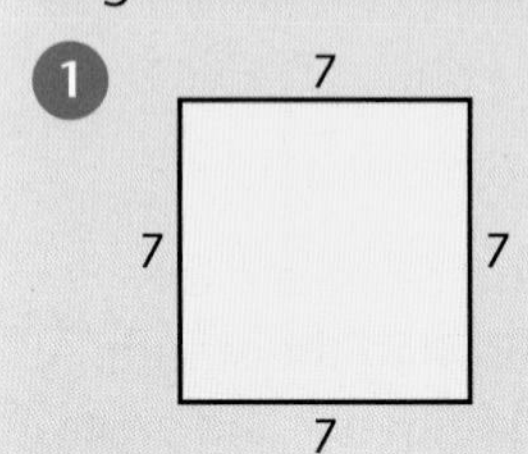

2
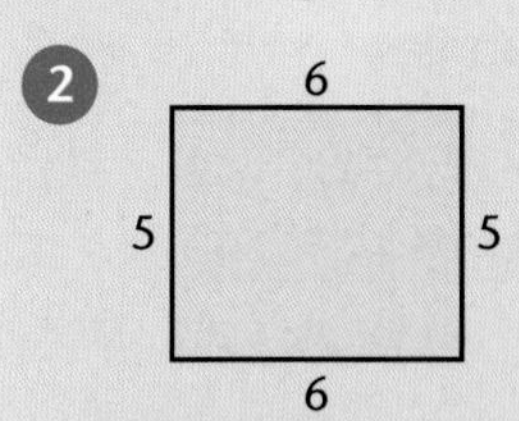

Construct each triangle and measure the length of the longest side to the nearest mm.

3 (3, 4)

4
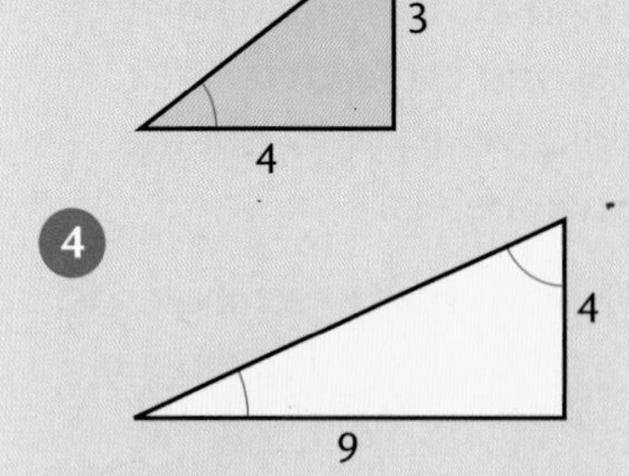

Construct each shape and measure the length of the diagonal to the nearest mm.

5 a square with a perimeter of 18 cm

6 a rectangle with a perimeter of 17 cm and a longest side of 6 cm

C

Construct each shape and measure the length of the diagonal.

1
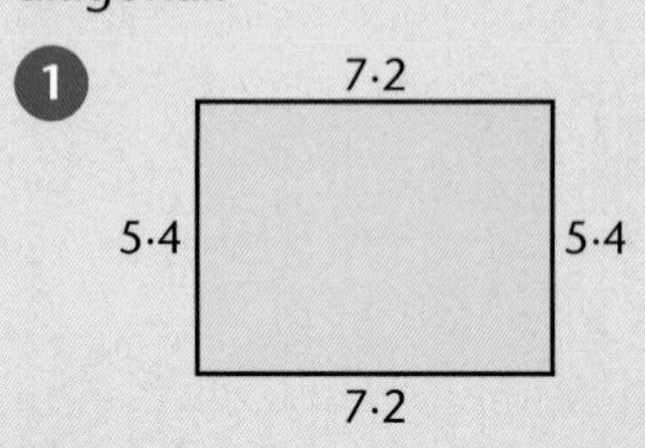

2 a square with a perimeter of 11·2 cm

Construct each triangle and measure the longest side.

3
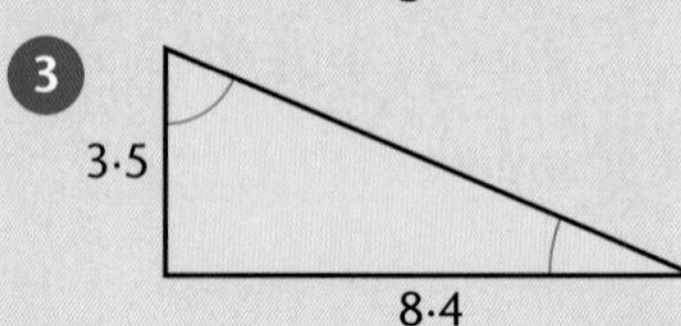

4
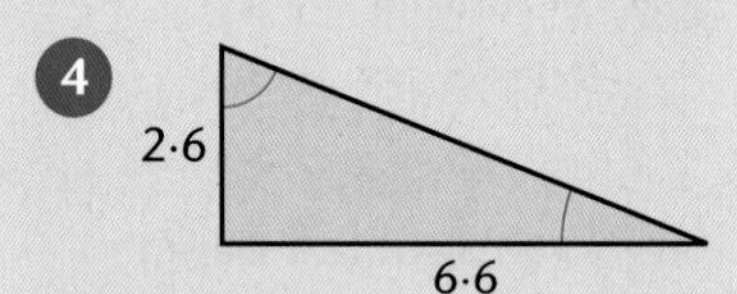

5 Construct the shape.

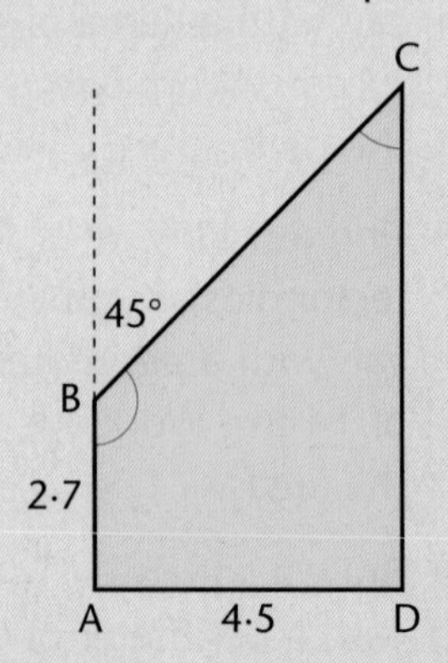

Find the length of:
a) CD **b)** BD.

I can reflect shapes in a mirror line.

Examples

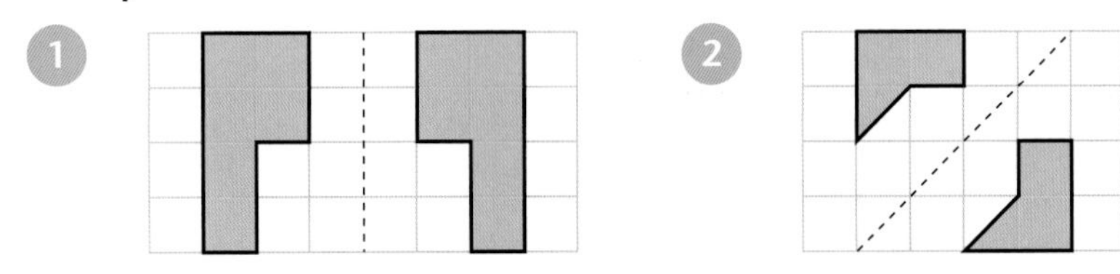

Use squared paper. Copy the shape and the mirror line. Sketch the reflection.

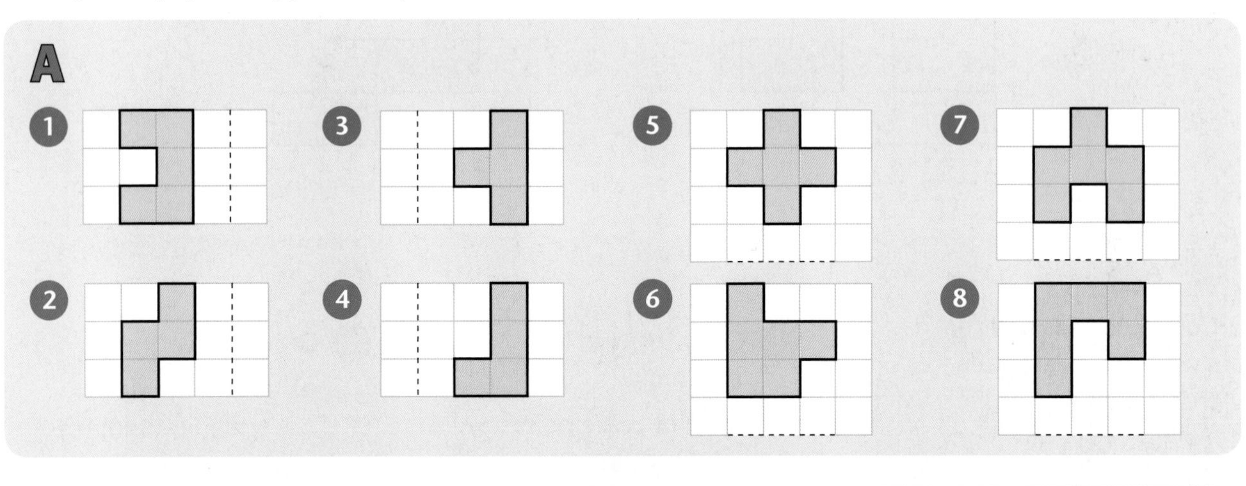

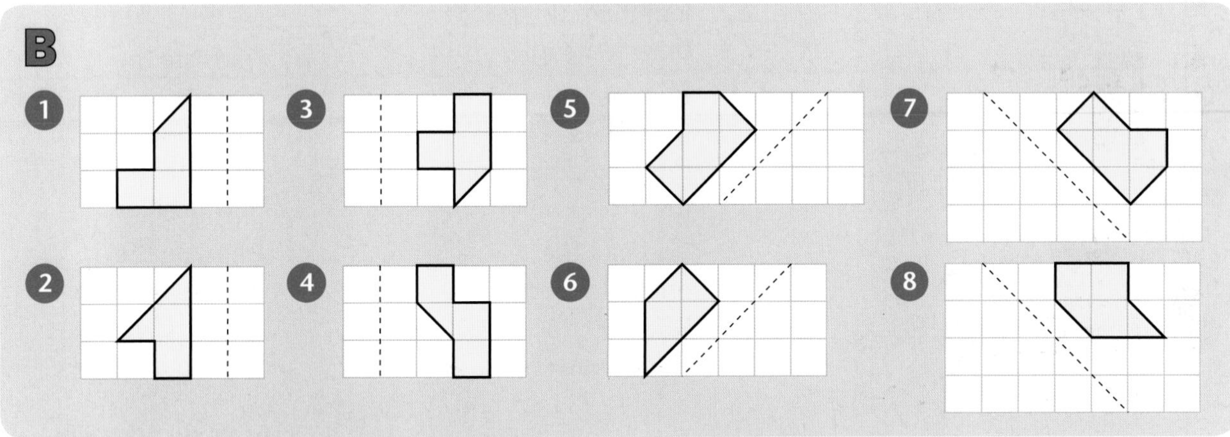

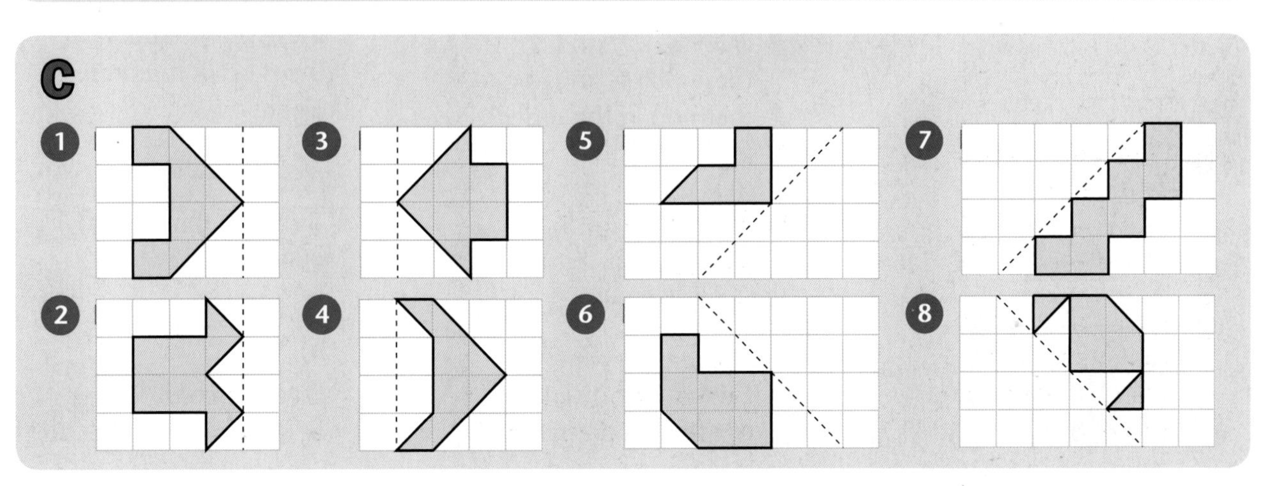

I can translate a shape and give the co-ordinates of the new position.

Examples Translate the shaded shape:

1. left 3 squares (L3)
2. up 2 squares (U2)
3. Right 2 Up 2 (R2 U2)
4. Right 2 Down 1 (R2 D1).

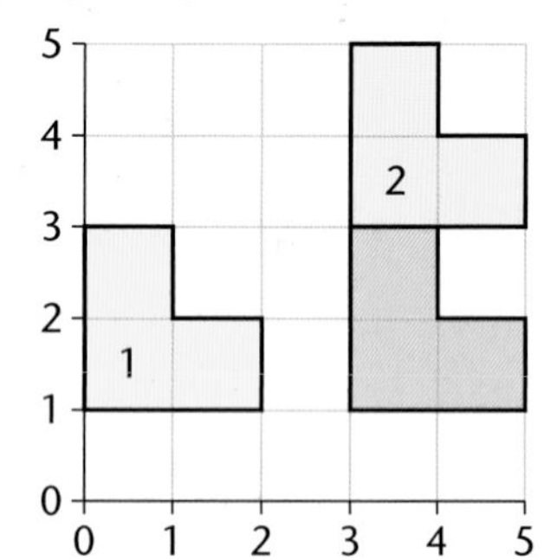

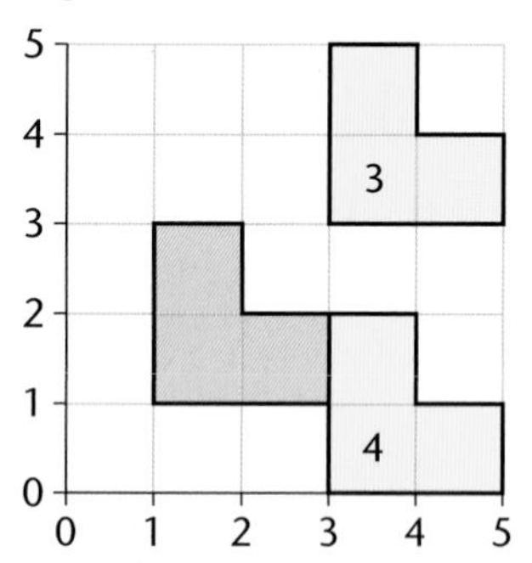

A

Copy the grids and the shapes. Translate each shape 3 times.

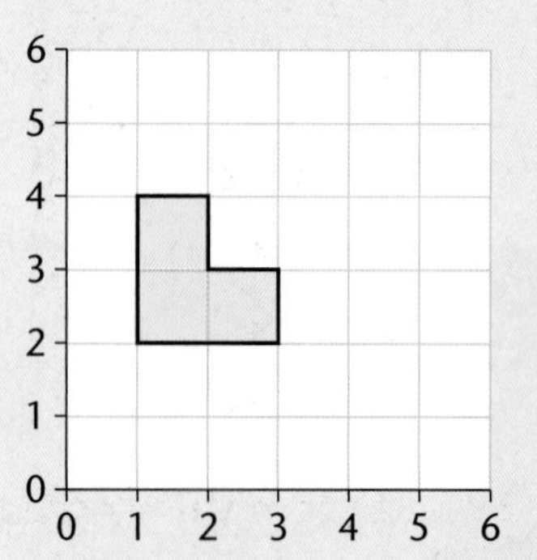

1 U2 2 R3 3 D2

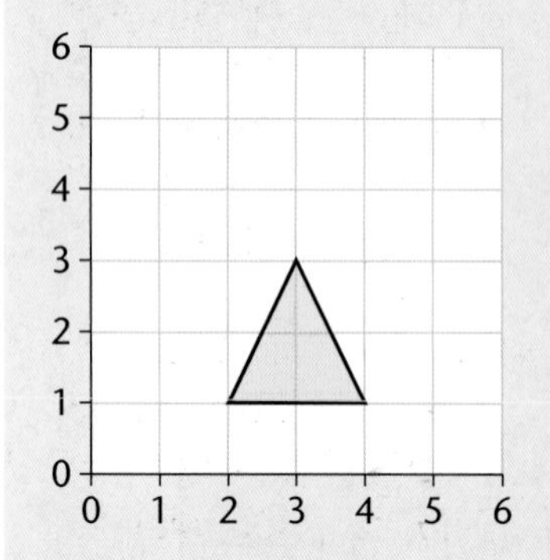

4 L2 5 R2 6 U3

B

1 Copy the grid in Section A.

a) Plot these points. (3, 4) (3, 6) (6, 4) Join them up to draw a triangle.

b) Translate the triangle L3. Give the co-ordinates of the new position.

c) Translate the original triangle D3. Give the new co-ordinates.

2 Draw a new grid. Plot these points and join them up in the order given. (0, 1) (2, 2) (2, 3) (0, 3) (0, 1) Translate the quadrilateral:

a) U2 b) R3.

Give the co-ordinates of the new positions.

C

1 Draw a new grid.

a) Plot these points and join them up to draw a triangle. (2, 4) (3, 6) (4, 5)

b) Translate the triangle L1 D4. Give the co-ordinates of the new position.

c) Translate the original triangle R2 D2. Give the new co-ordinates.

2 Draw a new grid. Plot these points and join them up in the order given. (3, 2) (4, 3) (6, 1) (5, 0) (3, 2) Translate the quadrilateral:

a) L1 U3

b) L3 U1.

Give the co-ordinates of the new positions.

I can solve problems involving ratio and proportion and scale the ingredients in recipes up or down.

Examples

There are 2 adults for every 3 children at a party. There are 18 children.
How many adults are at the party?

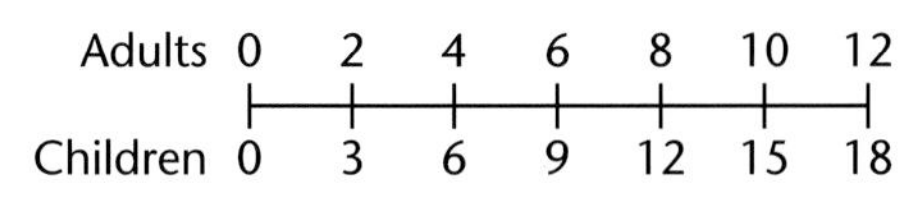

Answer *12 adults*

A recipe uses 500 g of meat for 4 people.
How much meat is needed for:

a) 1 person

b) 8 people?

Answers **a)** $500\text{ g} \div 4 = 125\text{ g}$

b) $500\text{ g} \times 2 = 1\text{ kg}$

1 

A necklace is made using this pattern of beads. Copy and complete the number line.

Red 0 5 10 15 50
Yellow 0 3 6 9 30

Use your number line.

2 Find how many red beads there are if there are:

a) 12 yellow beads

b) 21 yellow beads

c) 64 beads altogether?

3 How many yellow beads are there for every:

a) 25 red beads

b) 45 red beads?

4 How many yellow beads are there in every:

a) 48 beads

b) 80 beads

c) 56 beads?

B

CHEESE BISCUITS
200 g flour
40 g cheese
120 g butter
Makes 6 biscuits

1 Rewrite the above ingredients for:

a) 3 biscuits

b) 12 biscuits.

2 There are 4 adults on a bus for every 3 children. There are 21 children on the bus. How many adults are there?

3 There were 60 questions in a test. Rachel answered 3 in 5 correctly.
How many did she get right?

4 A jeweller mends 7 watches for every 2 he sells. In one month he mends 56 watches. How many does he sell?

C

BANANA SUNDAE
4 bananas
500 ml ice cream
200 ml cream
60 ml honey
Serves 4

1 Rewrite the above ingredients for:

a) 1 person

b) 3 people

c) 10 people.

2 Three in every fifty raffle tickets win a prize. 600 tickets are sold. How many win prizes?

3 Four hundred people attend a concert. There are seven children to every three adults. How many children are there?

4 In an orchard there are 5 times as many apple trees as pear trees. There are 300 trees altogether. How many are pear trees?

E3 PERCENTAGES OF QUANTITIES

I can find a fraction or a percentage of a number or a quantity.

Examples

10% of 40	30% of 40	5% of 40	3% of 400
$\frac{1}{10}$ of 40	(10% of 40) × 3	(10% of 40) ÷ 2	(1% of 400) × 3
40 ÷ 4	4 × 3	4 ÷ 2	($\frac{1}{100}$ of 400) × 3
4	12	2	4 × 3
			12

A

Find

1. $\frac{1}{5}$ of 35
2. $\frac{1}{3}$ of 27
3. $\frac{1}{6}$ of 24
4. $\frac{1}{4}$ of 32
5. 10% of 70p
6. 10% of £14
7. 10% of 1 metre
8. 10% of 250 g
9. There are 40 tins on a shelf. One fifth are sold. How many are left?
10. In June 2500 copies of a magazine are sold. In July sales increase by 10%. How many copies are sold in July?
11. A book cost £4. In a sale the price is cut by 10%. What is the new price?
12. Asif weighs 40 kg. Bruce weighs 10% more. What is Bruce's weight?

B

Find

1. $\frac{2}{3}$ of 21
2. $\frac{3}{4}$ of 80
3. $\frac{5}{8}$ of 48
4. $\frac{2}{7}$ of 56
5. 20% of 90p
6. 5% of £4·80
7. 30% of 2 litres
8. 60% of 30 cm
9. In the summer there was 120 mm of rainfall. In the autumn there was 40% more. How much rain fell in the two seasons altogether?
10. There are 60 people on a coach. Two fifths are men. 30% are women. How many children are on the coach?
11. A taxi driver earns £80 on Friday and sixty percent more on Saturday. How much does he earn in the two days altogether?

C

Find

1. $\frac{7}{9}$ of 54
2. $\frac{2}{15}$ of 300
3. $\frac{4}{7}$ of 91
4. $\frac{13}{20}$ of 800
5. 1% of £75
6. 3% of £180
7. 15% of 2·6 kg
8. 95% of 800 ml
9. There are 120 apples on a tree. Fifteen percent are picked and three eighths are blown off in the wind. How many apples are left on the tree?
10. As a special offer a 750 g packet of cereal has 20% more. How much cereal is in the packet?
11. A school has 200 pupils. On one day 4% were absent and one third of the rest were on a trip. How many children were in school?

I can find other fractions equivalent to a given fraction.

Examples

You can change a fraction into an equivalent fraction by multiplying or dividing (cancelling).

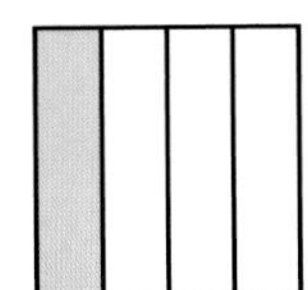

$\frac{1\,(\times 3)}{4\,(\times 3)} = \frac{3}{12}$

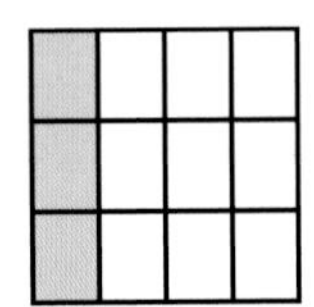

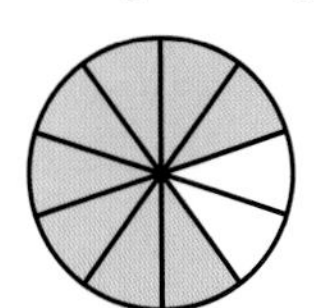

$\frac{4\,(\div 2)}{10\,(\div 2)} = \frac{2}{5}$

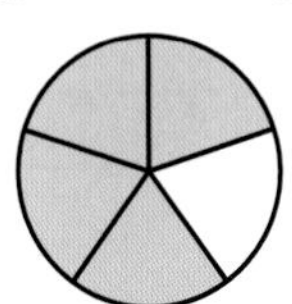

A

Write the equivalent fractions shown in each pair of diagrams.

1  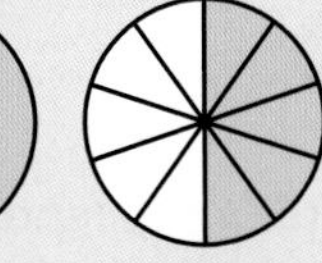

2 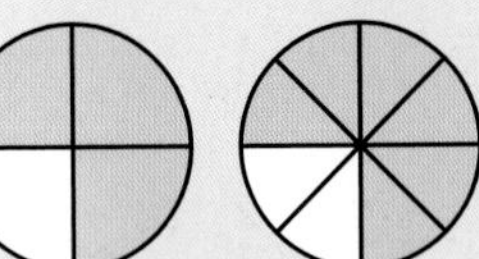

3 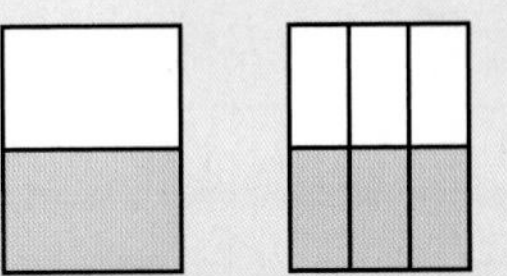

4 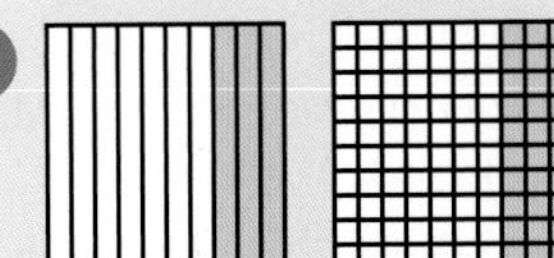

5 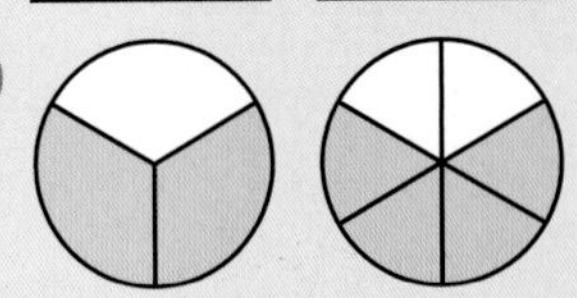

6 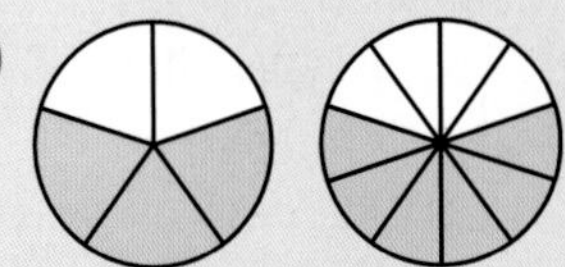

7 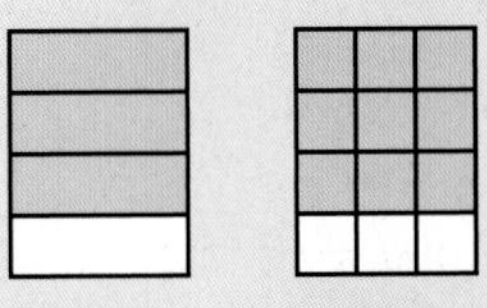

8 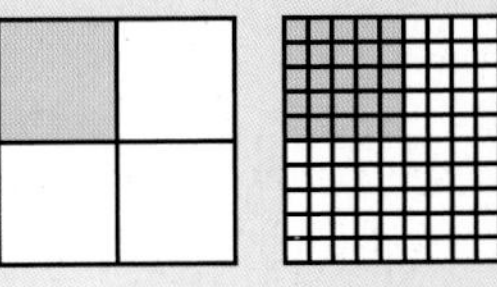

B

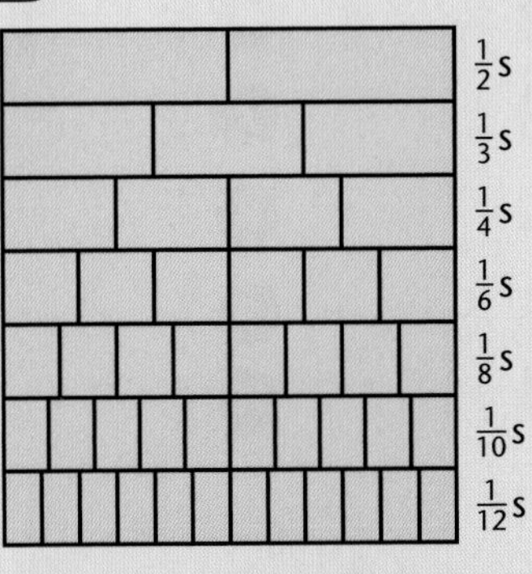

Use the fraction chart. Copy and complete these equivalent fractions.

1. $\frac{1}{2} = \frac{\square}{8}$
2. $\frac{1}{3} = \frac{\square}{6}$
3. $\frac{3}{5} = \frac{\square}{10}$
4. $\frac{5}{6} = \frac{\square}{12}$
5. $\frac{1}{4} = \frac{\square}{8}$
6. $\frac{6}{8} = \frac{\square}{12}$
7. $\frac{8}{12} = \frac{\square}{3}$
8. $\frac{2}{12} = \frac{\square}{6}$
9. $\frac{9}{12} = \frac{\square}{4}$
10. $\frac{5}{10} = \frac{\square}{8}$

Copy and complete these fraction chains.

11. $\frac{3}{4} = \frac{\square}{8} = \frac{\square}{12} = \frac{\square}{\square}$
12. $\frac{1}{6} = \frac{2}{\square} = \frac{3}{\square} = \frac{\square}{\square}$
13. $\frac{2}{5} = \frac{\square}{10} = \frac{\square}{15} = \frac{\square}{\square}$
14. $\frac{1}{8} = \frac{2}{\square} = \frac{3}{\square} = \frac{\square}{\square}$

C

Copy and complete these equivalent fractions.

1. $\frac{2}{3} = \frac{\square}{9}$
2. $\frac{1}{4} = \frac{\square}{20}$
3. $\frac{1}{2} = \frac{\square}{14}$
4. $\frac{1}{3} = \frac{\square}{18}$
5. $\frac{4}{5} = \frac{\square}{25}$
6. $\frac{9}{10} = \frac{\square}{100}$
7. $\frac{1}{5} = \frac{\square}{100}$
8. $\frac{2}{3} = \frac{\square}{15}$
9. $\frac{2}{5} = \frac{\square}{30}$
10. $\frac{1}{4} = \frac{\square}{60}$
11. $\frac{\square}{4} = \frac{9}{12}$
12. $\frac{\square}{5} = \frac{6}{15}$
13. $\frac{\square}{10} = \frac{36}{90}$
14. $\frac{\square}{6} = \frac{15}{18}$
15. $\frac{\square}{5} = \frac{60}{100}$
16. $\frac{\square}{7} = \frac{20}{35}$
17. $\frac{\square}{9} = \frac{8}{18}$
18. $\frac{\square}{3} = \frac{8}{12}$
19. $\frac{\square}{20} = \frac{40}{100}$
20. $\frac{\square}{8} = \frac{25}{40}$

Write three more fractions equivalent to:

21. $\frac{5}{13}$
22. $\frac{8}{36}$
23. $\frac{10}{40}$
24. $\frac{18}{33}$
25. $\frac{9}{16}$
26. $\frac{35}{40}$
27. $\frac{24}{60}$
28. $\frac{48}{150}$

I can use diagrams to compare and order fractions.

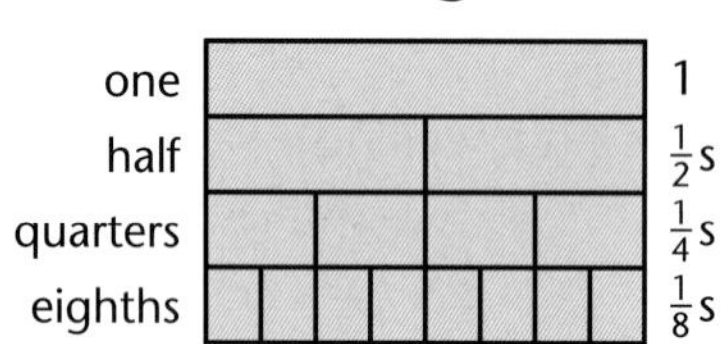

one — 1
half — $\frac{1}{2}$s
thirds — $\frac{1}{3}$s
sixths — $\frac{1}{6}$s

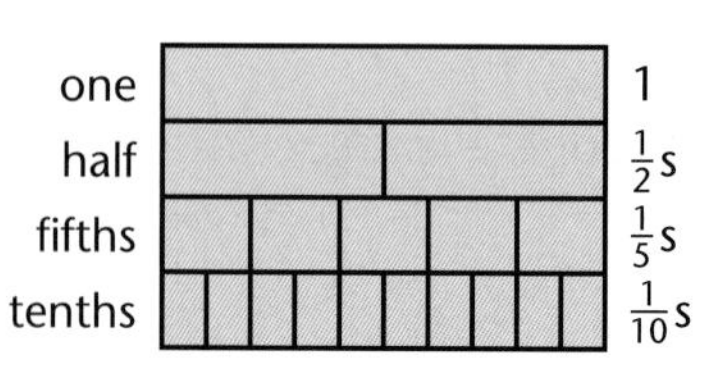

Use the fraction charts to find one half of:

1. $\frac{1}{2}$
2. $\frac{1}{4}$
3. $\frac{1}{3}$
4. $\frac{1}{5}$

Write down the larger fraction.

5. $\frac{1}{3}$ or $\frac{1}{2}$
6. $\frac{1}{6}$ or $\frac{1}{8}$
7. $\frac{2}{7}$ or $\frac{2}{9}$
8. $\frac{3}{5}$ or $\frac{3}{4}$
9. $\frac{1}{2}$ or $\frac{1}{10}$
10. $\frac{5}{100}$ or $\frac{5}{8}$
11. $\frac{1}{3}$ or $\frac{1}{100}$
12. $\frac{9}{12}$ or $\frac{9}{10}$

$\frac{2}{6}$	$\frac{2}{3}$	$\frac{4}{8}$	$\frac{4}{10}$	$\frac{3}{4}$
$\frac{3}{8}$	$\frac{5}{10}$	$\frac{3}{5}$	$\frac{1}{4}$	$\frac{3}{6}$

Which of the fractions in the box are:

13. equal to one half
14. less than one half
15. greater than one half?

B

Use the fraction charts to find one half of:

1. $\frac{2}{5}$
2. $\frac{2}{3}$
3. $\frac{6}{8}$
4. $\frac{8}{10}$
5. $\frac{3}{5}$
6. $\frac{3}{4}$
7. $\frac{2}{6}$
8. $\frac{1}{5}$
9. $\frac{1}{3}$
10. $\frac{4}{5}$

Write these fractions in order, smallest first.

11. $\frac{1}{2}, \frac{1}{4}, \frac{3}{4}, \frac{3}{8}$
12. $\frac{2}{6}, \frac{2}{3}, \frac{1}{2}, \frac{5}{6}$
13. $\frac{3}{5}, \frac{1}{2}, \frac{4}{10}, \frac{1}{5}$
14. $1\frac{1}{4}, \frac{3}{4}, 1\frac{1}{8}, \frac{1}{2}$
15. $1\frac{1}{2}, 1\frac{1}{3}, \frac{5}{6}, \frac{2}{3}$
16. $1\frac{2}{5}, \frac{7}{10}, \frac{1}{2}, 1\frac{3}{10}$

$\frac{50}{100}$	$\frac{5}{12}$	$\frac{10}{20}$	$\frac{4}{7}$	$\frac{12}{25}$
$\frac{6}{11}$	$\frac{45}{100}$	$\frac{4}{9}$	$\frac{25}{50}$	$\frac{9}{16}$

Which of the fractions in the box are:

17. equal to one half
18. less than one half
19. greater than one half?

C

Find one half of:

1. $\frac{3}{8}$
2. $\frac{7}{10}$
3. $\frac{5}{6}$
4. $\frac{1}{12}$
5. $\frac{9}{10}$
6. $\frac{1}{6}$
7. $\frac{7}{8}$
8. $\frac{33}{50}$

Write in ascending order.

9. $\frac{9}{16}, \frac{3}{4}, \frac{1}{2}, \frac{5}{8}$
10. $\frac{7}{12}, \frac{4}{9}, \frac{2}{3}, \frac{5}{6}$
11. $\frac{48}{100}, 1\frac{9}{20}, 1\frac{2}{5}, 1\frac{6}{10}$
12. $\frac{4}{6}, 1\frac{1}{2}, \frac{3}{4}, 1\frac{5}{12}$

Find the fraction which is halfway between each pair of numbers.

13. $\frac{1}{2}$ and 1
14. $\frac{1}{3}$ and $\frac{2}{3}$
15. $\frac{3}{5}$ and $\frac{4}{5}$
16. $\frac{1}{4}$ and $\frac{1}{2}$
17. $\frac{1}{3}$ and $\frac{1}{6}$
18. $\frac{3}{5}$ and $\frac{7}{10}$
19. $\frac{1}{2}$ and $\frac{3}{8}$
20. $\frac{2}{3}$ and $\frac{9}{12}$
21. $\frac{2}{5}$ and $\frac{9}{20}$
22. $\frac{1}{4}$ and $\frac{1}{3}$

I can express one amount as a fraction of another.

Examples

What fraction of 8 is 2?

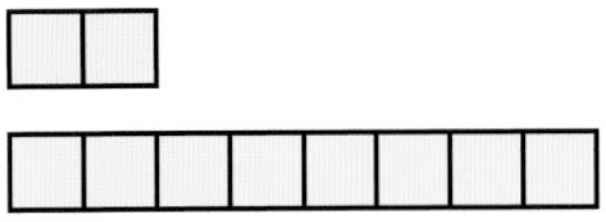

$8 = 4 \times 2$

2 is $\frac{1}{4}$ of 8

There are 40 beads in a necklace.
Eight beads are red. What fraction of the beads are red?

$40 \div 8 = 5$

Answer $\frac{1}{5}$ *of the beads are red.*

A

For each diagram copy and complete each number sentence.

1. $12 = \square \times 4$
2. 4 is $\square$ of 12

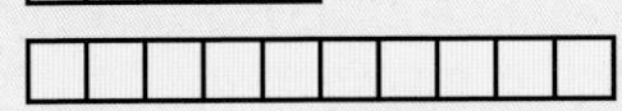

3. $10 = \square \times 5$
4. 5 is $\square$ of 10

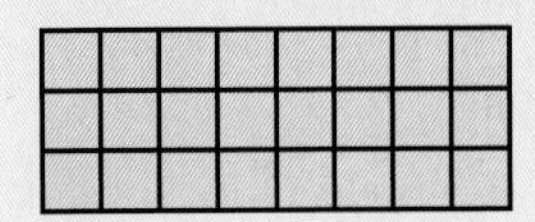

5. $24 = \square \times 8$
6. 8 is $\square$ of 24
7. 16 is $\square$ of 24

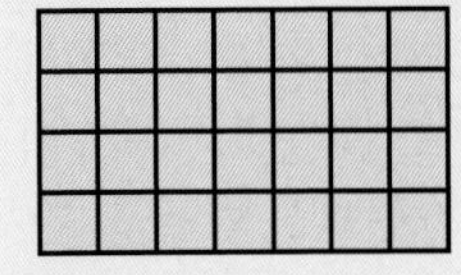

8. $28 = \square \times 4$
9. 4 is $\square$ of 28
10. 8 is $\square$ of 28

B

1. What fraction of 16 is:
   a) 2 c) 8
   b) 4 d) 1?
2. What fraction of 36 is:
   a) 3 c) 6
   b) 9 d) 18?
3. What fraction of £1 is:
   a) 50p c) 1p
   b) 30p d) 25p?
4. What fraction of 1 kg is:
   a) 600 g c) 50 g
   b) 750 g d) 10 g?
5. A bottle of lemonade holds 1 litre. 200 ml is poured out. What fraction is left?
6. Colin's book has 120 pages. He has read 40. What fraction has he read?
7. A baker makes 100 loaves. Seventy-five are sold. What fraction is left?

C

1. What fraction of 24 is:
   a) 6 c) 3
   b) 18 d) 9?
2. What fraction of 40 is:
   a) 10 c) 5
   b) 30 d) 25?
3. What fraction of £5 is:
   a) 1p c) £2
   b) £4·50 d) 5p?
4. What fraction of 2 m is:
   a) 10 cm c) 125 cm
   b) 50 cm d) 1 mm?
5. A netball team scored 36 goals. Shana scored 15 of them. What fraction of the team's goals did Shana score?
6. Jamil weighs 32 kg. His dad weighs 80 kg. What fraction of his dad's weight is Jamil's weight?
7. A running track is 400 m long. What fraction of a 10 km race is one lap of the track?

I can give equivalent fractions, decimals and percentages.

Examples

$\frac{1}{10} = 0{\cdot}1 = 10\%$
$\frac{2}{10} = 0{\cdot}2 = 20\%$
$\frac{3}{10} = 0{\cdot}3 = 30\%$
and so on

$\frac{1}{100} = 0{\cdot}01 = 1\%$
$\frac{2}{100} = 0{\cdot}02 = 2\%$
$\frac{3}{100} = 0{\cdot}03 = 3\%$
and so on

$\frac{1}{4} = 0{\cdot}25 = 25\%$
$\frac{1}{2} = 0{\cdot}5 = 50\%$
$\frac{3}{4} = 0{\cdot}75 = 75\%$

A

Write True or False.

1. $\frac{9}{10} = 0{\cdot}9$
2. $\frac{3}{4} = 0{\cdot}34$
3. $\frac{1}{10} = 1\%$
4. $\frac{1}{2} = 50\%$
5. $0{\cdot}3 = \frac{1}{3}$
6. $0{\cdot}25 = \frac{2}{5}$
7. $0{\cdot}7 = 70\%$
8. $0{\cdot}2 = 2\%$
9. $25\% = \frac{1}{4}$
10. $8\% = \frac{8}{100}$
11. $75\% = 0{\cdot}75$
12. $16\% = 1{\cdot}6$
13. Match each fraction with either a decimal or a percentage.

$\frac{1}{2}$	0·14
$\frac{4}{10}$	20%
$\frac{5}{100}$	0·25
$\frac{2}{10}$	50%
$\frac{14}{100}$	0·4
$\frac{1}{4}$	5%

B

Write as fractions.

1. 0·68
2. 0·5
3. 0·17
4. 0·3
5. 75%
6. 59%
7. 9%
8. 90%

Write as decimals.

9. $\frac{46}{100}$
10. $\frac{1}{4}$
11. $\frac{4}{100}$
12. $\frac{4}{10}$
13. 18%
14. 8%
15. 1%
16. 80%

Write as percentages.

17. $\frac{2}{10}$
18. $\frac{1}{4}$
19. $\frac{2}{100}$
20. $\frac{24}{100}$
21. 0·3
22. 0·03
23. 0·5
24. 0·35

Give the answer as a decimal.

25. $0{\cdot}5 + \frac{4}{10}$
26. $\frac{31}{100} - 0{\cdot}28$
27. $0{\cdot}8 - \frac{1}{2}$
28. $\frac{3}{4} - 0{\cdot}12$

Give the answer as a percentage.

29. $20\% + \frac{1}{2}$
30. $\frac{1}{4} + 53\%$
31. $94\% - 0{\cdot}3$
32. $\frac{7}{10} - 27\%$

C

Write in ascending order.

1. $\frac{3}{4}$ 43% 0·344
2. 0·91 19% $\frac{9}{10}$
3. $\frac{3}{5}$ 0·5 35%
4. 8% $\frac{81}{100}$ 0·188
5. $\frac{2}{7}$ 0·2 27%
6. 56% $\frac{5}{6}$ 0·556
7. 0·311 30% $\frac{1}{3}$
8. 11% 0·1 $\frac{101}{1000}$

Give the answer as a percentage.

9. $\frac{1}{2} + 0{\cdot}3$
10. $\frac{99}{100} - 0{\cdot}7$
11. $0{\cdot}61 + \frac{2}{10}$
12. $0{\cdot}22 - \frac{3}{100}$

Give the answer as a decimal.

13. $\frac{1}{10} + 32\%$
14. $38\% - \frac{1}{4}$
15. $5\% + \frac{1}{5}$
16. $\frac{3}{4} - 60\%$
17. A cake weighs 0·5 kg. One tenth is eaten on Monday. Twenty percent is eaten on Tuesday. How much is left in kilograms?

I can divide a three-digit number by a one-digit number.

Examples

$231 \div 6$

Estimate

$6 \times 30 = 180$

$6 \times 40 = 240$

$180 < 231 < 240$

$30 < \text{Answer} < 40$

$$\begin{array}{rl} 231 & \\ -\ \underline{60} & (6 \times 10) \\ 171 & \\ -\ \underline{60} & (6 \times 10) \\ 111 & \\ -\ \underline{60} & (6 \times 10) \\ 51 & \\ -\ \underline{48} & (6 \times 8) \\ 3 & \end{array}$$

Answer 38 r3

For a more efficient method of chunking start by subtracting this figure.

↓

$180 < 231 \div 6 < 240$

$$\begin{array}{rl} 231 & \\ -\underline{180} & (6 \times 30) \\ 51 & \\ -\ \underline{48} & (6 \times 8) \\ 3 & \end{array}$$

Answer 38 r3

A

Work out

1. $48 \div 2$
2. $112 \div 7$
3. $85 \div 5$
4. $102 \div 6$
5. $38 \div 3$
6. $152 \div 8$
7. $70 \div 4$
8. $126 \div 9$
9. $72 \div 5$
10. $84 \div 6$
11. $47 \div 3$
12. $112 \div 8$
13. $66 \div 4$
14. $118 \div 9$
15. $133 \div 7$
16. $136 \div 8$
17. There are eight cakes in each box. How many boxes can be filled from 104 cakes?
18. Six train tickets cost £96. How much does one ticket cost?
19. Kym has read one third of her book. The book has 57 pages. How many pages has she read?
20. Four friends share a prize of £58. How much should each person receive?

B

Work out

1. $138 \div 6$
2. $314 \div 7$
3. $250 \div 8$
4. $423 \div 9$
5. $347 \div 6$
6. $183 \div 7$
7. $224 \div 8$
8. $287 \div 9$
9. $201 \div 8$
10. $269 \div 7$
11. $377 \div 8$
12. $348 \div 9$
13. $290 \div 6$
14. $272 \div 7$
15. $310 \div 8$
16. $420 \div 9$
17. There were 245 passengers on a plane. One seventh of the passengers got off at Paris. How many flew on to Rome?

18. Eight magazines weigh 536 grams. How much does one weigh?

C

Work out

1. $292 \div 4$
2. $407 \div 9$
3. $346 \div 6$
4. $434 \div 7$
5. $455 \div 8$
6. $393 \div 5$
7. $572 \div 9$
8. $401 \div 7$
9. $168 \div 14$
10. $294 \div 21$
11. $342 \div 16$
12. $526 \div 23$
13. $610 \div 19$
14. $550 \div 26$
15. $760 \div 22$
16. $800 \div 35$
17. A school needs 450 exercise books. How many packs of 24 will the school need to order? How many books will be left over?
18. The 728 children in a school are divided equally into 28 classes. How many children are there in each class?
19. A pack of 18 bags of crisps weighs 630 g. How much does one bag weigh?

E3 ROUNDING UP OR DOWN

I can make sensible decisions about rounding up or down after division.

Examples

How many £6 tickets can I buy with £87?
$87 \div 6 = 14$ remainder 3
Answer *14 tickets can be bought.*

An egg box holds 6 eggs.
How many boxes do I need to hold 87 eggs?
$87 \div 6 = 14$ remainder 3
Answer *15 boxes are needed.*

1. Yoghurts are sold in packs of 4. How many packs can be made from 70 yoghurts?
2. One lorry can carry 8 containers. How many lorries are needed to carry 100 containers?

3. There are 40 straws in each packet. How many packets can be made up from 300 straws?
4. A car can carry 3 children as passengers. How many cars are needed to carry 50 children?
5. Ten CDs can be stored in a rack. How many racks are needed to store 213 CDs?
6. How many complete hours are there in 200 minutes?

B

1. Nine children can sleep in a large tent. How many tents are needed for 150 children?
2. Video tapes are sold in packs of 8. How many packs can be made from 300 tapes?
3. The tables at a wedding reception seat 6 people. How many tables are needed if there are 200 guests?
4. How many complete weeks are there in 150 days?
5. Hayley saved £30 each week towards her holiday. How many weeks did it take her to save £500 she needed?

6. There are 150 footballers at a tournament. How many 11-a-side teams can be made?

C

1. A garden centre can fit 8 plants on each tray. How many trays are needed to display 500 plants?
2. One lorry can carry seven containers. How many trips are necessary to transport 400 containers?
3. Cough sweets are sold in packets of 12. How many packets can be made up from 200 sweets?
4. There are beds for 24 patients in each ward of a hospital. How many wards are needed for 350 patients?
5. A loaf of bread has 22 slices. A cafe needs 300 slices of bread for sandwiches. How many loaves does the cafe owner need to buy?
6. Cakes cost 45p. How many can be bought for £12?
7. Pencils are packed into boxes of 15. How many boxes can be filled from 365 pencils?

I can write a remainder as a fraction and as a decimal.

Examples

REMAINDERS AS FRACTIONS

$77 \div 4 = 19\frac{1}{4}$ $(1 \div 4 = \frac{1}{4})$

$53 \div 10 = 5\frac{3}{10}$ $(3 \div 10 = \frac{3}{10})$

REMAINDERS AS DECIMALS

$77 \div 4 = 19{\cdot}25$ $(1 \div 4 = 0{\cdot}25)$

$53 \div 10 = 5{\cdot}3$ $(3 \div 10 = 0{\cdot}3)$

MONEY

£77 ÷ 4 = £19·25

£53 ÷ 10 = £5·30

A

Give the remainder as a fraction

1. 33 ÷ 2
2. 73 ÷ 5
3. 19 ÷ 3
4. 137 ÷ 10
5. 27 ÷ 4
6. 21 ÷ 2
7. 33 ÷ 5
8. 37 ÷ 4
9. 23 ÷ 3
10. 62 ÷ 5

Give the remainder as a decimal.

11. £17 ÷ 2
12. £77 ÷ 10
13. £29 ÷ 4
14. £28 ÷ 5
15. £23 ÷ 4
16. £27 ÷ 2
17. £19 ÷ 4
18. £57 ÷ 5
19. £12 ÷ 10
20. £39 ÷ 5
21. A rope is 31 metres long. It is cut in half. How long is each length in metres?
22. Five people share a prize of £17. How much should each person receive?
23. Two friends share the cost of a meal. The bill is £23. How much should each person pay?

B

Give the remainder as a fraction.

1. 83 ÷ 4
2. 39 ÷ 7
3. 73 ÷ 9
4. 38 ÷ 6
5. 136 ÷ 25
6. 109 ÷ 5
7. 43 ÷ 8
8. 173 ÷ 10
9. 641 ÷ 100
10. 26 ÷ 7

Give the remainder as a decimal.

11. 47 ÷ 2
12. 127 ÷ 4
13. 131 ÷ 5
14. 427 ÷ 10
15. 93 ÷ 4
16. £4·80 ÷ 3
17. £9·20 ÷ 4
18. £12·00 ÷ 5
19. £9·10 ÷ 2
20. £8·10 ÷ 6
21. A CD player costs £76. The price is reduced by one tenth. What is the new price?
22. It takes 115 litres of water to fill four identical fish tanks. How much water does each tank hold?

C

Copy and complete.

1. $\square \div 7 = 12\frac{2}{7}$
2. $\square \div 8 = 4\frac{7}{8}$
3. $\square \div 9 = 8\frac{1}{9}$
4. $\square \div 6 = 15\frac{5}{6}$
5. $\square \div 100 = 14\frac{91}{100}$
6. $\square \div 6 = 26\frac{1}{6}$
7. $\square \div 10 = 16\frac{7}{10}$
8. $\square \div 9 = 19\frac{1}{9}$

Give the answer as a decimal. Round to one decimal place where necessary.

9. 94 ÷ 4
10. 137 ÷ 10
11. 94 ÷ 5
12. 90 ÷ 7
13. 52 ÷ 3
14. 111 ÷ 9
15. 79 ÷ 5
16. 87 ÷ 6
17. Toni cycles 25 km in one hour. How far does she cycle in 1 hour 15 minutes?
18. Eight tins of sardines weigh 1 kg. What is the weight of 5 tins in kilograms?

Write in words.

1. 75 240
2. 320 108
3. 1 407 850
4. 2 090 016

Give the value of the underlined digit.

5. $12\underline{9}\,417$
6. $1\,\underline{5}83\,000$
7. $\underline{4}5\,936$
8. $\underline{3}\,506\,200$

Work out

9. 249 × 10
10. 3000 × 10
11. 4180 × 10
12. 37 × 100
13. 1500 × 100
14. 461 × 100
15. 42 000 ÷ 10
16. 300 000 ÷ 10
17. 6020 ÷ 10
18. 23 000 ÷ 100
19. 58 600 ÷ 100
20. 200 000 ÷ 100

Use these digits.

6 9 2 5

21. Make the largest possible number.
22. Make the smallest possible number.

Round to the nearest 100.

23. 863
24. 1247
25. 2970
26. 4652

Round to the nearest 1000.

27. 7394
28. 14 516
29. 26 298
30. 19 730

Approximate by rounding to the nearest 10.

31. 462 + 87
32. 536 + 243
33. 86 − 38
34. 162 − 93
35. 39 × 5
36. 48 × 7

37. What number is shown by each arrow?

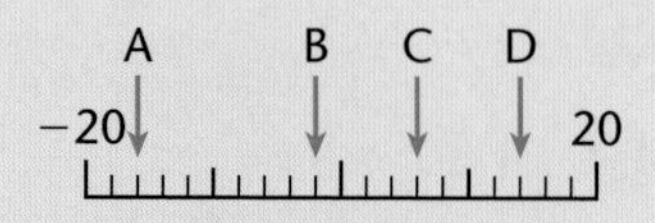

Look at the number line above. What is the difference between:

38. A and B
39. B and C
40. C and A
41. D and B?

42. Write in order, smallest first.

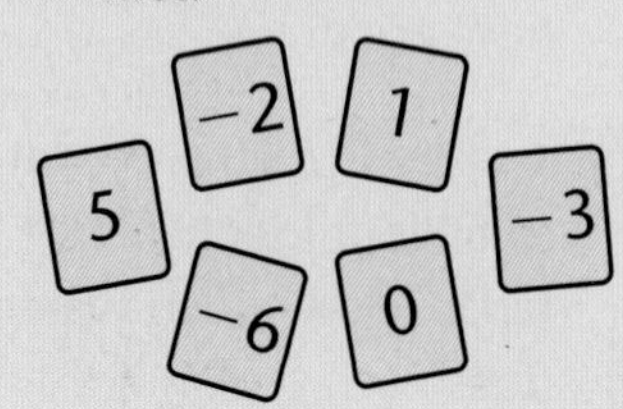

21 28 36 45 56 60

Which of the above numbers are multiples of:

43. 3
44. 4
45. 7
46. 15?

Find two numbers that are multiples of both:

47. 2 and 9
48. 3 and 8
49. 4 and 7
50. 5 and 6.

Find all the factors of the following numbers.

51. 22
52. 28
53. 30
54. 36
55. 27
56. 42
57. 40
58. 105

Work out

59. 4^2
60. 7^2
61. 10^2
62. 8^2

Copy the sequence. Write the next four terms.

63. 33 40 47 54
64. 0·1 0·3 0·5 0·7
65. −2 −5 −8 −11
66. 99 90 81 72
67. 15 30 45 60
68. −10 −8 −6 −4
69. 80 72 64 56
70. 250 300 350 400

Copy and complete these equivalent fractions.

1 $\frac{1}{2} = \frac{\square}{4}$

2 $\frac{1}{4} = \frac{\square}{8}$

3 $\frac{1}{2} = \frac{\square}{6}$

4 $\frac{1}{2} = \frac{\square}{10}$

5 $\frac{2}{5} = \frac{\square}{10}$

6 $\frac{2}{3} = \frac{\square}{6}$

7 $\frac{3}{4} = \frac{\square}{8}$

8 $\frac{4}{5} = \frac{\square}{10}$

Place in order, smallest first.

9 $\frac{3}{4}$, $\frac{1}{2}$, $\frac{5}{8}$

10 $\frac{2}{5}$, $\frac{1}{2}$, $\frac{3}{10}$

Change to mixed numbers.

11 $\frac{7}{2}$

12 $\frac{9}{4}$

13 $\frac{11}{3}$

14 $\frac{8}{5}$

15 $\frac{19}{8}$

16 $\frac{25}{6}$

17 $\frac{37}{10}$

18 $\frac{249}{100}$

Change to improper fractions.

19 $2\frac{2}{3}$

20 $4\frac{3}{4}$

21 $7\frac{1}{10}$

22 $3\frac{5}{6}$

23 $5\frac{3}{8}$

24 $1\frac{37}{100}$

25 $6\frac{2}{5}$

26 $4\frac{7}{9}$

Give the value of the underlined figure.

27 $1{\cdot}\underline{9}2$

28 $1\underline{6}{\cdot}38$

29 $39{\cdot}2\underline{7}$

30 $42{\cdot}\underline{5}$

31 $2\underline{5}{\cdot}43$

32 $7{\cdot}\underline{1}9$

33 $53{\cdot}0\underline{6}$

34 $18{\cdot}\underline{7}$

35 Write the numbers shown by the arrows as decimal fractions.

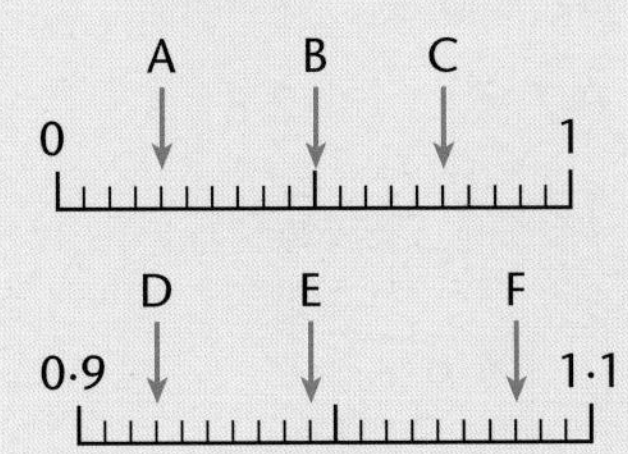

Arrange in order, smallest first.

36 4·72 2·7 4·27 2·47

37 5·91 1·9 1·59 5·19

38 6·8 3·8 3·68 6·38

39 5·7 5·37 5·73 5·3

Round to the nearest:

metre

40 3·1 m

41 2·8 m

42 7·3 m

43 4·5 m

44 9·6 m

pound

45 £11·90

46 £6·20

47 £29·74

48 £87·48

49 £4·50

Write each shaded area as:

a) a fraction

b) a decimal

c) a percentage.

50 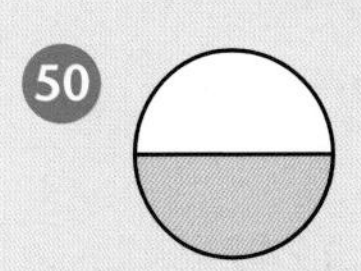

51 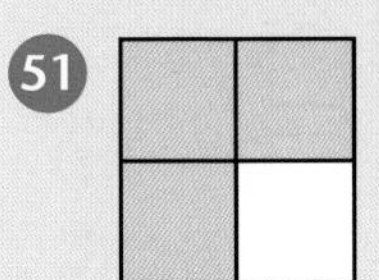

52 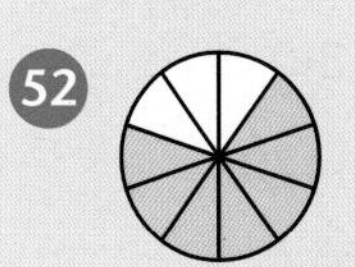

53 

54 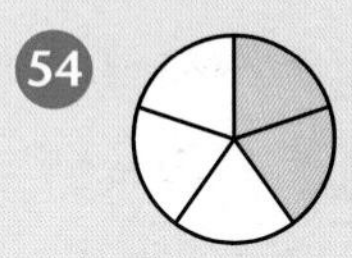

55 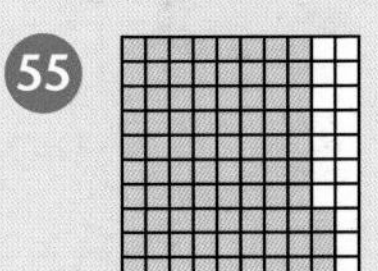

Find

56 $\frac{1}{4}$ of 200

57 $\frac{3}{4}$ of 200

58 $\frac{1}{10}$ of 240

59 $\frac{2}{3}$ of 18

60 $\frac{1}{6}$ of 30 cm

61 $\frac{9}{10}$ of 1 m

62 $\frac{21}{100}$ of £1

63 $\frac{4}{5}$ of 60p

Find

64 10% of 70

65 25% of 36

66 20% of 80

67 30% of £5·00

68 75% of 60p

69 60% of £2·00

70 50% of £5·50

CALCULATIONS REVIEW

Copy and complete.

1. 460 + 270 = □
2. 55 + 38 = □
3. 6·3 + □ = 7·0
4. 38 + □ = 100

5. □ + 500 = 1247
6. □ + 49 = 126
7. 7·9 − 0·6 = □
8. 117 − 61 = □

9. 600 − □ = 514
10. 8·4 − □ = 8·0
11. □ − 340 = 470
12. □ − 57 = 215

Work out

13. $\begin{array}{r}438\\+275\\\hline\end{array}$
14. $\begin{array}{r}564\\+327\\\hline\end{array}$
15. $\begin{array}{r}849\\+286\\\hline\end{array}$
16. $\begin{array}{r}774\\+598\\\hline\end{array}$
17. $\begin{array}{r}783\\-139\\\hline\end{array}$
18. $\begin{array}{r}548\\-375\\\hline\end{array}$
19. $\begin{array}{r}892\\-436\\\hline\end{array}$
20. $\begin{array}{r}961\\-728\\\hline\end{array}$

Use a written method to find the totals.

21. 356 + 9 + 1408 + 27
22. 48 + 3271 + 7 + 685
23. £2·61 + 92p + £1·35
24. 73p + £5·84 + 29p

Use a written method to find the differences between each pair of numbers.

25. 1957 and 392
26. 63 and 1546
27. £5·38 and £2·94
28. 7·5 and 28·1

Copy and complete.

29. 14 × 21 = □
30. 32 × 6 = □
31. 0·7 × □ = 2·8
32. 12 × □ = 0

33. □ × 6 = 54
34. □ × 3 = 1·8
35. 420 ÷ 7 = □
36. 9 ÷ 1 = □

37. 48 ÷ □ = 6
38. 150 ÷ □ = 30
39. □ ÷ 5 = 4·0
40. □ ÷ 10 = 3·1

Work out

41. $\begin{array}{r}128\\\times\ \ 6\\\hline\end{array}$
42. $\begin{array}{r}254\\\times\ \ 9\\\hline\end{array}$
43. $\begin{array}{r}537\\\times\ \ 8\\\hline\end{array}$
44. $\begin{array}{r}369\\\times\ \ 7\\\hline\end{array}$

Copy and complete.

45. $7\overline{)114}$
46. $6\overline{)172}$
47. $9\overline{)131}$
48. $8\overline{)278}$

Copy and complete.

49. $\begin{array}{r}48\\\times\ 17\\\hline\\\hline\\\hline\end{array}$
50. $\begin{array}{r}75\\\times\ 36\\\hline\\\hline\\\hline\end{array}$

Work out

51. 5·4 × 3
52. 3·6 × 7
53. 8·7 × 5
54. 6·9 × 6
55. 2·8 × 8
56. 7·5 × 4

Work out and give the remainder as a fraction.

57. 40 ÷ 7
58. 263 ÷ 10
59. 67 ÷ 9
60. 51 ÷ 8
61. 89 ÷ 4
62. 77 ÷ 6

Work out and give the remainder as a decimal.

63. 85 ÷ 2
64. 319 ÷ 10
65. £7·20 ÷ 4
66. £8·00 ÷ 5
67. £3·90 ÷ 2
68. £5·40 ÷ 10

69. How many seconds are there in one hour?
70. There are 14 sweets in each packet. How many packets can be made from 300 sweets?
71. A school has 243 pupils. 128 are boys. How many girls are there?
72. Sara has 127 marbles. Tina has 39 fewer. How many do they have altogether?

Copy and complete.

1. 4·3 km = ☐ m
2. 5870 m = ☐ km
3. 194 cm = ☐ m
4. 2·6 m = ☐ cm
5. 0·5 cm = ☐ mm
6. 79 mm = ☐ cm
7. 3·82 m = ☐ cm
8. 7800 m = ☐ km
9. 6·25 kg = ☐ g
10. 2·3 kg = ☐ g
11. 3740 g = ☐ kg
12. 500 g = ☐ kg
13. 1·4 litres = ☐ ml
14. 3·860 litres = ☐ ml
15. 2900 ml = ☐ litres
16. 480 ml = ☐ litres

Work out the measurement shown by each arrow.

17.

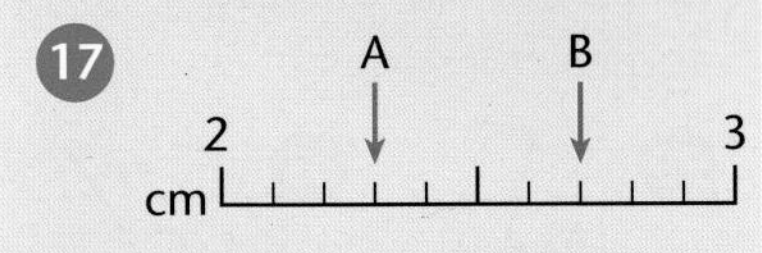

18.

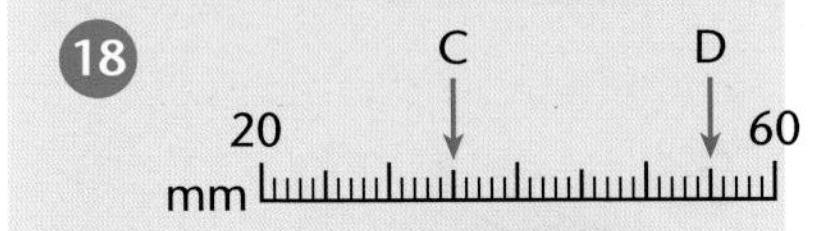

19. 20.

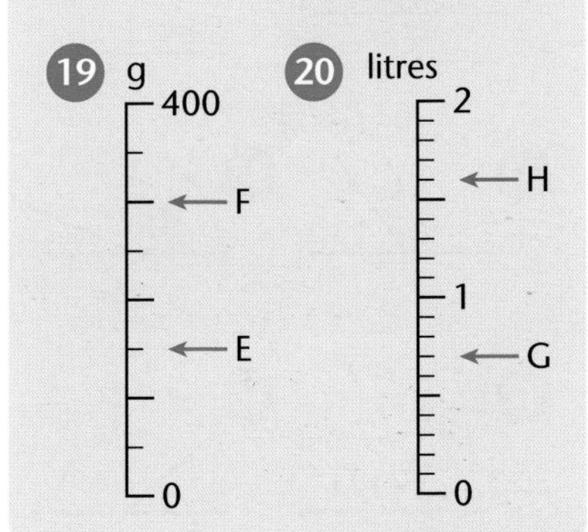

21. A bottle contains 2 litres of cola. Six 200 ml cups are filled from the bottle. How much cola is left?

22. There is 48 cm between the top of a wardrobe and the ceiling. The room has a height of 2·2 metres. How tall is the wardrobe?

23. One tin of peas weighs 300 g. What do fifteen tins weigh in kilograms?

24. A roll of wire is 6 metres long. How many 30 cm lengths can be cut from the roll?

25. What is the area of the rectangle?

26. What is the perimeter of the rectangle?

27. Work out the area and perimeter of these shapes:
    - **a)** rectangle 6 cm × 4 cm
    - **b)** square 7 cm sides

28. A square field has a perimeter of 400 metres. What is the area of the field?

Copy and complete.

29. 36 months = ☐ years
30. 2 years = ☐ weeks
31. 42 days = ☐ weeks
32. 3 days = ☐ hours
33. $6\frac{1}{2}$ hours = ☐ mins.
34. 300 seconds = ☐ mins.
35. 4 centuries = ☐ years
36. $2\frac{1}{2}$ hours = ☐ mins.

July 1st falls on a Friday.
On what day will these dates fall?

37. July 12th
38. July 23rd
39. August 7th
40. June 16th

41. Copy and complete the table showing 12-hour and 24-hour clock times.

12-HOUR CLOCK	24-HOUR CLOCK
4:25 pm	
10:30 am	
7:15 pm	
	08:42
	21:06
2:55 am	
	11:37
	17:21
7:49 am	
	23:11

Write the names of each of these 2-D shapes.

1, 5

2, 6

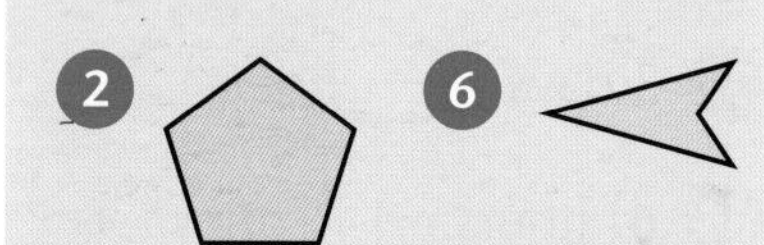

3, 7

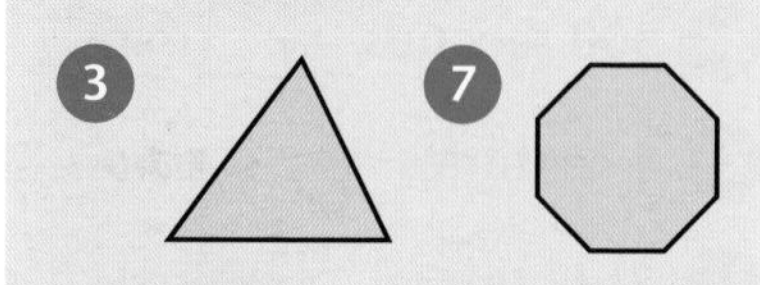

4, 8

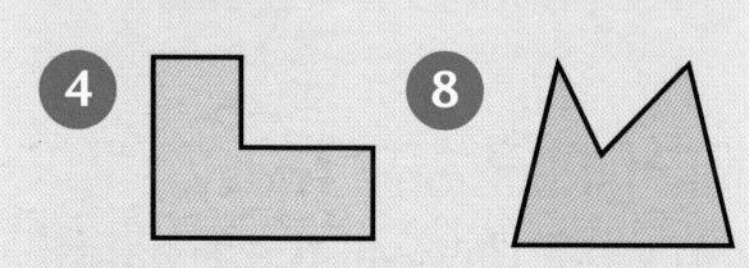

9 Which of the above shapes:

a) are concave

b) have parallel lines

c) are regular?

Use squared paper.
Copy the shape and the mirror line and sketch the reflection.

10, 11

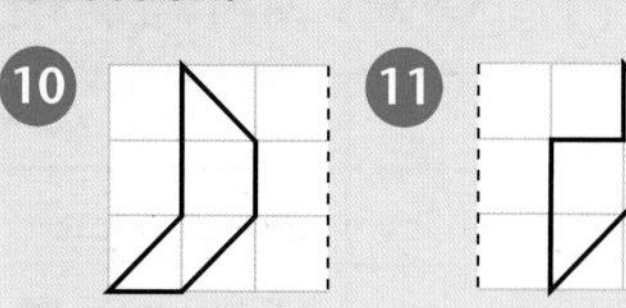

12

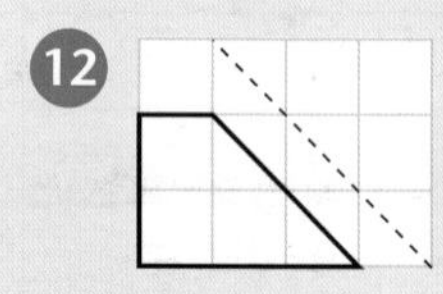

13

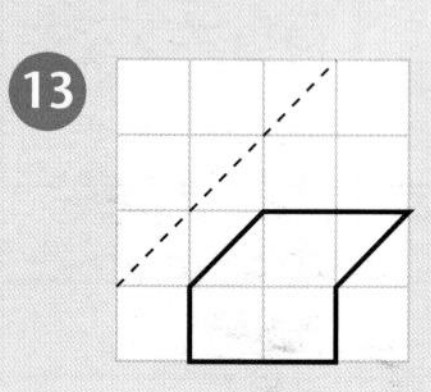

For each 3-D shape write.

a) the name of the shape

b) the number of faces

c) the number of edges

d) the number of vertices.

14, 15

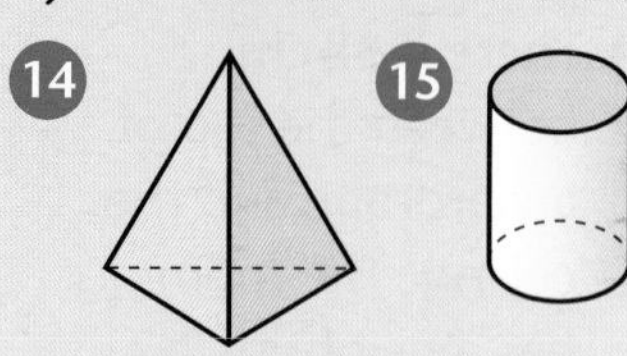

16

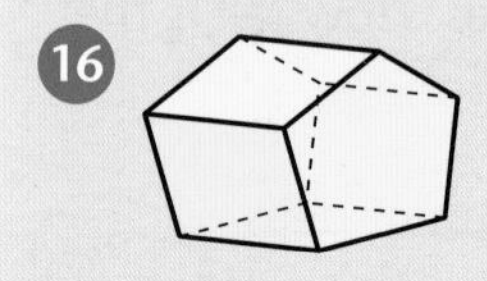

17, 18

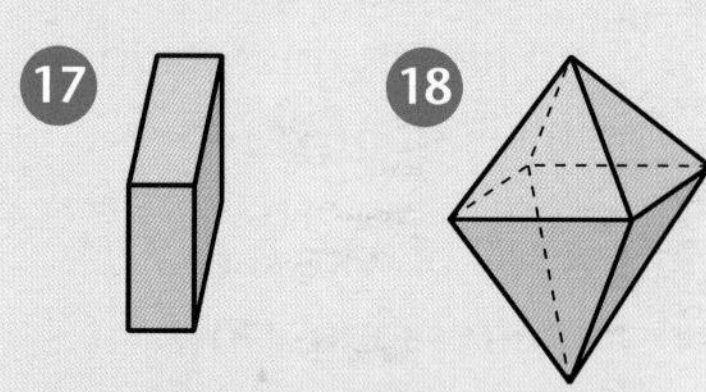

19

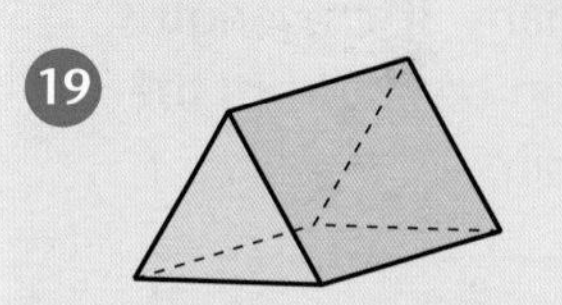

20, 21

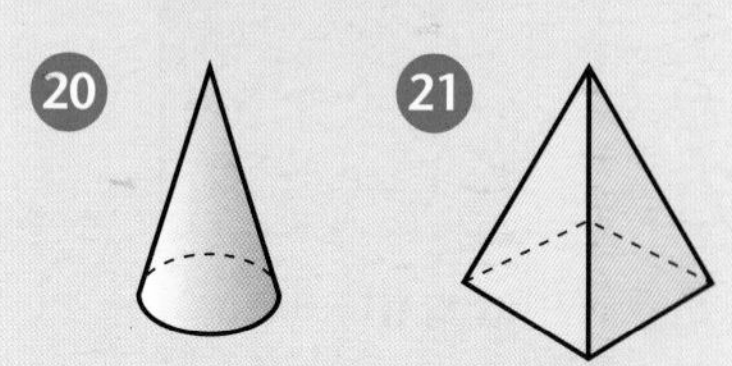

How many cubes are needed to build each shape?

22, 23

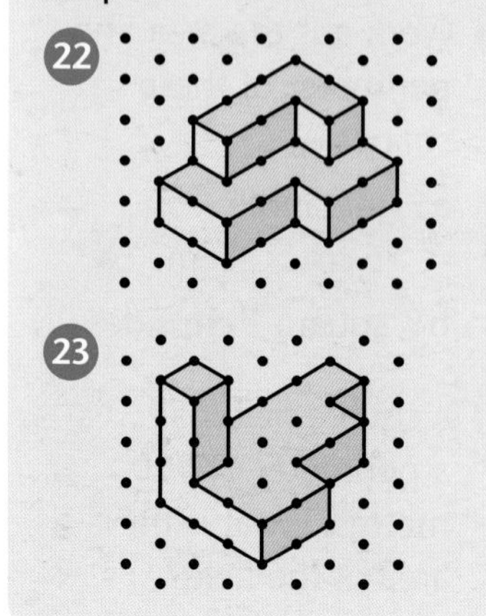

24 Copy the grid.

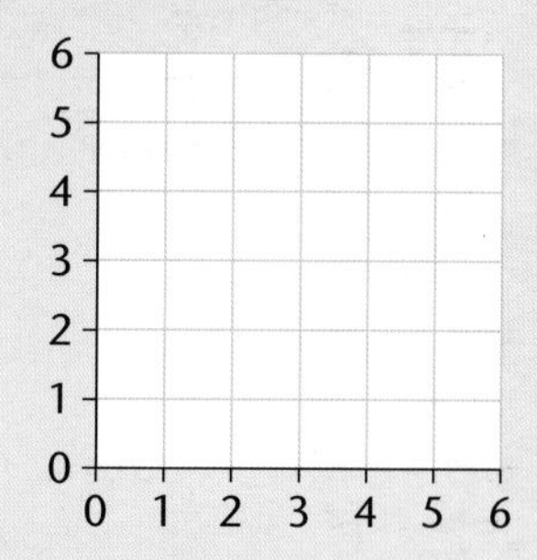

Plot these points and join them up in this order.
(1, 1) (3, 3) (3, 1) (1, 1)

Translate the shape twice.

a) Right 2 squares

b) Up 3 squares

Use a protractor to draw these angles. Write acute or obtuse by each angle.

25 65°

27 95°

26 150°

28 15°

Calculate the missing angles.

29, 33

30, 34

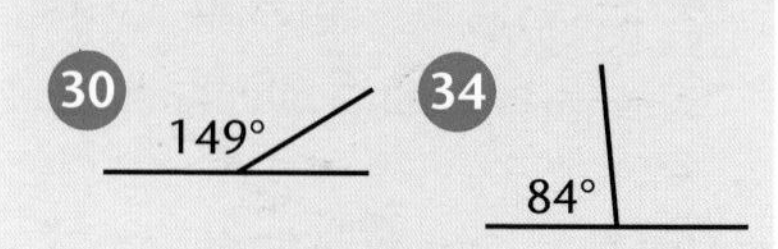

31, 35

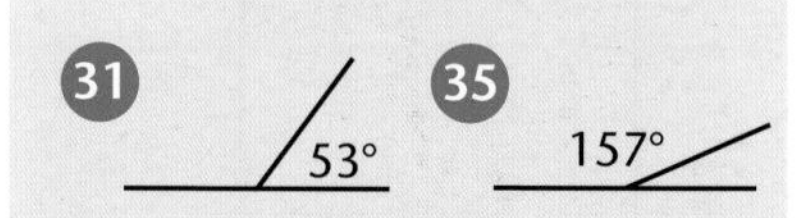

32, 36

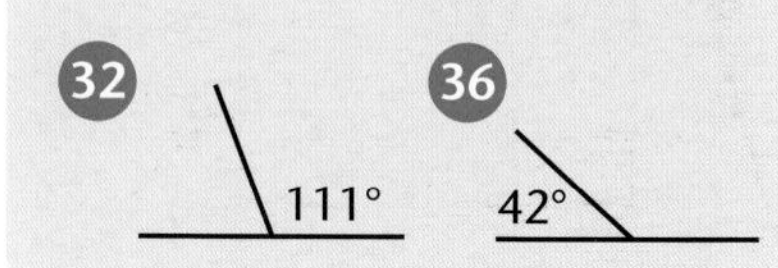

1 This line graph shows the average daily maximum temperature recorded in one week.

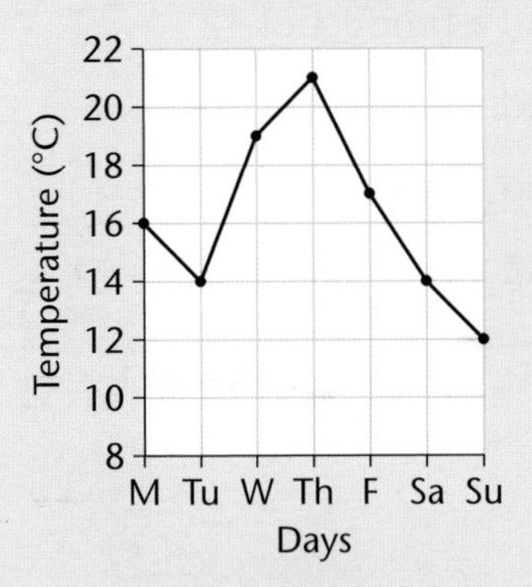

a) What was the highest temperature?

b) What was the temperature on Friday?

c) Which day saw the largest rise in temperature?

d) What temperature was the mode?

2 Use the table to draw a line graph showing Emma's marks in her weekly tables test.

Week	Mark
1	7
2	9
3	12
4	13
5	15
6	14
7	17
8	17
9	18
10	19

3 This bar chart shows the numbers of children absent in Year 5 in one term.

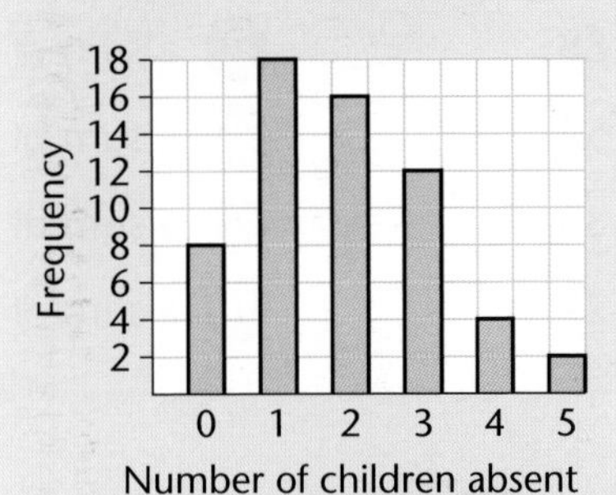

a) What was the largest number of children absent in one day?

b) On how many days were 2 children absent?

c) On how many days were there more than 3 children absent?

d) On how many days were there less than 2 children absent?

e) What was the modal number of children absent?

f) How many days were there in the term?

g) Draw how you think the bar chart might look for a term in which there was less illness. Keep the number of days the same.

4 This bar line chart shows the lengths of time spent at a zoo by the visitors on one day.

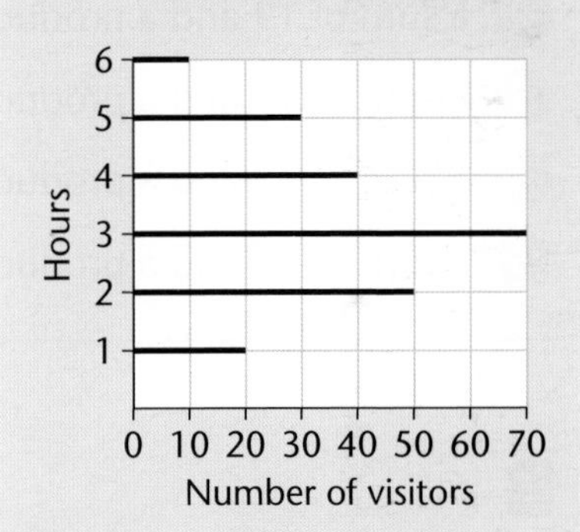

a) How many visitors spent four hours at the zoo?

b) What was the longest time spent at the zoo?

c) What was the modal number of hours spent at the zoo?

d) How many people spent more than 4 hours at the zoo?

e) How many people spent less than 3 hours at the zoo?

f) How many people visited the zoo altogether?

Find a pair of numbers with:

1. a sum of 13 and a product of 36
2. a sum of 19 and a product of 88
3. a sum of 15 and a product of 56
4. a sum of 12 and a product of 36
5. a sum of 12 and a product of 27
6. a sum of 29 and a product of 180
7. a sum of 17 and a product of 42
8. a sum of 25 and a product of 100
9. a sum of 15 and a product of 54
10. a sum of 18 and a product of 45.

B

Find the number.

1. below 40
   a prime number
   the sum of its digits is 11
2. a square number
   a 2-digit number
   the sum of its digits is 10
3. a 2-digit number
   a prime number
   the product of its digits is 12
4. a multiple of 50
   a 3-digit number
   a multiple of 11
5. a multiple of 7
   a 2-digit number
   the product of its digits is 30
6. a prime number
   a factor of 51
   a 2-digit number
7. a multiple of 9
   a 2-digit number
   the sum of its digits is 18
8. a square number
   a 2-digit number
   the product of its digits is 8

C

1. Use a calculator.
   Find two consecutive numbers with a product of:

   a) 121 b) 182 c) 870 d) 462 e) 272 f) 1056 g) 342 h) 1332 i) 1560

2. Use a calculator.
   Find a pair of prime numbers with a product of:

   a) 65 b) 69 c) 85 d) 119 e) 533 f) 473 g) 111 h) 217 i) 1769

3. 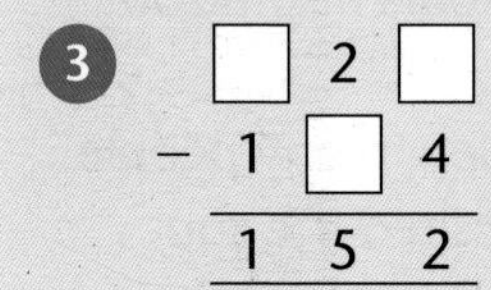

4. 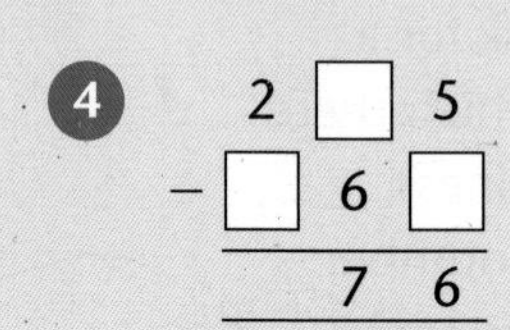

5. 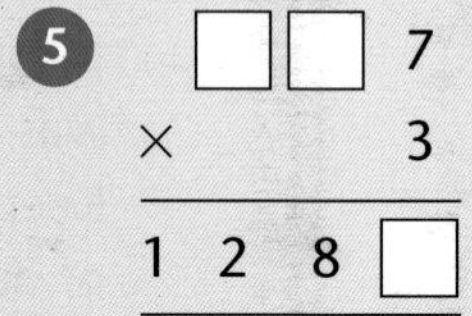

6. 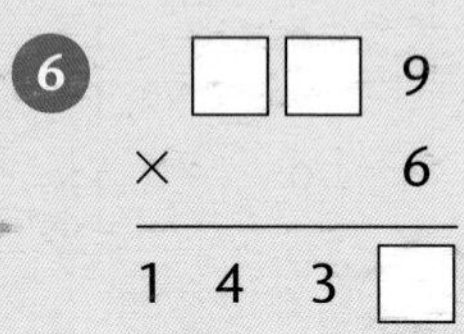